In Defense of America

(The Red Volume)

PETE MITCHELL
BILL PERKINS

ANDERSON – NOBLE PUBLISHING
LONG BEACH, CALIFORNIA
www.Anderson-Noble.com

Visit our Web site at **www.ModernDayHeroes.com** for more information on the subjects covered in this book.

Although the authors and publisher have made every effort to ensure the accuracy and completeness of information contained in this book, we assume no responsibility for errors, inaccuracies, omissions, or any inconsistency herein. Any slights of people, places, or organizations are unintentional.

ISBN 0-9754819-9-1

Library of Congress Control Number: 2004092373

We would like to thank the many publishers and individuals who granted us permission to reprint the cited material. All copyrighted material was used by permission.

Published in the United States of America by
Anderson – Noble Publishing, LLC
6285 East Spring Street, Suite 387
Long Beach, Ca 90808-4000

Cover by Pete Mitchell.
Cover photo by Pete Mitchell, all rights reserved.
Modern Day Heroes® is a registered trademark of Pete Mitchell and Bill Perkins.

ATTENTION CORPORATIONS, UNIVERSITIES, COLLEGES, AND PROFESSIONAL ORGANIZATIONS: Quantity discounts are available on bulk purchases of this book for educational, gift purposes, promotional, or as premiums for increasing magazine subscriptions or renewals. Special books or book excerpts can be created to fit specific needs. Write to Director of Special Projects, Anderson – Noble Publishing, LLC, 6285 East Spring Street Suite 387, Long Beach, California, 90808-4000, for information on discounts and terms. For faster service, email dsp@anderson-noble.com or dsp@ModernDayHeroes.com. You can also call (800) 551-HERO.

Dedication

America was born out of defiance of tyranny and great personal sacrifice. A group of 56 men signed their names on a death warrant we now know as the Declaration of Independence. The spirit of those 56 men still lives on today. We carry a deep sense of pride in the men who have, do, and will fight to keep us and our families safe from the evils in the world today. This book is dedicated to those who have fought for freedom and have returned home having sacrificed their sight, their hearing, their limbs, their bodies, and their minds for an America that both loves and embraces them, and at the same time, longs for a day when their duties will no longer be needed.

These are their stories...

With Strength, Honor, and Pride,
Pete Mitchell and Bill Perkins

Contents

5: The Unthinkable Evil, The Unforgettable Heroes
(Continued)

7: Heroes Remembered
(Continued)

8: In Defense of America   211

8: In Defense of America
(Continued)

Preface -
Note to the Reader

Pete Mitchell and Bill Perkins

For many, the United States is not so much a place, but an ideal. It is an ideal that holds that the individual is imbued with the liberty to do as he wishes. It is this very liberty that has allowed Americans to be innovators in technology. It is this very liberty that has allowed Americans to walk on the moon. It is also this very liberty that allows Americans to choose to do little, while others are so very productive. However, the great irony of the United States is that the very liberty, which so many hold dear, is won through a virtue that some hold to be the antithesis of liberty. It is the virtue that perhaps best defines what it means to be a hero. It is also the virtue that often most benefits those who do not possess it. It is the virtue of individual sacrifice.

The concept of sacrifice is seemingly incongruous with America, especially in context with her prosperity. Most citizens around the world have the notion that Americans never sacrifice, that they live in perpetual weal with nary a thought to the struggles that many face on a daily basis. However, an examination of the history of the United States paints a very different picture. From the very founding of this nation, Americans have been willing to pay the wages of liberty, wages that are paid in blood and sacrifice.

The tradition of sacrifice began even before the time of our Founding Fathers, when persecuted Europeans left the material comforts of home to seek religious freedom in the new world. Flocks of Pilgrims who desired to separate from the Church of England

11

thought it a worthwhile sacrifice to give up the safety of hearth and home for the potential to worship their God as they saw fit. Groups of Puritans followed, also seeking the freedom of worship. More groups followed, all with distinct views on deity and religious practice, but united by the sacrifice they made of leaving kith and kin behind.

Further on, the Founding Fathers of the United States placed their lives, their liberty, and their sacred honor on the line for the, at the time, potential benefit of throwing off the yoke of British tyranny and establishing a sovereign nation. It is easy to view these men with casualness in the comforts of our homes over 200 years later. However, the assurance of victory in their endeavors was far from certain. The sacrifice that these men made in terms of time, money, and blood is immeasurable. Yet, it is undeniable that the sacrifices endured by the Founding Fathers and the brave men who fought along side them brought into existence the wonderful country that we live in.

The United States continued the tradition of sacrifice in one of her darkest moments, the War Between the States. Unlike previous conflicts in her short history, this war pitted brother against brother, father against son, countryman against countryman. The sacrifice on both sides was tremendous. Fortunes were lost, families were divided, and the loss of life was greater than any other armed conflict in the history of the Western Hemisphere.

Many in the United States again sacrificed when they were called to battle in World War II. This group of men saw warfare on a level unprecedented through the scope of human history. On land, sea, and air, Americans fought against the menace of global fascism in places far from home. The cost was high and the places liberated were not American. However, Americans heard the call to sacrifice and, to the benefit of the world, Americans answered.

The virtue of sacrifice is not a thing of the past. We continue to see it in the actions of many Americans in recent history and today. Brave soldiers left behind their lives of comfort to help the tiny nation of Kuwait when Iraq invaded in the early 1990s. While perhaps not as large as the scale of WWII, the cost of sacrifice was no less real. Just like their predecessors, some who answered the call did not come home to enjoy the fruits of sacrifice.

More recently Americans have continued the tradition of sacrifice in Mogadishu, Afghanistan, and Iraq. While the enemy is a more fluid, nebulous force, the sacrifice is the same. Whether fighting large nation-states or ever moving terrorist cells, Americans continue to give up the quiet lives they prefer to lead and sacrifice for the safety and well-being of others.

The tragedy of sacrifice, specifically the sacrifice of soldiers who pay with their lives, is that those who do it do not ever witness the benefit. Further, there is no way to personally thank those who have laid down their lives for us. The best we can do is to honor their memories and attempt to live lives of productivity and virtue so that their sacrifices are not in vain. It is to the memory of all American heroes, and the sacrifices they have made for all of us, that this book is dedicated.

Introduction

> "Now where men are not their own masters and independent, but are ruled by despots, they are not really militarily capable, but only appear to be warlike...For men's souls are enslaved and they refuse to run risks readily and recklessly to increase the power of somebody else. But independent people, taking risks on their own behalf and not on behalf of others, are willing and eager to go into danger, for they themselves enjoy the prize of victory. So institutions contribute a great deal to military valor." - Hippocrates

Doug DeCinces
Former 3rd Baseman for the California Angels and Baltimore Orioles

It is a curious, yet common axiom that states, "History is written by the winners." While the veracity of this maxim has been debated, an underlying question is often ignored; why do certain places routinely seem to win? Historians, sociologists, pseudo-scientists, and others have constructed elaborate theories in an attempt to find an answer, and, in truth, there is probably no simple singular reason. However, one factor that has played a key role in the continuous tradition of victory, in the Western world in general and America in particular, is the role of government.

Since antiquity a peculiar form of government indigenous to the West has allowed for the rise of philosophical inquiry, free market economies, and decisive shock battle. The form of government is democracy. Originating in the tiny poleis of Greece, democracy established the tradition of rule by the people. This seemingly small political convention has had enormous influence on the progression of history, especially on the battlefield.

Throughout history the dominant form of government has been tyranny. Simple in its directness, efficient in its focus, tyranny

15

put absolute power in the hands of an individual. There was no rule of law, no written constitutions, just the will of the tyrant. Tyrants throughout history have held different titles; in Egypt they were known as Pharaohs, Persia had Shahs, the Mongols had Khans, and the list goes on. However, no matter the title, no matter the epoch, no matter the place, the tyrant's will was law. However, in certain places (although always in the West) groups of people banded together with different thoughts on government. Thoughts that would allow for private ownership of property with laws to protect those rights, written constitutions that would guarantee standardized forms of conduct, and attempts to maximize individual liberty. These ideas, which would blossom into what we call democracy, are seemingly unrelated to battle, yet would have devastating impacts on how and why soldiers would fight.

A prime example of the dynamism of democratic ideas on the battlefield is evidenced at the Battle of Salamis. In 480 BC, things were looking bleak for the confederation of Greek poleis. After repeated defeats at the hands of emperor Xerxes' forces, the Greeks were reeling. With the Spartan defeat at the Battle of Thermopylae, the Persian forces marched upon Athens. The Athenians were forced to leave their city and many fled to the island of Salamis to watch their beloved Athens burn and put their last vestiges of hope in the Greek fleet.

Some Greeks must have wondered what else could be expected? How could a tiny confederation of peoples numbering in population no more than 1 million persons and encompassing an area of less than 50,000 square miles stand against the collective might of an empire that ranged over 1 million square miles and boasted a population of over 70 million? The answer would lie in the dynamism of democracy.

As Athens was burning, Xerxes sent his armada to wipe out the remainder of Greek resistance at Salamis. Historians differ on the numbers, but anywhere from 600 to 1,000 triremes (Herodotus asserts the greater number) sailed towards the narrow straights for Xerxes confident of crushing a numerically inferior (the Greeks were able to field a force of little more than 300 triremes) foe. So confident of victory was Xerxes, in fact, that he had a throne placed on a nearby hill so that he could savor the imminent Persian victory and serve as a reminder to his admirals that the emperor was watching. Little could he have known that the Battle of Salamis was to be the beginning of the end of Persian occupation in Greece.

With a crew of roughly 200 sailors per trireme, the Battle of Salamis was a fight of epic proportions. 60,000 Greeks fought against a Persian force of 120,000 to 200,000. By days end, more than 200 Persian ships were sunk, compared to only 40 for the Greeks. Additionally, most of the Persian crews perished when their triremes sank because of their inability to swim. Xerxes, no doubt disgusted by the miserable defeat he witnessed, called for what remained of his fleet to begin the slow process of returning to Persia.

How does one account for Greek victory against such overwhelming odds? Several reasons are applicable, but most noteworthy was the role of democracy. Xerxes forces, even his officers, were not free in any Western sense of the word. All in Persia were chattel, slaves of the emperor. By contrast, the Greeks were free citizens, fighting for their individual farms, families, and way of life. Further, the will and words of Xerxes was law. There was no discussion of strategy, no personal initiative against the orders of the emperor, no room for dissent and analysis. By contrast, the Greek forces were led by soldiers who had been democratically chosen. They were subject to review and dismissal. Additionally, Greek soldiers were aware that poor performance would not lead to summary execution by a capricious emperor. The ability to act freely was the difference for the Greeks at Salamis. The requirement to obey the emperor without question was the downfall of the Persians at Salamis. Herodotus, in his account of Greek democratic dynamism, perhaps put it best stating, "As long as the Athenians were ruled by a despotic government, they had no better success at war than any of their neighbors. Once the yoke was flung off, they proved the finest fighters in the world."

Some assert that fighting for their homes or way of life doesn't adequately demonstrate the superiority of democracy over tyranny. Some argue that it is intuitive that men would fight more bravely or with more desire when fighting in protection of their homes. However, this argument ignores other examples that demonstrate the superiority of democracy over tyranny in terms of battle. The Battle for Tenochtitlan brilliantly illustrates the point.

In 1518, Hernan Cortes and a small compliment of Spanish conquistadors departed from the island of Hispanola to explore the

Yucatan. In the course of a little less than 2 years, Cortes had subjugated and allied with several indigenous tribes with his eyes on the Aztec empire and the riches that it possessed. In 1520, with his indigenous allies, but only 1,200 Spanish troops, Cortes began his occupation of Tenochtitlan, the capital of the Aztec empire. Over the course of the next year, Cortes would appropriate vast amounts of gold from the Aztecs, hold the Aztec emperor Montezuma captive, be forced to flee the Aztec capital while incurring tremendous losses, yet manage to rally and regroup for a final siege that eradicated the Aztec empire and began the long domination of Spain in Latin and South America.

Much like the Greeks at the Battle of Salamis the Spanish were vastly outnumbered. Tenochtitlan was a city of 250,000, while Cortes never had more than 1,200 Conquistadores at any given time. However, unlike Salamis where the Greeks were fighting for hearth and home, Cortes was half a world away from Spain, seeking riches and honors. Again, the question of how a numerically inferior force could so decisively move to victory is before us.

The difference between democracy and tyranny provides a convincing answer. The most obvious distinction is drawn in the simple observation that the Spaniards were in Mexico, not the Aztecs in Spain. This came about through democratic means. Individual citizens, free to explore and free to reap the benefits had the impetus to expand. The Aztec means of government provided no such liberty. Further, as Cortes was forced to flee Tenochtitlan during La Noche Triste, him and his men used up and/or lost valuable gunpowder, cannon, and harquebuses. The King of Spain had issued a decree forbidding the manufacture of gunpowder in the New World. Exercising personal initiative, however, Cortes began the manufacture of gunpowder in order to resupply his troops for another assault on the Aztec capital. This initiative in the face of authority is indicative of democracy, where the individual is free to petition and protest the actions of his government. This kind of defiance would have earned any Aztec a place on the sacrificial alter in Tenochtitlan. Finally, in the face of defeat, Cortes allowed his men to choose whether to carry gold, thereby making them less mobile and more likely to not escape Tenochtitlan, or to leave the treasure behind, better equipping them to escape, but ensuring they would return as paupers. Further, after escaping the Aztecs, he allowed his men to decide whether to return and conquer or to leave. This kind of liberty is never found under tyranny, only in a democracy where the rights of individuals are held as significant.

Democracy has continued to make the difference in more modern examples as well. At the outbreak of World War II, the Japanese naval fleet was numerically and qualitatively superior to the American fleet. However, Imperial Japan would make few changes in the quality of her weapons of war, whereas the upgrades made in the American war machine by wars end would have been unthinkable at the outset. Further, America's ability to produce weapons of war was an extension of her democratic ideals. As citizens banded together for the war effort, more efficient means of production were rewarded with lucrative contracts, personal innovations to improve weaponry were greeted with congratulations, not suspicion, and review and analysis of failures on the battlefield were seen as a means toward progress and improvement, not disloyalty and subversiveness.

In our current times, democracy is proving again that it is superior to tyranny. As our soldiers bravely fight against the tyranny of terrorism, the democracy on which our military is so firmly founded has repeatedly demonstrated it is up to the task. At present, an all-volunteer military, something a tyranny could never even fathom, is taking the fight to the farthest reaches of the earth. The weapons and technology they bring with them are the product of a democratic society that encourages inquiry, rewards innovation, and secures these beliefs under the rule of law. The men and women who fight on behalf of America do so at their own free will. They do so out of a patriotic love for their country and their fellow man. Democracy is the reason America abounds with stories of heroes, because it is the ability to choose what one wishes to do that is provided by a democracy that makes the sacrifices made by those individuals so heroic.

Chapter 1

The Sacrifice of Yesterday

The American Heroes
of D-Day

American heroes... Well, the 300,000 soldiers, sailors and Marines that made the ultimate sacrifice in liberating Europe from Nazis' death grip were heroes. And the rest of their comrades sure were, too.

I'll just be a little partial to all those junior and not so junior officers that jumped into occupied France in SOE/OSS teams to link up with Resistance fighters weeks before D-Day. As I said to a [friend] whose relatives died in Sainte-Mère-l'Eglise, if jumping from a perfectly functional airplane into a country occupied by hostile forces don't make you a hero, then what does?

And these SOE/OSS operatives had no military unit to back them up; it was solitary heroism all along.

Yves Chaineau
Poitiers, France

U.S. Representative Jim Greenwood -
gave this speech on June 17, 2002 at a ceremony he hosted to present World War II Veterans with the Jubilee of Liberty Medal. The "Jubilee of Liberty" medal is awarded to Veterans who served at Normandy between June 6, 1944 (D-Day), and August 31, 1944. While the medals were first awarded at the D-Day 50th Anniversary ceremony held in France in 1994, the French Government has extended permission to present this medal to those Normandy Veterans from the United States who were unable to attend the original ceremony.

Good morning ladies and gentlemen, and thank you for being here to help the commissioners and me to honor the American heroes of D-Day.

We are grateful to the Harry C. Wilson VFW post here in Warminster for hosting this special ceremony.

Most especially, I want to thank the D-Day Veterans, as it is your victory that we celebrate.

You are living monuments of arguably the greatest invasion in world history.

With the benefit of hindsight and with the knowledge that the Normandy invasion was an enormous success, many of us may not comprehend just how risky the operation was.

The architects of the D-Day invasions – people like Winston Churchill and Dwight Eisenhower -- understood the enormous gamble they were taking, which is why Churchill dubbed the mission "Operation Overlord": it was so ambitious in size and objective that, once begun, there was no turning back.

The allies assembled a tremendous armada of five thousand, three hundred thirty-three (5,333) ships carrying an invasion force of approximately one hundred seventy-five thousand (175,000) men.

To put this in perspective, consider our more recent war in Afghanistan: by May of this year [2002] – nearly eight months after the terrorist attacks of September eleventh – the total number of American personnel in Afghanistan totaled six thousand (6,000) troops; that's less than three percent of the D-Day invasion force.

For D-Day's mammoth operation to succeed, overwhelming challenges would need to be overcome.

First, the allies had to outfox German intelligence and keep the details of the invasion a secret. The Germans knew that an attack was coming, but they did not know where or when it would come.

Imagine mobilizing 5,000 ships and 175,000 men across an ocean, all the while keeping your arrival a surprise. In all likelihood, such a feat will never again be replicated.

Most of the allied soldiers, in fact, did not know their destination until they were en route to Normandy through the English Channel.

The channel, a dangerously unpredictable body of water, posed another challenge to the thousands of ships. The tumultuous rides caused sea sickness in many of these men, men who were simultaneously trying to brace themselves as they prepared for battle.

Some troops, such as the 4th infantry division, were forced to spend an extra day at sea because the ocean was too rough for the landing. Bottled like sardines in a can, the restless crew was forced to wait, as one private described, in a "stench of vomit."

And the waiting, the anticipation, must have been maddening. While an incredible tempest of fear and eagerness and adrenaline filled the hearts of every passenger, the soldiers had no choice but to wait it out. Minutes seemed like hours, and hours felt like lifetimes.

Eventually, the hour arrived.

The allied troops neared the landing point greeted by the deafening sounds of bombardments from the German guns and from the firing of their own ships. It was painfully loud and terrifying. Even General Omar Bradley said that he had "never heard anything like it" in his entire life.

At 6:31 am, June 5, 1944, the first landing began at Utah beach.

As for the events of the next few hours, most of us can only try to comprehend what our brave men experienced.

The beaches themselves were bristling with traps. Anticipating the attack, German Field Marshal Erwin Rommel had filled the beaches with mines, barbed wire, and tank traps. By the time the allies landed, there were roughly half a million of these obstacles in place, waiting to ensnare the invaders.

Even more daunting were the Germans themselves: eighty thousand (80,000) troops and one Panzer division that showered the allies with incessant firepower.

The Germans had perched their long-range guns in high, well-fortified positions on the beach. In fact, from their superior vantage point, the German gunners could see the allied ships through the cloud cover before the ships could see the guns.

Yet, our men stormed the hazardous beaches through the mines, the wire, the gun fire, and the explosions.

The best visual recreation we have into these horrible moments is the opening scenes of the movie, "Saving Private Ryan."

Director Steven Speilberg overwhelms us with the blood and confusion that surrounded the Americans.

The film helps us to begin to understand how difficult it must have been to function amidst such chaos.

It shows what it was like to have your buddy standing beside you one minute and then, right before your eyes, to see him taken away forever.

We see how the cries of the wounded would long remain unanswered, because few doctors accompanied the first wave.

In spite of all the horror, the allies did not yield. They did not turn back. Instead, they dove head first into a thicket of danger. They overcame the Germans, they overcame their fears, and they did their job.

The allied commanders, leaders like Eisenhower and Churchill, designed "Operation Overlord" and made the bold decision to invade. But it was the soldiers like you who made the invasion work and "D-Day" a day for all ages.

You trained vigorously. You made a treacherous journey to a foreign land, without knowing where you were going, and without the promise of ever returning home.

You risked everything. And you did your job.

You, Veterans of Normandy, are living history. We are grateful for what you have done for us, and grateful for this chance to honor you. For as columnist Bob Greene of the Chicago Tribune has said:

"they are leaving us now, the men and women of these war years; soon we, their children, will be all alone in the world they saved for us."

As we were painfully and cruelly reminded on 9-11, there is much evil and danger in this world, a world that needs saving again.

As we face this challenge together, we take this day to remember you, Normandy Veterans, and the great feats of which Americans are capable. Guided by your example, strengthened by the legacy of sacrifice and courage that you have given us, we will roll on.

We salute you, we thank you, and we ask that God bless America.

America wants to hear the story of your experience or the experience of someone you know from World War II. Share your story with us at -   www.ModernDayHeroes.com

The Forgotten War

American heroes are those men and women whose character - by nature - jettisons selfish desires for the virtue of serving family, neighbor, community and country.

Byron de Arakal
Costa Mesa, CA

U.S. Representative Ron Kind –

gave this speech on July 21, 2003 regarding House Resolution 212. This resolution properly recognized the service and sacrifice of the 22 nations, thousands of American service members, and millions of South Korean citizens who stood together half a century ago in defense of the principle of freedom.

I rise today in strong support of H. Con. Res. 212, offered by my friend and colleague, Representative Sam Johnson.

This resolution properly recognizes the service sacrifice of the 22 nations, thousands of American service members, and millions of South Korean citizens who stood together half a century ago in defense of the principle of freedom.

The Korean Conflict is often referred to as the Forgotten War. Yet, this war is only "forgotten" by those who have not been blessed with the teachings of history – not by the millions of Americans whose lives have been touched in so many ways by those committed to opposing tyranny and injustice, regardless of the sacrifices required.

America entered the Korean War with a military made up of a mix of war-scarred servicemen and women toughened by the hard lessons of Guadalcanal, Okinawa and Normandy, as well as a new generation of soldiers and sailors who had only seen war on the silver screen, and a newly created Air Force.

After three long, bloody years, the fighting ended. We had rebuilt a military that became, even by today's standards, one of the most coherent fighting forces in the world. The alliance, consisting of units from 22 nations, supported an armistice that prevented the potential death of millions more in a savage, spreading war, and permitted South Korea to flourish into a miracle of freedom that we witness today.

Tragically, nearly 37,000 American soldiers fell on the fields of battle and lost their lives in the Korean War.

There were also far too many who were taken prisoner or met an unknown fate, whose ranks of over 8,000 remain today unaccounted for, but never forgotten. Indeed today, this nation continues to search for every missing warrior who fought to preserve the freedom we cherish; we seek and demand the fullest possible accounting of America's fallen heroes.

It is our solemn promise that we will never forget or forsake them.

Nor will we forget the Veterans who returned home to help reshape this nation and the world. And while some returned to parades and fanfare, many returned quietly without public recognition and the "thanks" they deserved.

On July 27, 2003, our nation will commemorate the 50th anniversary of the armistice with North Korea – giving us the opportunity to reaffirm our appreciation and extend the gratitude some soldiers never received. Many Americans, including the thousands of Veterans and their families from that war, will take a moment to remember the meaning of their service: whether they rest in Korea, remain unaccounted for, or have returned home to their families and the freedom they fought to defend.

More than 1.5 million Americans served during the Korean War. Today, Americans are still there on-point, still defending freedom in Korea. Soldiers, sailors, airmen, and Marines serve alongside their South Korean counterparts, astride what has been called the world's most dangerous border.

We pause today to recall with gratitude the sacrifices of all Veterans who have served the causes of democracy and freedom. To the Veterans of the Korean War and their families, we especially offer our thanks. The world could be a significantly less friendly place if you had not stepped forward selflessly when you were needed. Thank you.

Mr. Speaker, from Korea to Iraq, let's not forget the sacrifices our men and women in uniform, and indeed their families, have made on behalf of this great country.

Remember too, that on any given day, there are Americans on guard, demonstrating and defending democracy and freedom in over 100 countries around the world.

God bless our service members, our Veterans and their families.

God bless America.

Our Military Men and Women: Heroes Past, Present, and Future.

Victory or Death

Our history is brimming with examples of American heroes. It is one of the principle reasons we are one of the greatest nations in the history of the world. To me, the American hero is an ordinary person who does an extraordinary act, or over time, lives an extraordinary life.

I believe one of the key aspects of the American hero is that his conduct both goes to the heart of who we are as human beings and transcends purely national concerns. It may be personal, such as the man who jumped into the Potomac River to save that aircraft crash victim; or it may be that soldier who gave his life on the beaches of Normandy. In each case they put another person, or human value, ahead of their self interest.

There is not a major decision in my life that I can recall where I have not relied on American heroes as a beacon to guide my way or a source of comfort in my moments of despair. God has truly blessed us, and may it always be so.

> Duf Sundheim
> Palo Alto, CA

U.S. Representative Pete Sessions

Inscribed on the Korean War Veterans Memorial in Washington, DC, is a quote by a Korean War-era Air Force officer named William describing the motivation of his fellow soldiers and airmen. "They went not for conquest and not for gain, but only to protect the anguished and innocent," he said. "They suffered greatly and by their heroism in a thousand forgotten battles they added a luster to the codes we hold most dear: duty, honor, country, fidelity, bravery, integrity..."

These words together define the virtues that many of us think of when we envision our heroes, and the codes William spoke of, bond the many who have served our nation in her short history. I was born just two years after the armistice that ended the Korean War, and I was fortunate to learn of heroes at an early age. For me, the lesson was personal: William is my father, Judge William S. Sessions.

But just five months before my birth, President Dwight D. Eisenhower had seen to it that the heroism my father spoke of was to live on as a part of America's national identity. On October 8, 1954, Eisenhower issued his now famous Veterans Day Proclamation.

In it, he stated: "Now, therefore, I, Dwight D. Eisenhower, President of the United States of America, do hereby call upon all of our citizens to observe Thursday, November 11, 1954, as Veterans Day. On that day let us solemnly remember the sacrifices of all those who fought so valiantly, on the seas, in the air, and on foreign shores, to preserve our heritage of freedom, and let us re-consecrate ourselves to the task of promoting an enduring peace so that their efforts shall not have been in vain."

Now, in 2004, as we approach the 50th anniversary of our nation's first observance of Veterans Day, Americans cannot fail to recognize the great progress of the last half-century. We have seen technological advances, cultural shifts, and changes in the global balance of power from which the United States has emerged in as the world's sole superpower. Undeniably, we owe much of this success to the brave men and women who have served in uniform.

Veterans Day itself was originally known as Armistice Day, a holiday honoring Veterans of World War I. However, in 1954, following World War II and the Korean War, America recognized the need to honor our nation's heroes of all generations. The 83rd Congress amended Armistice Day to recognize not only our Veterans of World War I, but all American Veterans who served in defense of our country and freedom around the world.

Like my father, an Air Force flight training officer, Eisenhower was a serviceman himself. He knew service and sacrifice firsthand. He knew the stories of his brothers-in-arms, the stories of their families left behind, and the price many paid for freedom. He also knew that similar sacrifices had been made by past generations and would continue to be required of future generations in defense of freedom and democracy.

In designating Veterans Day, Eisenhower ensured that future generations would always have a reason to learn about the price our heroes paid for the freedoms we enjoy. In learning this lesson, they learn also that they and the generations that follow may be called to similar duty.

So many of our sons and daughters, brothers and sisters, friends and loved ones are serving at this very moment, doing their duty with distinction like so many have before them. Newspaper headlines and television news alerts remind us that the world is still a dangerous place. A clear-eyed realism has replaced the euphoria that greeted the end of the Cold War.

Heroism must never go unnoticed in such a world. Heroes will always be needed to heed the call of service. Sir Winston Churchill is known to have called World War II our "finest hour." But no victory, even one as hard-fought as that of World War II, is permanent. Peace must be preserved by each new generation.

We are fortunate in America that in each new generation, we have men and women who are willing to put their lives on the line to protect and nurture peace, freedom, and democracy. Their patriotism, spirit, and pride in our nation are tangible manifestations of the belief that America is worth fighting for. They exemplify the very ideals that motivate so many sons and daughters of other lands to dream of being Americans.

America should never be outdone in honoring those who paid the ultimate price to purchase the freedoms other nations envy. No other nation has sacrificed so much of its human treasure to secure not only its own freedom, but also that of other nations. No other nation has so many of its honored dead buried in so many cemeteries in so many foreign lands. Foe after foe have thought Americans too soft to fight and too selfish to sacrifice. Each has been proven wrong.

My own home state of Texas gained its independence from Mexico thanks to men who dedicated themselves to fighting for freedom. Texas has been honored by the service of many brave men, including Sam Houston, James Bowie, and William Barrett Travis.

While holding off a much larger Mexican force at the Alamo nearly 170 years ago, Travis sent for reinforcements, but pledged his intent to die in pursuit of a just cause should the battle be lost.

"Then, I call on you in the name of liberty or patriotism and everything dear to the American character to come to our aid with all dispatch." He continued, "If this call is neglected, I am determined to sustain myself as long as possible and die like a soldier who never forgets what is due to his honor and that of his country."

Like so many American soldiers, Travis knew that the price of freedom could be high, but he also knew that the cost of not fighting for his beliefs would be worse than death itself. He signed his plea: "Victory or Death, William B. Travis."

Such powerful sentiment in fighting for the virtues of freedom and liberty is not just a thing of the past. Today, American men and woman put themselves in harm's way here at home and around the globe. They are committed to using the genius and resourcefulness of our great nation to ensure that the values that led America and the West to democracy will be allowed to take root in places like Iraq and Afghanistan. The United States' success in these endeavors will mark new milestones in the great history of liberty.

The fight for liberty isn't easy and it isn't cheap – but it is important, and it will make life for our children and grandchildren much safer. American servicemen and servicewomen today, like my father and those who served in his generation, know this. The freedom and democracy that we now enjoy was neither ordained by God, nor achieved by theorists, but won and preserved through blood and iron on the fields of Dunkirk, the beaches of Normandy, the hills of Afghanistan, and the streets of Baghdad. As Americans, it is our duty to honor our protectors as they honor us with their service each and every day. Let us remember, always, those who fight the good fight.

Korean War Veterans – share your stories with us at -
www.ModernDayHeroes.com
Lest the world forget "...the sacrifices of all those who fought so valiantly, on the seas, in the air, and on foreign shores, to preserve our heritage of freedom..."
- President Dwight D. Eisenhower

I Don't Want My Son
to be a Quitter

An American hero is someone willing to sacrifice their life for all Americans, even those who protest against the very people who are fighting to protect them.

Harmony Allen
Alexandria, VA

U.S. Representative Randy Cunningham

On January 19, 1972, I was flying a mission over North Vietnam when I shot down my first MiG. This was the first MiG kill in over two years for the United States. When I got back to the ship, the flight deck was alive. There were arms waving and hastily made signs of congratulations. Before I could climb down out of the cockpit, Willie White, my ordanencemen, nearly knocked over Admiral Cooper, leaped up on the F-4 , shook my hand and said, "Mr. Cunningham, we got our MiG today, didn't we?" There were tears of excitement in his eyes, and rightfully so. On that day his Sidewinder missile, his effort in making sure it was connected properly, his inspection of all the systems, allowed that missile to perform effectively.

Willie White reminded me that he and thousands of other men working on that ship, right down to the cooks and boiler tenders, made it possible for us to carry out our mission-- that there is no substitute for teamwork. My time as a military aviator taught me many valuable life lessons like this one, and made other lessons ring true.

My love for airplanes began long before I shot down that first MiG. As a boy in Shelbina, Missouri, building model airplanes with my father, I daydreamed about being a pilot, controlling my own plane. At 15, I took my first flight. I knew immediately that I was born to fly. Years later when I flew my first solo, I knew that flying would forever be a part of who I was, who I wanted to become. But as I trained to become a fighter pilot I learned that it would take more than desire, it would take significant dedication, confidence and perseverance.

My father once told me that, "Quitting becomes a way of life and I don't want my son to be a quitter." I thought of that saying often throughout my flight career, especially during my time in flight school in Pensacola, Florida. On one particularly grueling day of training, my drill sergeant asked me if I was going to quit. Part of me wanted to, but I remembered my father's words. I said, "No sir. I've got a silver dollar in my back pocket that I'm going to spend."

Once you are commissioned as an officer, tradition holds that you give a silver dollar to the first non-commissioned officer to salute you. My father gave me a silver dollar before I left for flight school as a reminder not to quit. I still carry that very silver dollar in my back pocket today. Both my drill instructor and my father instilled in me the dedication I would need as a combat fighter pilot. This dedication would carry me through many dogfights and battles, all the way to the aviation hall of fame.

For years, people have asked me how I was able to shoot down five MiGs, three in one day. My response: "You fight like you train." My training was second to none. I can honestly say, though we were outnumbered, our intense air combat training had instilled confidence in us. My Navy training is the reason I'm alive today, and I thank the Navy officials who had enough foresight to offer us an energetic tactical flight program.

Today, as a member of Congress, I carry the military's teamwork, dedication, and confidence with me. I often rely on these qualities when I am working on the difficult task of bridging party lines or trying to get legislation passed. Our military aviation program developed these values within me and they are essential to achieving one of my top priorities: strengthening the military and keeping our forces prepared.

Military training and preparedness is the backbone of our national security. That is why I fight so hard in Congress to properly fund today's military. Unfortunately, since the early 90's, inadequate budgets, extended deployments, and a reduced force have caused major havoc on our military readiness. Delayed acquisition forced personnel to rely on aging equipment, and peace keeping missions overseas meant putting more wear and tear on aging systems that are already operating far beyond their planned lifetime.

President Bush has taken some bold steps to begin the restoration of our military, and Congress has lent its full support. But it is going to take time to achieve that goal, and the continued commitment and funding even as we take on the added and unforeseen costs of fighting the global war on terrorism.

The challenges are real. While U.S. forces today have many of the most advanced technologies, our international competitors -- allies and adversaries alike – have moved forward aggressively while we were ramping down military investments over the past decade. As a result, we cannot match them pound for pound in every technological capability, and we are increasingly losing our longstanding edge in others. That is why we must continue to prioritize training and readiness. That is what has always separated U.S. forces from their competitors, and it is what will ensure our victory in the war on terrorism.

I cannot accept anything less than providing our forces with every tool at our disposal to ensure their success. It is that fighter pilot spirit that guides my personal life and work today and inspires me to keep charging forward. I have always possessed a desire to fly. Aviation is not only my life, it taught me to how to live. It taught me about life and death, good and evil, victory and defeat, and most importantly, being prepared.

A Witness to the Heroism of Many

Silent soldiers, coming back to a silent country; in my mind I still see the young men coming home from war. To have given up so much only to get so little in return, yet despite that, their love for their country is a lesson that each one of us should learn. To those soldiers of my time, Vietnam, I salute you for everything you sacrificed. You will always be my heroes.

K. Pearson
Wilmington, NC

Ronnie Guyer, Vietnam Veteran

"Aloha" Ronnie fought in the Battle of the Ia Drang Valley (1965) made famous by the men who fought there with honor and bravery and immortalized by the Paramount Pictures movie "We Were Soldiers", staring Mel Gibson.

In a new time of war, in a new century, with an enemy that is now just around the corner and up our streets, big time, I am so very proud of the way President George W. Bush and Vice-President Dick Cheney so quickly defined this new threat to our freedom after the attacks of September 11, 2001, and then moved to defeat it.

The 20th Century was the war century that saw the defeat of world Communism and Totalitarianism because so many heroes fought for it so unselfishly.

President Bush has also defined the 21st century as the freedom century by his promising to bring freedom to the oppressed peoples and cultures of the world as America's own best self-defense against future terrorist attacks here at home. This is heroism in the truest sense to me.

As a Vietnam Veteran I never expected to be blessed to live long enough to witness a sitting President commit the United States to bringing about freedom's return to Communist Vietnam, North Korea, Cuba and freedom's arrival to all the countries of the Middle East as America's answer to the world after being viciously attacked in a new century.

I have also been so blessed over my lifetime to have been a witness to the heroism of so many on behalf of others.

As a participant in the Vietnam War's 1st major battle between invading North Vietnamese Communists and American forces in the Valley of Death, that was the Ia Drang valley of Novmeber 1965, I found myself surrounded by Congressional Medal of Honor caliber individuals, some already so recognized for that battle and others soon to be.

But the heroic link I feel so closely bonded to from long ago, and the events of September 11, 2001, would be the heroic actions of one Cyril "Rick" Rescorla, himself so deserving of the Presidential Medal of Freedom Award.

It is Lt. Rick Rescorla's Ia Drang photograph that appropriately graces the cover of the book written about our 1965 battle of the Ia Drang valley titled *We Were Soldiers Once and Young*. This book was written by the American Commander at the battle Lt. Col. Harold G. Moore (now Lt. General Retired), and the UPI war coorespondent at the battle, Joseph L. Galloway. I was one of Lt. Col. Moore's Radiomen in Vietnam.

"Braveheart" star Mel Gibson portrays Lt. Col. Moore in the outstanding Randall Wallace motion picture production of "We Were Soldiers" about our battle based on the Moore-Galloway book. It is Lt. Rick Rescorla that is depicted in this movie picking up an old French/North Vietnamese bugle after the battle, which I have also been blessed to hold. I have named Rick's bugle a symbol of clarity.

Rescorla's heroism in saving the lives of his men while under repeating Communist human wave assaults on their positions in the fight at Landing Zone X-Ray in the Ia Drang valley is indexed on 35 pages of the book. Now that's a hero.

In the battle of the Ia Drang valley Lt. Rick Rescorla sang Cornish hymns (Rick was originally from Cornwall, England) and "God Bless America" to his men to empower them to fight back for victory. They succeeded against overwhelming odds with surprisingly few casualties.

After Rick Rescorla returned home, he went on to earn a Master's degree and Law degree. He then went on to become the Morgan Stanley brokerage house's 1st Vice-President for Security, housed in the 20 middle floors of New York City's World Trade Center Tower 2.

After the World Trade Center bombing in 1993 it was Rick Rescorla who had gotten everyone out of Tower 2. He went back in for stragglers and became known as the last man out. He had even predicted this terrorist attack of 9-11 ahead of time and thus had drilled his employees in regular Tower 2 evacuations.

After accurately predicting air attacks on the World Trade Center after the 1993 bombing, Rescorla continued to drill Morgan Stanley employees under him in regular evacuation drills unceasingly.

After the first jetliner piloted by terrorists slammed into Tower 1 on September 11, 2001, Rick Rescorla immediately started moving everyone out of Tower 2, thus giving 3,700 Morgan Stanley employees an extra 18 minutes head start before the second jetliner hit Tower 2. He calmed them by again singing "God Bless America'" and Cornish hymns to them, just like he did the men of Ia Drang long ago.

Rick was on his way back up Tower 2's stairwell to search for any stragglers in his final search when all came crashing down on him.

Rick Rescorla = A Man for the Ages. And a man whose keen intuitive sense is now being sorely missed in our new world wide War on Terrorism as former CIA Director James Woolsey has proclaimed Rick Rescorla the example for all the rest of us to follow to victory now. Sound familiar?

There is something else that has been really tugging at my heart for over 3 decades. It is the silent heroism of some of my fellow Vietnam Veterans, who, not surprisingly, couldn't handle being so horribly abused upon their return home, that many ended up as a large part of our nation's homeless population as a result.

While some in America called *us* the *terrorists* and *rapists* as opposed to those we were fighting against in a then free South Vietnam, Mel Gibson, on the other hand, was inspired while filming our real story of love and sacrifice to finally make his ultimate love story "The Passion of the Christ."

I wonder who got the story right.

Sign the petition to get Rick Rescorla the Presidential Medal of Freedom at:
www.petitiononline.com/pmfrick/petition.html
or use the link at:
www.ModernDayHeroes.com

They spilled their blood for a confused nation. The Vietnam Veteran fought in a war understood by few, but they fought for a country they loved. Tell us about your experience in Vietnam at-

www.ModernDayHeroes.com

"God Bless America" -
The Story of a P.O.W.

I'm not quite sure what a hero is, but I can tell you what a hero is not. A hero is not some sorry excuse of a man who enlists, or for that matter, is drafted by the nation to serve his country and defend his family from tyranny and death, and then turns his back on his unit and whimpers those "magic" words, "I'm a conscientious objector."

> Dean Kelly
> Long Beach, CA

President George W. Bush -
awarded, posthumously, the Medal of Honor to Vietnam War hero Captain Humbert Roque "Rocky" Versace on July 8, 2002. He is buried in an unmarked grave somewhere in Vietnam. This is the first Medal of Honor to be given to an Army P.O.W. for his actions while a prisoner.

Good afternoon, and welcome to the White House. It's a -- this is a special occasion. I am honored to be a part of the gathering as we pay tribute to a true American patriot, and a hero, Captain Humbert "Rocky" Versace.

Nearly four decades ago, his courage and defiance while being held captive in Vietnam cost him his life. Today it is my great privilege to recognize his extraordinary sacrifices by awarding him the Medal of Honor.

I appreciate Secretary Anthony Principi, the Secretary from the Department of Veteran Affairs, for being here. Thank you for coming, Tony. I appreciate Senator George Allen and Congressman Jim Moran. I want to thank Paul Wolfowitz, the Deputy Secretary of Defense; and General Pete Pace, Vice Chairman of the Joint Chiefs;

Army General Eric Shinseki -- thank you for coming, sir. I appreciate David Hicks being here. He's the Deputy Chief of Chaplains for the United States Army.

I want to thank the entire Versace family for coming -- three brothers and a lot of relatives. Brothers, Dick and Mike and Steve, who's up here on the stage with me today. I appreciate the classmates and friends and supporters of Rocky for coming. I also want to thank the previous Medal of Honor recipients who are here with us today. That would be Harvey Barnum and Brian Thacker and Roger Donlon. Thank you all for coming.

Rocky grew up in this area and attended Gonzaga College High School, right here in Washington, D.C. One of his fellow soldiers recalled that Rocky was the kind of person you only had to know a few weeks before you felt like you'd known him for years. Serving as an intelligence advisor in the Mekong Delta, he quickly befriended many of the local citizens. He had that kind of personality. During his time there he was accepted into the seminary, with an eye toward eventually returning to Vietnam to be able to work with orphans.

Rocky was also a soldier's soldier -- a West Point graduate, a Green Beret, who lived and breathed the code of duty and honor and country. One of Rocky's superiors said that the term "gung-ho" fit him perfectly. Others remember his strong sense of moral purpose and unbending belief in his principles.

As his brother Steve once recalled, "If he thought he was right, he was a pain in the neck." [Laughter.] "If he knew he was right, he was absolutely atrocious." [Laughter.]

When Rocky completed his one-year tour of duty, he volunteered for another tour. And two weeks before his time was up, on October the 29th, 1963, he set out with several companies of South Vietnamese troops, planning to take out a Viet Cong command post. It was a daring mission, and an unusually dangerous one for someone so close to going home to volunteer for.

After some initial successes, a vastly larger Viet Cong force ambushed and overran Rocky's unit. Under siege and suffering from multiple bullet wounds, Rocky kept providing covering fire so that friendly forces could withdraw from the killing zone.

Eventually, he and two other Americans, Lieutenant Nick Rowe and Sergeant Dan Pitzer, were captured, bound and forced to walk barefoot to a prison camp deep within the jungle. For much of the next two years, their home would be bamboo cages, six feet long, two feet wide, and three feet high. They were given little to eat, and little protection against the elements. On nights when their netting was taken away, so many mosquitoes would swarm their shackled feet it looked like they were wearing black socks.

The point was not merely to physically torture the prisoners, but also to persuade them to confess to phony crimes and use their confessions for propaganda. But Rocky's captors clearly had no idea who they were dealing with. Four times he tried to escape, the first time crawling on his stomach because his leg injuries prevented him from walking. He insisted on giving no more information than required by the Geneva Convention; and cited the treaty, chapter and verse, over and over again.

He was fluent in English, French and Vietnamese, and would tell his guards to go to hell in all three. Eventually the Viet Cong stopped using French and Vietnamese in their indoctrination sessions, because they didn't want the sentries or the villagers to listen to Rocky's effective rebuttals to their propaganda. Rocky knew precisely what he was doing. By focusing his captors' anger on him, he made life a measure more tolerable for his fellow prisoners, who looked to him as a role model of principled resistance.

Eventually the Viet Cong separated Rocky from the other prisoners. Yet even in separation, he continued to inspire them. The last time they heard his voice, he was singing "God Bless America" at the top of his lungs.

On September the 26th, 1965, Rocky's struggle ended [in] his execution. In his too short life, he traveled to a distant land to bring the hope of freedom to the people he never met. In his defiance and later his death, he set an example of extraordinary dedication that changed the lives of his fellow soldiers who saw it firsthand. His story echoes across the years, reminding us of liberty's high price, and of the noble passion that caused one good man to pay that price in full.

Last Tuesday [July 2, 2002] would have been Rocky's 65th birthday. So today, we award Rocky -- Rocky Versace -- the first Medal of Honor given to an Army POW for actions taken during captivity in Southeast Asia. We thank his family for so great a sacrifice. And we commit our country to always remember what

Rocky gave -- to his fellow prisoners, to the people of Vietnam, and to the cause of freedom.

Now, Major, please read the citation.

[The citation is read, and the Medal is presented.] [Applause.]

The Society

In my opinion, an American hero is a person who thinks more highly of others than he does of himself. He is ready to lend a hand to help, even if it means putting his life on the line. The underlying motive beneath his behavior is love. In this day and age, when everyone is so self-involved, it's a rare and precious trait indeed.

Nancy Arant Williams
Stover, MO

Governor Mike Huckabee

Hello, this is Gov. Mike Huckabee with a comment from my corner of the Capitol. When we look back on the year 2001, a highlight for many Arkansans will be the celebration we held in October along the banks of the Arkansas River in downtown Little Rock. All who were there that Sunday night were touched by the *Salute To Arkansans In Uniform*. We were able to honor active military personnel, members of the National Guard, members of the Reserves, police officers, firefighters, ambulance service employees, doctors, nurses and other emergency service personnel. The horrible terrorist attacks of Sept. 11 on New York and Washington gave us a renewed appreciation for our men and women in uniform. We realized once more that freedom isn't free. That goes for those in the armed forces along with those who provide security here at home. A day to honor those in uniform was especially meaningful for me since my father was a firefighter at Hope. One of the best visits I've had in years was the one I made on a Sunday afternoon soon after the Sept. 11 attacks. The destination was the New York Fire Department's Ladder Company 3, Battalion 6, which lost seven men in the attacks on the World Trade Center.

Arkansans always have been known for answering the call to duty in a time of crisis. This was a chance for us to honor our Veterans in addition to those currently in uniform. We asked those with uniforms to wear them that Sunday to church. Churches across Arkansas set aside special times during their morning services to honor these men and women. Many of them came in uniform that night. Others wore red, white and blue. I've been impressed with what has occurred in our country since Sept. 11. We can't change what happened that horrible day. We can never bring back the thousands of innocent Americans who perished. But it seems we're now working together to ensure they didn't die in vain. We remember those who fought in World War II as the Greatest Generation. Now, we're engaged in a full-fledged war on terrorism and appear determined to be remembered as a generation also known for its greatness.

Earlier this month on Veterans Day, we had another chance to honor those who have served this country. I'm delighted to announce the director of our state Department of Veterans Affairs, Nick Bacon, recently was elected as the national president of the Congressional Medal of Honor Society. Nick is a true American hero and will now lead an organization made up of other heroes. The Medal of Honor is the highest award that can be given to an American for bravery on the battlefield. Of the more than 3,400 Medals of Honor awarded since its inception during the Civil War, about 170 recipients are still alive. Less than 1,200 Medals of Honor have been awarded since the start of World War II due to a changed order of precedence for military decorations. You can see what a rare honor this is. The Congressional Medal of Honor Society was chartered by Congress in 1958. The goal of the society is to educate and inspire the youth of this country with the message that no obstacle is too big to overcome if you have a winning attitude.

Nick distinguished himself while serving as an Army Staff Sergeant on Aug. 26, 1968, west of Tam Ky, Vietnam. When his company came under fire from an enemy bunker, Nick quickly organized his men and led them forward in an assault. He advanced on the hostile bunker and destroyed it with grenades. As he did so, several of his fellow soldiers, including the platoon leader, were struck by machine-gun fire and fell wounded in an exposed position. Nick immediately assumed command of the platoon and assaulted the hostile gun position, killing the entire machine-gun crew by himself. When another platoon moved to Nick's location, its leader also was wounded. Without hesitation, Nick took charge of the additional platoon and continued the fight. He killed four more enemy soldiers and silenced an anti-tank weapon. Due to his leadership, the members of both platoons accepted his authority without question. Continuing to ignore intense hostile fire, he climbed on the exposed deck of a tank and directed fire into the enemy position while several wounded men were evacuated. As a result of his efforts, his company was able to move forward, eliminate the enemy positions and rescue the men who had been trapped.

Fortunately, few of us will ever be in a battle such as the one Nick was in that late summer day in 1968. Yet we're all in this domestic battle against terrorism. If you were to ask Nick Bacon, his message to his fellow Arkansans would be to move forward with our lives rather than allowing ourselves to be consumed by fear. As we move into the Christmas season, we should remember the perseverance and faith in God exhibited by Nick Bacon and thousands like him throughout our country's history. Until next week, this is Gov. Mike Huckabee.

**Have a Medal of Honor story? Tell us at -
www.ModernDayHeroes.com**

Honor the Sacrifices

Heroes are those whose actions, in the defense of others, place them in danger of injury or death. Risking one's life to help another, without thought of personal gain, is a heroic deed.

C. E. (Chuck) Cassity
Costa Mesa, CA

U.S. Representative James A. Leach

Memorial Day is an occasion for reflection. Particularly this year.

The first Memorial Day was celebrated in 1868 when Commander in Chief John A. Logan of the Grand Army of the Republic issued a general order setting aside May 30 of that year "for the purpose of strewing with flowers or otherwise decorating the graves of comrades who died in defense of their country during the late rebellion."

Thus its other name, Decoration Day, calls to mind that it is a day to remember those whose sacrifice in this nation's struggles have preserved the way of life we are so prone to take for granted.

There is much to remember.

The 20th century was one of almost continuous warfare. It was hoped World War I would be the war to end wars. But it was followed by World War II and then the Cold War and the more contained but no less heroic Korean, Vietnam, and Gulf wars. Each left scars on successive generations of Americans.

At the end of the century the hope was that the enormous toll these conflicts had exacted had purchased Americans the right to celebrate. The 21st century began with our values -- democracy, individual rights, free markets -- vindicated.

The atrocities of last September [2001] brought a rude awakening. American sacrifices have been noted by the world, but the cause of freedom knows no respite. Human history is the story of struggle. Violence, to date, has been an integral part of the human condition. What changes are circumstances.

This Memorial Day finds the United States standing alone as the preeminent power in a world for which the two great "isms" of hate -- fascism and communism -- are now fast becoming footnotes in the story of humankind. Instead of a world divided between East and West, America faces a more troubling division -- that between the "haves" and the "have nots," not simply in economic terms, but in terms of that most precious of human commodities, hope.

What is different in terms of security is that a free society is so totally vulnerable to terrorism.

There are many lessons of 9/11, but one that stands out is that it is easy to destroy. A few can inflict great havoc on many. Anarchy is terrorism's fellow traveler.

More sobering still is the premise that, for the first time in history, weapons exist that jeopardize life itself on the planet. And access to these weapons is becoming wider, not only between nations states, but potentially by terrorist organizations accountable to no government.

Just as the invention of gunpowder made possible the nation-state because it made the castle-based feudal system indefensible, so terrorism makes modern civilization vulnerable.

As an instrument of envy and fanatical hatred, terrorism cannot be guarded against simply by maintaining a strong army. Its causes must be understood and dealt with at their roots.

This Memorial Day we honor the sacrifices of the past. We can best do that by recommitting the enormous material and spiritual resources bequeathed to us by that past to addressing the causes of the despair that gives rise to the desperation, the disease, the hunger, the perceived lack of respect that are robbing so many in the world of their future.

We can lead because we have the means. But our leadership has meaning principally because of the models of sacrifice that generations of Americans have provided their country. We are in their debt.

You Stood Watch

An American hero is someone who selflessly risks, sacrifices, or gives of his well-being to uplift, care for, or rescue a person or people in need.

Andrew Parris
Lakewood, CO

Gordon R. England, Secretary of the Navy

In 1918, at the 11th hour, of the 11th day, of the 11th month, the guns of World War I fell silent. After years of bloody struggle, "the war to end all wars" had at last come to a close. This is the genesis of Veterans Day. Throughout the 20th century, more wars, suffering, and sacrifice followed this devastating conflict.

In 1954, President Dwight Eisenhower issued a proclamation calling on the nation to "solemnly remember the sacrifices of all those who fought so valiantly, on the seas, in the air, and on foreign shores, to preserve our heritage of freedom, and let us reconsecrate ourselves to the task of promoting an enduring peace so that their efforts shall not have been in vain."

Today the words of Eisenhower retain their deep, profound meaning.

Your service abroad and at home calls for many sacrifices, but we have fought hard to not only preserve our freedom and way of life, but to bring freedom to the oppressed. We continue to engage throughout the world, and by working to rebuild Iraq and Afghanistan we are helping to bring hope for the future and an enduring peace.

You can take pride in the knowledge that future generations will pause on this day to remember your contributions to peace. They will remember how you defeated brutal tyrants in Afghanistan and Iraq, removing the enemy with one hand and restoring hope with the other. They will remember your countless acts of compassion and service around the world from bringing stability to the Liberia to fighting fires in California and helping your neighbors in the wake of hurricane Isabel. They will remember that you stood watch at the front lines in America's defense and defeated every threat.

As we remember those who have gone before us, so too will you be remembered by generations yet unborn. I am deeply honored to stand with those who serve the cause of Freedom. Our nation is grateful to you and your families for your service and sacrifice. May God bless our Veterans, and may God continue to bless the United States of America.

Share your story with us at -
www.ModernDayHeroes.com
"As a Veteran of years of service, the answer you seek is very simple.

A hero is a person who is willing to pay the ultimate price for the sake of others...without regret, hesitation, remorse. A person who seeks not glory, fame or fortune but gives it all cause they care. That is a hero."
– Anonymous Veteran

You Must Be a Veteran

I think a modern day hero is an individual who lives a life of integrity demonstrated by uncompromising, principled and value driven life choices that impact others in a profound way.

Carlos Martinez
Costa Mesa, CA

U.S. Representative John Shimkus

How many of you have pulled all night duty just to be rewarded with a full day's work ahead of you?

Then you must be a Veteran.

How many of you have stood guard in the sun, rain, snow, and sleet sometimes during the same shift?

Then you must be a Veteran.

How many of you have received cookies from home in 1,000 pieces broken precisely in enough pieces to feed your brigade?

Then you must be a Veteran.

How many of you have been called everything but your name and this was on a good day?

Then you must be a Veteran.

How many of you have slept under a starry sky on another continent, wondering if these are the same stars you used to see at home?

Then you must be a Veteran.

How many of you have saluted and stood when Old Glory marches in front of you?

Then you must be a Veteran.

How many of you have carried a casket of a friend with the flag draped over it, understanding that someday you too will have that same honor?

Then you must be a Veteran.

I too am a proud Veteran and a member of American Legion Post 365 in Collinsville. As a West Point graduate I am a Major in the Army Reserve.

I am concerned that we as citizens have lost our bearings as to our responsibility. In the military we used the Code of Conduct to keep us on track of our overall responsibilities, especially in adversity. Now it might be time for a Citizen Code of Conduct. Some would say we as a society are experiencing great adversity. I'll use the Military Code of Conduct as a draft for the Citizen Code of Conduct. I've carried this in my wallet longer than I can remember.

Military Code of Conduct	Citizens Code of Conduct
I am an American fighting man. I serve in the forces which guard my country and our way of life. I am prepared to give my life in their defense.	I am an American citizen. I am blessed with this opportunity to live in a free and bountiful land. I accept the rights and responsibilities of citizenship.
I will never surrender of my own free will. If in command, I will never surrender my men while they sill have the means to resist.	I will not allow the corrosive elements of cynicism, distrust, and hatred to destroy my feelings for my country. I will do all in my power to promote the good and welfare of the state and her citizens.
If I am captured, I will continue to resist by all means available. I will make every effort to escape and aid others to escape. I will accept neither parole nor special favors from the enemy.	The cornerstones of this great country are faith in God, individual responsibility, and charity toward others. Even when assaulted by materialism, power, prestige and immortality I will remember the God who made me and cares for me.

Military Code of Conduct	Citizens Code of Conduct
If I become a prisoner of war, I will keep faith with my fellow prisoners. I will give no information or take part in any action which might be harmful to my comrades. If I am senior, I will take command. If not, I will obey the lawful orders of those appointed over me and will back them in every way.	I will play this game of life by the rules. I will not lie, cheat, or steal, nor will I tolerate those who do. I will lead by example, always building up my fellow citizens, not tearing them down.
When questioned, should I become a prisoner of war, I am required to give only name, rank, service number, and date of birth. I will evade answering further questions to the utmost of my ability. I will make no oral or written statements disloyal to my country and its allies or harmful to their causes.	When I stumble, I will remember that this is America – the land of the free and the home of the brave, the land of endless opportunities. I will stay loyal to my forefathers who from the sweat of their brow became successful. I too will succeed.
I will never forget that I am an American fighting man, responsible for my actions, and dedicated to the principles which made my country free. I will trust in my God and in the United States of America.	I will never forget that I am a United States citizen responsible for my actions, and dedicated to the principles which made my country free. I will trust in my God and in the United States of America.

Good citizenship is promoted by Veterans. I salute you for your efforts. Keep up the good work.

The History of Heroes

Have you ever seen an American hero? They don't wear signs and they won't tell you that they are a hero. Here in America you can see them everywhere, but they are unrecognizable unless there is a catastrophe. Instantly you would then see the heroes we've raised right here in America. Simple, plain, standing strong.

An American hero doesn't think of himself/herself when there is calamity, chaos, or violence. An American hero selflessly runs to the rescue without thought of pain, death or humiliation. An American hero doesn't need praise or adoration. An American hero is just doing what comes natural: risking it all for someone, anyone when the need arises. Standing up for what is right is part of being an American.

An American hero keeps his/her head and doesn't panic. He/she makes quick, lightning fast decisions that save the lives of others, usually strangers. When the work is done is when they will cry.

This kind of person dwells in most Americans. You see it when there is peril, destruction or death, like on 9/11. Big hearted people from all walks of life risking their lives to save the lives of others. To stop hurt, unfairness and pain is all they want to do.

Most American heroes have no idea that they are American heroes. Luckily for us they just ARE fearless, strong and God fearing American heroes. Thank God!

Leslie McIsaac
Orange, CA

U.S. Representative Ron Kind

Last year, on Veterans Day, I held an event that brought together local school children with a number of their area war

Veterans. The purpose was to give the students a chance to meet some of those who served in battle, and learn first-hand of the courage, triumphs and horrors Americans' have faced in this country's wars. Students often tell me that history is their hardest subject in school, but I stood and watched the kids absorb the stories the Veterans told them of their time in service. What these students received was more than just a chronicle of a tumultuous time, but history made personal by a cast of everyday people who we asked to do extraordinary things under extraordinary circumstances.

Sadly, future generations will not have the same benefit we have in hearing directly from those who helped shape our nation's future through their honor, courage, and commitment during times of war. Today, 19 million American Veterans are still alive. Of the 4.7 million who served in WWI, there are only 3,400 Veterans still among us. From the 16.5 million Americans who served in WWII, 6 million remain, but 1500 pass away each day. Clearly, we should take steps to preserve our Veterans' eye-witness accounts to history before they become forever lost to time.

That is why I authored the Veterans Oral History Project, HR 5212. This broadly supported, bipartisan legislation will encourage war Veterans, their families, Veterans groups, communities and students to video-tape the recollections of Veterans' time in service, and forward the tapes to the Library of Congress. This legislation also encourages Veterans to share copies of written materials, such as diaries and letters home. The Library of Congress will create an easily accessible electronic archive of these written documents and oral histories for future use by families, students, historians, and all interested in U.S. history.

We all owe a huge debt of gratitude to those tough and courageous men and women who ensured the freedoms that Americans enjoy today. Their stories exemplify how men and women are often sustained during their wartime service by the simple ideals of patriotism, family, and duty. Current technology gives us a unique opportunity to capture the memories of these Veterans and preserve them as a vital part of our nation's history. If we are to truly honor our Veterans, we should preserve their memories for future generations. I hope Congress will act quickly to pass my legislation so we can begin to collect this important part of our nation's history.

The Veterans Oral History Project, HR 5212, was authored by Representative Ron Kind and introduced in the Senate By Senator Chuck Hagel. This legislation established the Veterans' Oral History Project, authorized by Congress in 2001 to be maintained by the Library of Congress. The project's purpose is to collect the oral histories of our Veterans and those who served to support them during their service to our country. The project collects and preserves videotaped interviews, photocopies of any written material and photographs they may have kept from their wartime experiences. More information can be found at:

www.loc.gov/folklife/vets/
or link to it at:
www.ModernDayHeroes.com

To give your life to the cause of freedom is the definition of nobility. But those who have lost their lives for our country's sake are not the only heroes of our past and present. Those that have paid a price far greater than death itself, are those that hold the physical and mental scars of war as they continue to walk with us today.

Some would argue, from a powerful position, that our soldiers who have lost a limb or have been marked by burns on their body and continue with us still today, with a flag on their heart and a singular passion for our country on their mind, are a breed of hero that inspires our country and leaves a powerful sense of fear in our enemies.

These great men are the heroes America still needs to hear from today. Contact us with your story at -
www.ModernDayHeroes.com

Darkest of Hours

An American hero is one who holds responsibility to community, country and faith ahead of himself and acts accordingly.

Tim DeCinces
Costa Mesa, CA

President Ronald Reagan -
shared these thoughts with the Baptist Fundamentalism Annual Convention on April 13, 1984 at the District of Columbia Convention Center. He was introduced by the Reverend Jerry Falwell.

Reverend Falwell, ladies and gentlemen, thank you very much, for there are no words to describe a welcome such as you've given me here. It's a real pleasure to be with so many who firmly believe that the answers to the world's problems can be found in the Word of God.

I'm only sorry I can't spend the entire evening with you, but I'm expected across town. [Laughter.] But tonight, believe me, I came here with some trepidation, and your warm welcome didn't exactly make me feel any easier, because I'm going to do something that I haven't done before. I'm not going to talk to you about some of the things we've talked about before and some of the things that we've tried to accomplish and that we haven't yet. With regard to that, I will only say let us all heed the words of an old Scotch ballad, ``For those defeats that we've had so far, we are hurt; we are not slain. We'll lie us down and rest a bit, and then we'll fight again."

What I'm going to do -- and I know you're not supposed to apologize any time you start speaking for what you're going to say -- but I know that even you, whose calling it is to keep the rest of us, if possible, on the right path, in these days of cynicism, in these days when there are people that in the guise of separating church and state would go so far as to say we should not even have chaplains in the military service -- I know that there are times when all of us wonder whether we're being effective. And tonight, I'd like to share an account that I received that shows how God works in our lives even in the darkest of hours.

This report concerns the Marines in Beirut, brave men who believed that the goal we sought in that place was worthy of their best and gave their best. In the end, hatred centuries old made it impossible for Lebanon to achieve peace when we and so many others hoped it would. But while they were there, those young men of ours prevented widespread killing in Beirut, and they added luster, not tarnish to their motto, "Semper Fidelis."

I'm going to read to you another man's words. And they're words that, perhaps, answer what I said a moment ago about whether we sometimes were shaken in our faith and in our beliefs. On that October day when a terrorist truck bomb took the lives of 241 marines, soldiers, and sailors at the airport in Beirut, one of the first to reach the tragic scene was a chaplain, the chaplain of our 6th Fleet, Rabbi Arnold E. Resnicoff. And here is what he finally felt urged at the end of that day to put down in writing of the experiences of that day.

He said, "I, along with Lieutenant Commander George 'Pooch' Pucciarelli, the Catholic chaplain attached to the Marine unit, faced a scene almost too horrible to describe. Bodies and pieces of bodies were everywhere. Screams of those injured or trapped were barely audible at first, as our minds struggled to grapple with the reality before us -- a massive four-story building, reduced to a pile of rubble; dust mixing with smoke and fire, obscuring our view of the little that was left.

"Because we'd thought that the sound of the explosion was still related to a single rocket or shell, most of the Marines had run toward the foxholes and bunkers while we, the chaplains, had gone to the scene of the noise, just in case someone had been wounded. Now, as the news spread quickly throughout the camp -- news of the magnitude of the tragedy, news of the need for others to run to the aid of those comrades who still might be alive, Marines came from all directions. There was a sense of God's presence that day in the small miracles of life which we encountered in each body that, despite all odds, still had a breath within. But there was more of His presence, more to keep our faith alive, in the heroism and in the humanity of the men who responded to the cries for help. We saw Marines risk their own lives again and again as they went into the smoke and the fire to try to pull someone out or as they worked to uncover friends, all the while knowing that further collapse of huge pieces of concrete, precariously perched like dominos, could easily crush the rescuers.

"There was humanity at its best that day and a reminder not to give up the hope and dreams of what the world could be in the tears that could still be shed by these men, regardless of how cynical they had pretended to be before, regardless of how much they might have seen before.

"Certain images will stay with me always," he writes. "I remember a Marine who found a wad of money amidst the rubble. He held it at arm's length as if it were dirty and cried out for a match or a lighter so that it could be burned. No one that day wanted to profit from the suffering of catastrophe. Later the chaplains would put the word out that the money should be collected and given to us, for we were sure that a fund for widows and orphans would ultimately be established. But at that moment, I was hypnotized with the rest of the men and watched as the money was burned.

"Working with the wounded -- sometimes comforting, simply letting them know help was on the way; sometimes trying to pull and carry those whose injuries appeared less dangerous in an immediate sense than the approaching fire or the smothering smoke -- my kippa was lost. That is the little headgear that is worn by rabbis. The last I remember it, I'd used it to mop someone's brow. Father Pucciarelli, the Catholic chaplain, cut a circle out of his cap -- a piece of camouflaged cloth which would become my temporary headcovering. Somehow he wanted those Marines to know not just that we were chaplains, but that he was a Christian and that I was Jewish. Somehow we both wanted to shout the message in a land where people were killing each other -- at least partially based on the differences in religion among them -- that we, we Americans still believed that we could be proud of our particular religions and yet work side by side when the time came to help others, to comfort, and to ease pain.

"Father Pucciarelli and I worked that day as brothers. The words from the prophet Malachi kept recurring to me -- words he'd uttered some 2,500 years ago as he had looked around at fighting and cruelty and pain. 'Have we not all one Father?' he had asked. 'Has not one God created us all?' It was painfully obvious, tragically obvious, that our world still could not show that we had learned to answer, yes. Still, I thought, perhaps some of us can keep the question alive. Some of us can cry out, as the Marines did that day, that we believe the answer is yes.

"Before the bombing, Pooch -- that's his name for the other chaplain with him -- and I had been in a building perhaps a hundred yards away. There'd been one other chaplain, Lieutenant Danny Wheeler, a Protestant minister who'd spent the night in the building which was attacked. Pooch and I were so sure that he was dead that we had promised each other that when the day came to return to the States we would visit his wife together. Suddenly, Pooch noticed Danny's stole, what he used to call his Protestant tallith. Because it was far from the area Danny was supposed to have been in, there was cautious hope that perhaps he had been thrown clear, that perhaps he had survived. Later, Danny would tell the story of his terror. He was under the rubble, alive, not knowing what had happened and not knowing how badly he was hurt. Then he heard voices of the Marines searching near his stole. And his cry for help was answered with digging, which lasted 4 hours before he was dragged out alive.

"Danny told me later that I treated him like a newborn baby when he came out; that I counted his fingers and toes, trying to see that he was whole. I didn't realize that I was so obvious, but the truth is that we couldn't believe that he was in one piece. I hugged him as they brought over a stretcher. I can still hear his first words. Wracked with pain, still unsure of his own condition, he asked how his clerk was. Like so many of the men we would save that day, he asked first about others.

"These men, the survivors, still had no idea of the extent of the damage. They still thought that perhaps they'd been in the one area of the building hit by a rocket or mortar. We would wait until later to sit with these men and tell them the truth, to share with them the magnitude of the tragedy. After the living were taken out there was much more work to be done. With the wounded, with those who had survived, there was the strange job of trying to ease a gnawing feeling of guilt that would slowly surface, guilt that they -- -- "

[At this point, the President was interrupted by persons chanting, "Bread, not bombs!"]

Wouldn't it be nice if a little bit of that Marine spirit would rub off, and they would listen about brotherly love?

[Applause. The chanting continued.]

I was talking about the guilt that was felt by the men who were alive; the guilt that they had somehow let down their comrades by not dying with them. That is something that happens a great deal in combat.

"So, our job," he said, "was to tell them how every life saved was important to us; how their survival was important to our faith and our hope. They had to give thanks with us that they still had the gift and the responsibility of life which would go on -- -- "

[The chanting continued.]

I've got more decibels at work for me than they have.

[Applause. At this point, there was some commotion in the audience.]

I think they're leaving. [Applause] Well, back to the chaplain. [Laughter]

"With others, the Marines who stayed behind to continue the job of digging -- a terrible, horrifying job of collecting human parts for identification and for eventual burial -- there was the job of comforting them as they mourned.

"Thankfully, the self-defense mechanism within us took over from time to time and we were able to work without reacting to each and every horror that we would encounter. But suddenly something would trigger our emotions, something would touch our humanity in a way impossible to avoid. For some it would be the finding of a friend's body, someone filled with life only days before. For others, it would be a scrap of paper or a simple belonging, a birthday card or a picture of someone's children which would remind them that this was no abstract body count of 240 military casualties. This was a tragedy of people where each was unique and each had a story. Each had a past and each had been cheated of a future. As the Mishnah puts it, 'Each was a world.' We were not digging up 240. We were digging up one plus one plus one.

"I have a personal memory of two things which brought to my mind images of life, images which haunt me still. One was a packet of three envelopes tied together with a rubber band. On top, under the band, was a note which read, 'To be mailed in case of death.' The other was a Red Cross message delivered the next morning. The American Red Cross is the agency used by many Navy families to communicate medical news from home. This message was a birth announcement. A baby had been born, and we were to deliver the good news. Only now, there was no father whom we could congratulate, no father to whom the news could be conveyed. That message stayed on the chaplains' desk for days. Somehow we couldn't throw it away, so it stayed on the desk and without mentioning it, we all seemed to avoid that desk.

"I stayed in Beirut for 4 more days before finally returning to Italy and to my family. During those days, as the work went on, a Marine here or there would send a silent signal that he wanted me, that is, a chaplain, near. Sometimes it was to talk. Sometimes it was so that he could shrug his shoulders or lift his eyes in despair. Sometimes it was just to feel that I was near. For despite the struggles I might be feeling on a personal level, I was a chaplain and, therefore, a symbol that there was room for hope and for dreams, even at the worst of times.

"In our tradition, of course, when we visit the home of a mourner during Shiva, the first week following the death of a loved one, visitors follow a simple rule: If the mourner initiates the conversation, the visitor responds. Otherwise, you sit in silence, communicating concern through your very presence, even without words. Somehow I applied those rules during those days of digging. When a soldier or sailor said something, I responded. Otherwise, I stood by.

"During all of my visits to Beirut, I, along with the other chaplains, spent much time simply speaking with the men. Informal discussions, whether going on while crouched in a foxhole or strolling toward the tents set up for chow, were just as important as anything formal we might set up.

"I remember the first time I jumped in a foxhole, the first time the shells actually fell within the U.S. area. Looking around at the others in there with me, I made the remark that we probably had the only interfaith foxholes in Beirut. The Druze, the Muslims, Christians, all had theirs. The Jewish forces in the Israeli Army had theirs. But we were together. I made the comment then that perhaps if the world had more interfaith foxholes, there might be less of a need for foxholes altogether.

"To understand the role of the chaplain -- Jewish, Catholic, or Protestant -- is to understand that we try to remind others, and perhaps ourselves as well, to cling to our humanity even in the worst of times. We bring with us the wisdom of men and women whose faith has kept alive their dreams in ages past. We bring with us the images of what the world could be, of what we ourselves might be, drawn from the visions of prophets and the promises of our holy books. We bring with us the truth that faith not only reminds us of the holy in heaven, but also of the holiness we can create here on Earth. It brings not only a message of what is divine, but also of what it means to be truly human.

"It's too easy to give in to despair in a world sometimes seemingly filled with cruelty and brutality. But we must remember not just the depths to which humans might sink, but also the heights to which they may aspire.

"That October day in Beirut saw men reach heroic heights -- indeed, heights of physical endurance and courage to be sure, but heights of sacrifice, of compassion, of kindness, and of simple human decency as well, and, even if the admission might bring a blush to the cheeks of a few of the Marines, heights of love.

"Long ago the rabbis offered one interpretation of the Biblical verse which tells us that we're created in the image of God. It does not refer to physical likeness, they explained, but to spiritual potential. We have within us the power to reflect as God's creatures the highest values of our Creator. As God is forgiving and merciful, so can we be; as He is caring and kind, so must we strive to be; as He is filled with love, so must we be.

"Because of the actions I witnessed during that hell in Beirut, I glimpsed at least a fleeting image of heaven, for in the hearts and hands of men who chose to act as brothers, I glimpsed God's hand as well. I did not stand alone to face a world forsaken by God. I felt I was part of one created with infinite care and wonderful, awesome potential.

"We live in a world where it's not hard to find cause for despair. The chaplain has the challenge to bring to those who often see terror at its worst, some reason for hope. We need to keep faith and to keep searching, even in the worst of times. Only then may we find strength enough to keep believing that the best of times might still be."

These were the words of Lieutenant Commander Resnicoff. I read them because I just felt that all of us -- and I know how much you do of this -- let us strive to live up to the vision of faith that Chaplain Resnicoff saw that day, and let us never stop praying and working for peace.

Thank God, and thank you, and God bless you all.

**Have a story of a military chaplain? Share the story at -
www.ModernDayHeroes.com**

Chapter 2

The Heroes
at Home

To Protect and Serve

The definition of what makes a hero is constant--it never changes.

A hero knows what is right and does it. They have the willingness and courage to stand against great opposition. They do not think of themselves, but of others.

A hero loves truth with all of their heart, soul, and might. Their entire being is guided by truth. A hero is unselfish and humble.

Modern examples of American heroes are our Founding Fathers, Booker T. Washington, Dr. King, Clarence Thomas, and Condoleezza Rice. They are excellent examples of what we all can be.

Rev. Jesse Lee Peterson
Author of *Scam: How the Black Leadership Exploits Black America*

U.S. Senator Mike DeWine

I rise today to pay tribute to a dear and cherished friend -- a mentor and a role model -- former Yellow Springs, Ohio, chief of police of 34 years, Jim McKee, who passed away on January 18, 2003, at the age of 73.

Raised in Springfield, Ohio, Jim McKee moved to Yellow Springs when he was 18 years old, fresh out of high school, in search of a job. During his first year in Yellow Springs, Jim held a number of different positions, working in a shoe repair shop and later at Mills Lawn Elementary School. It was in First Grade at Mills Lawn Elementary School where I first met my future wife Frances, but it was also at Mills Lawn where I first met Jim McKee.

Jim was the person who kept things going at Mills Lawn. I remember how much respect, love, and admiration the students had for Jim. He had an incredible ability to connect with people. I saw it as a child. I remember he would gather the students together and talk to them about how we needed to keep the place looking good and how important that was. I remember how we looked up to him and how much we respected him.

Eventually, Jim McKee took a job at Wright Patterson Air Force Base near Yellow Springs. But by 1957, Jim decided he needed to move on and do something he had always dreamed of doing -- and that was to get involved in law enforcement. This was his chance, his opportunity. Before long, he was realizing that dream. The village of Yellow Springs hired him as a police officer. He joined a department of two officers and a chief. Within two short years and in recognition of his talent and his hard work, Jim McKee was appointed chief of police.

In this new leadership position, Jim McKee soon found himself dealing with issues he probably did not think he was going to be dealing with -- issues of historic importance, because at that time, the civil rights movement was beginning to sweep our country. The civil rights movement had reached my hometown of Yellow Springs, a small community in southwest Ohio, and it reached us there sooner than most other parts of the country.

Jim McKee was one of the few African-American chiefs of police in the State of Ohio. Jim McKee guided my hometown with great skill through a very difficult period of time. As one of the few African-American chiefs of police in the State -- really one of the few in the country at the time -- Jim McKee faced his own civil rights issues early on in the movement. Everybody in Yellow Springs -- a community then and now of great diversity and a community that then and now embodies a person's right to free speech -- everybody in Yellow Springs respected and liked Jim McKee. That made all the difference in the world.

Whether Jim realized it or not during this tumultuous era, Jim was, in fact, playing a part in our American history. Jim McKee kept the peace, maintained order, and all the while respected people's freedom of speech, their right to demonstrate, and their civil rights. He did it in a professional way.

I remember when Dr. Martin Luther King came to Yellow Springs to deliver the commencement address at Antioch College. Chief McKee, of course, provided his security detail. Years later, recalling this experience with Dr. King, Chief McKee had this to say:

"At the time, there were rumors they were out to get him. I saw him do his nonviolent teachings. I drove around in the car with him for two days. He was a perfect Christian gentleman, and I was frightened to death because I was providing his security. We told people he was staying at the Antioch Inn, but in fact he was right across the street from where I live -- in the home his wife, Coretta, lived in as a student at Antioch years before. You would think they would have figured it out, with all the police cruisers parked out front. I was never so glad to see a plane take off."

Despite whatever concerns Jim McKee may have had, the chief performed his duties with a great sense of professionalism, with honor, and with courage.

Though he dealt with significant issues on the national stage, Chief McKee dedicated his career to Yellow Springs and to keeping the community he loved so much safe and free from crime. As Members of the Senate know -- or may not know -- Yellow Springs is not a large city. It is a village. It is a small village, where people know their neighbors and watch out for one another. Even today, I believe there are probably only about eight or so police officers on the force. Chief McKee, as the local police chief, was really an icon in his own community. He was greatly admired and respected as an officer, as a protector, but most of all as a friend.

Though I first met him as a First Grader, I had the opportunity later on to reconnect with Jim. Our lives came together again when I became assistant county prosecuting attorney and he was by that time the dean of the chiefs of police in Greene County. We worked on a number of cases that arose out of Yellow Springs, several very difficult rape cases. We worked on several of those cases together. During this time, I learned a great deal about how Chief McKee treated people and how he dealt with some of the most tense situations. Perhaps most importantly, though, I saw his great sense of humanity toward both victims and suspects.

Chief Jim McKee taught me there is much more to police work than arrests and convictions. He taught me about the human component in police work. He taught me about people and about compassion. I remember one instance, in particular, when I saw and learned about how Jim McKee dealt with a man who had been in an auto accident. This man was involved in a horrible thing, as many accidents are, but he came out of it. He walked out of the accident, but the other person in the other vehicle did not and the other person died. This particular person was actually a suspect, and he could have been charged. The police were looking at and trying to decide whether to charge him.

Actually, later on there was a grand jury that was convened. The grand jury had to make a decision whether this person was going to be charged and would have to stand trial. Eventually, they decided not to charge him, but Jim did not know that at the time. I saw how Jim dealt with this man and showed this man, who was going through great anguish at the time, a man who was really a suspect, and I saw how Jim worked him through this, how he talked to him, and how he showed great kindness to him.

That is how Jim McKee treated everyone -- with great kindness and with great compassion -- all the time being a professional, all the time doing his job. It was this compassion that set Jim McKee apart. He cared deeply about people and just knew how to deal with them.

At the end of Chief McKee's distinguished 36-year career in law enforcement, I had the honor of attending his farewell banquet. I was Lieutenant Governor at the time and was there to pay tribute to the chief on behalf of the entire State of Ohio, and on behalf of Governor, then-Governor George Voinovich. At this reception and this dinner, I was struck by the sheer outpouring of respect and admiration and appreciation for Chief McKee's work and for his selfless contributions to our community. It was clear at this reception how important Chief McKee was to the people, to the village of Yellow Springs, and to the entire law enforcement community across the State of Ohio. I was proud to be part of this memorable event.

Following his retirement from the force in 1993, Chief McKee remained active in the community until the day he died. He was a key member of the Yellow Springs Men's Group, an organization dedicated to studying issues important to the day-to-day lives of Yellow Springs residents. Through this organization, the James A. McKee scholarship fund was established in 2002 as a tribute both to Jim and to his legacy of community involvement.

In the recent days following Jim's death, a number of newspapers ran articles about his life and his legacy. As I read through these tributes, I was especially taken with a statement from my friend, Paul Ford, who had known Chief McKee since 1949. This is what Mr. Ford said:

> "We've lost a good citizen, a good friend, and a humanitarian. Once you met Jim, you were a friend."

Indeed, Jim McKee was my friend and someone for whom I had great affection and admiration. This quote really gets to why Chief McKee was so special to the community of Yellow Springs and to all of us who knew him. He dedicated his life to serving the people of Yellow Springs. He worked to keep his community safe and free from crime.

Mr. President, when I think about Jim McKee and his life's work as a police officer and protector of the community, I am reminded of a Bible passage from Matthew, "Blessed are the peacemakers for they shall be called the children of God." Indeed, Chief Jim McKee was a peacemaker and a protector and just a good and decent hard-working man. He was a kind person, a kind human being who always tried to do the right thing for his family, for his community, and for his nation.

My wife, Fran, and I extend our heartfelt sympathy and our prayers to the entire McKee family -- to his wife of 54 years, Naomi; his four daughters, Bari McKee-Teamor, Karen McKee, Jean McKee, and Sandra McKee-Smith; his son, Jimmy; his five grandchildren; and his one great-grandson.

Jim McKee loved his family. He cared deeply for them. I know they, like all of us, will miss him tremendously. Thank you, Jim, for all you did for Yellow Springs and for our nation. You will be remembered always in our minds and in our hearts.

Brave, Courageous, Fearless, and Tough as Nails

An American hero is someone who is willing to give up their own safety or sense of well-being in order to protect someone else's right to free speech, liberty or guarantee of equality. It is putting yourself at risk for a principle that is greater or more noble than life itself.

Susan Sullam
Baltimore, MD

U.S. Senator Mike DeWine

I rise today to pay tribute to Steve Young -- an Ohioan who dedicated his life to keeping our communities safe and free from crime. Steve was a well-known and well-respected figure in the law enforcement community, who was elected by his peers to serve as the National President of the Fraternal Order of Police. He held this post until his death from cancer last week on January 9th [2002]. He was just 49 years old.

Steve grew up in Upper Sandusky, Ohio, and was a graduate of Upper Sandusky High School. He joined the Marion City Police Department in 1976, and spent his entire law enforcement career as an active duty officer there. It was in Marion that Steve first became a member of the FOP, joining FOP Lodge #24. Steve later went on to serve as President of this Lodge and in the Year 2000, he received the prestigious lifetime honor of President Emeritus.

Leadership in the law enforcement community came naturally to Steve, as his hard work and dedication earned him the respect and admiration of his peers. Steve went on to become active in the Ohio State Lodge of the FOP and served first as Vice President and then as President -- representing Ohio's 24,000 law enforcement officers. Through the Ohio State Lodge, Steve helped to create the Ohio Labor Council. This council created a model for improved management-labor negotiations in police forces -- a model that now has been adopted in at least 14 other states.

Steve's leadership in the Ohio law enforcement community and his expertise in labor issues earned him a national reputation. In 2001, after serving for four years as National Vice President, Steve was unanimously elected to serve as the National President of the FOP. In this capacity, Steve represented over 300,000 law enforcement officers and worked to protect the interests of our nation's finest. This was a job he loved and one that he did with great dignity and pride.

Mr. President, while Steve Young had an incredibly successful career with multiple accomplishments, I would also like to take a few moments today to discuss my personal connection with Steve. I had the privilege of knowing not just Steve Young the officer, but also Steve Young the man. Steve was a dear friend for many years. He was someone in whom I had great trust and was fortunate to be able to call on him as a trusted adviser.

Whether it was when I was Lt. Governor of Ohio or as a United States Senator, I had the opportunity to work with Steve for many years, and I relied heavily on his advice and expertise. I consulted with him regularly on criminal justice issues and his keen insights have helped shape nearly every piece of crime legislation that I have written. Steve made a lasting impression on law enforcement both in Ohio and across our nation. From pension plans to crime fighting technology, Steve's foresight and vision have helped bring law enforcement into the 21st century.

One of the last times I saw Steve, he was here in Washington in July for a Judiciary Committee hearing. I'm fortunate that I had a chance to spend a few brief moments with him. That meeting reminded me of Steve's humility. He was a humble man -- he had no airs about him. He was quiet and self-effacing. He didn't put on a show or try to impress people with his position or his power within the FOP. People felt comfortable around him, because he was comfortable around them. He liked people and they liked him back.

At the same time, though, his affable nature didn't hide the fact that Steve Young was also a very strong man -- brave, courageous, fearless, and tough as nails. After all, he was a policeman

-- and exactly the kind of policeman I would have wanted by my side when I was a county prosecutor -- the kind of policeman I would have wanted helping me if I were a victim of a crime -- the kind of policeman I would have wanted protecting my children and my grandchildren and my entire family. That was Steve Young, Mr. President -- a model for all of law enforcement.

Because Steve was so humble and unassuming about his work and his position as the President of the FOP, many people don't realize just how many leaders relied on him for guidance and counsel. President Bush listened to him. In fact, the President called Steve shortly before his death to seek his wisdom and guidance. That shows how much respect President Bush had for him and how much he appreciated Steve's work and service to our nation.

As I read through so many of the tributes written about Steve after his death, I was especially struck by a statement given by Chuck Canterbury, the FOP's National Vice President. Mr. Canterbury said:

> "In his eleven years as President of the Ohio State Lodge, four years as National Vice President and his all-too brief term as National President, Steve woke up each morning and went to work for the citizens of Marion City and the rank-and-file officers in every region of the country. He was as dedicated a man, an officer, and a friend as I have ever known."

Mr. President, I couldn't agree more. This quote illustrates why Steve Young was so special to so many people. He was a humble, dedicated man, who devoted his career to working for the good of his fellow officers, for the good of Ohio, and for the good of this nation. Steve's commitment to our communities was evident in everything he did. Criminals were caught because of him -- and crimes were prevented. He was a protector. He was a leader. He was a good, decent, hard-working man for whom I have great respect and admiration.

As I think about Steve's short, but full life, I am reminded of a very familiar passage from the Bible -- a passage from St. Paul's second letter to Timothy, in which St. Paul said, "...the time of my departure has come. I have fought the good fight. I have finished the course. I have kept the faith."

There is no question, Mr. President -- Steve Young fought the good fight. He finished the course. He kept the faith. Steve lived a life of great achievement, both public and private, and we will miss him deeply.

My wife, Fran, and I extend our heartfelt sympathy and our prayers to the entire Young family -- especially to his wife, Denise; his sons, Staten and Steven; his sisters, Gloria, Kay, and Deborah; and his mother, Lillian. Our thoughts are also with all of the police officers in Steve's extended family.

The heroes here at home deserve more acknowledgement than they often get. The Police in our communities deserve our respect for a job that is dangerous and often thankless. Have a story of a local hero that you think others should hear?

Share the story with us at –
www.ModernDayHeroes.com

Chapter 3

One Giant Leap

Slipped the Surly Bonds of Earth

Being an American has always stood for that rugged individual who has the chance, through hard work, luck, and a little planning, to succeed. An "American hero", however, is beyond mere success. It is taking the successes or failures that you have and still making a positive contribution to the people around you, no matter the cost to yourself.

Brian McCullough
Newport Beach, CA

President Ronald Reagan –
addressed the nation on the explosion of the space shuttle Challenger on January 28, 1986. The President spoke at 5 p.m. from the Oval Office at the White House. The address was broadcast live on nationwide radio and television.

Ladies and gentlemen, I'd planned to speak to you tonight to report on the state of the Union, but the events of earlier today have led me to change those plans. Today is a day for mourning and remembering. Nancy and I are pained to the core by the tragedy of the shuttle Challenger. We know we share this pain with all of the people of our country. This is truly a national loss.

Nineteen years ago, almost to the day, we lost three astronauts in a terrible accident on the ground. But we've never lost an astronaut in flight; we've never had a tragedy like this. And perhaps we've forgotten the courage it took for the crew of the shuttle. But they, the Challenger Seven, were aware of the dangers, but overcame them and did their jobs brilliantly. We mourn seven heroes: Michael Smith, Dick Scobee, Judith Resnik, Ronald McNair,

Ellison Onizuka, Gregory Jarvis, and Christa McAuliffe. We mourn their loss as a nation together.

For the families of the seven, we cannot bear, as you do, the full impact of this tragedy. But we feel the loss, and we're thinking about you so very much. Your loved ones were daring and brave, and they had that special grace, that special spirit that says, ``Give me a challenge, and I'll meet it with joy.'' They had a hunger to explore the universe and discover its truths. They wished to serve, and they did. They served all of us. We've grown used to wonders in this century. It's hard to dazzle us. But for 25 years the United States space program has been doing just that. We've grown used to the idea of space, and perhaps we forget that we've only just begun. We're still pioneers. They, the members of the Challenger crew, were pioneers.

And I want to say something to the schoolchildren of America who were watching the live coverage of the shuttle's takeoff. I know it is hard to understand, but sometimes painful things like this happen. It's all part of the process of exploration and discovery. It's all part of taking a chance and expanding man's horizons. The future doesn't belong to the fainthearted; it belongs to the brave. The Challenger crew was pulling us into the future, and we'll continue to follow them.

I've always had great faith in and respect for our space program, and what happened today does nothing to diminish it. We don't hide our space program. We don't keep secrets and cover things up. We do it all up front and in public. That's the way freedom is, and we wouldn't change it for a minute. We'll continue our quest in space. There will be more shuttle flights and more shuttle crews and, yes, more volunteers, more civilians, more teachers in space. Nothing ends here; our hopes and our journeys continue. I want to add that I wish I could talk to every man and woman who works for NASA or who worked on this mission and tell them: ``Your dedication and professionalism have moved and impressed us for decades. And we know of your anguish. We share it.''

There's a coincidence today. On this day 390 years ago, the great explorer Sir Francis Drake died aboard ship off the coast of Panama. In his lifetime the great frontiers were the oceans, and an historian later said, ``He lived by the sea, died on it, and was buried in it." Well, today we can say of the Challenger crew: Their dedication was, like Drake's, complete.

The crew of the space shuttle Challenger honored us by the manner in which they lived their lives. We will never forget them, nor the last time we saw them, this morning, as they prepared for their journey and waved goodbye and ``slipped the surly bonds of earth'' to ``touch the face of God.''

The Risk of Life

I think the last couple of years have taught us that heroes come in all shapes and sizes and that there are countless people surrounding us, in all walks of life who are performing heroic acts through their courage, sacrifice and determination.

Rodell Mollineau
Washington, D.C.

U.S. Senator Bill Nelson

Once again we are tragically reminded of the perils of space exploration.

Gus Grissom understood that peril 36 years ago when -- shortly before he and two fellow astronauts died in the Apollo fire -- he said, "The conquest of space is worth the risk of life."

New Hampshire schoolteacher Christa McAuliffe and the six astronauts aboard the ill-fated Challenger space shuttle understood and accepted the risk, too. Like Grissom, McAuliffe and the eight other earlier casualties of our nation's space program, the seven astronauts who died over Texas yesterday were willing to accept that risk in exchange for the great benefits their brave exploration of the heavens could achieve for all mankind.

Like so many other Americans, I'll never forget seeing the Challenger launch into the clear blue Florida sky on Jan. 28, 1986. Just 10 days earlier, as chairman of the House space subcommittee, I had returned from six days on the 24th flight of the space shuttle Columbia. Staff members and I gathered around the television in my Washington office, and I was explaining each step of the launch sequence when the terrible explosion occurred.

Yesterday morning, the skies were equally blue as Columbia soared 200,000 feet over Texas toward its scheduled landing at the

Kennedy Space Center in Florida after 16 days of scientific research in space.

It will be a while before we know what caused the sudden, horrific ending of its flight and the tragic deaths of the six Americans and the first Israeli astronaut aboard.

Today, our hearts and prayers go out to their loved ones left behind. And as we once again extend our respect and gratitude to the families of fallen astronauts, we must rededicate ourselves to making future exploration of this final frontier as safe as humanly possible.

We already can thank the space program for spawning more than 1,300 technological advances -- including CAT scans, kidney dialysis machines and the artificial heart.

Now, with the International Space Station, continued research may one day lead to a cure for cancer and many other findings on behalf of the good life here on Earth.

That is the cause for which 17 space explorers have now given their lives. That is the cause for which all our astronauts have risked their lives for nearly four decades now. And that is the cause that took this nation to the moon in 1969.

Our next destination can still be Mars, but we've got to put a higher priority on ensuring the safety of those who might journey there. Our nation recommitted itself to making manned space flight as safe as possible after the Challenger explosion. But these efforts have lagged amid the budget pressures and cuts of recent years. Now, in the wake of this new tragedy, we need to make a new commitment. And we must live up to it.

As Gus Grissom said, the conquest of space is worth it.

With President George W. Bush directing the space program to find a way to build a station on the moon and then go to Mars, do you think America should attempt such a goal?
Let us know your thoughts at -
www.ModernDayHeroes.com

Not One of Them is Missing

An American hero is one who sacrifices for the good of the community with no thought to their own well-being. Their total focus is to make the world a better place to live for others.

Andy Polk
Monroe, NC

President George W. Bush –
addressed the nation from the Cabinet room with regard on the loss of Space Shuttle Columbia.

My fellow Americans, this day has brought terrible news and great sadness to our country. At 9:00 a.m. this morning, Mission Control in Houston lost contact with our Space Shuttle Columbia. A short time later, debris was seen falling from the skies above Texas. The Columbia is lost; there are no survivors.

On board was a crew of seven: Colonel Rick Husband; Lt. Colonel Michael Anderson; Commander Laurel Clark; Captain David Brown; Commander William McCool; Dr. Kalpana Chawla; and Ilan Ramon, a Colonel in the Israeli Air Force. These men and women assumed great risk in the service to all humanity.

In an age when space flight has come to seem almost routine, it is easy to overlook the dangers of travel by rocket, and the difficulties of navigating the fierce outer atmosphere of the Earth. These astronauts knew the dangers, and they faced them willingly, knowing they had a high and noble purpose in life. Because of their courage and daring and idealism, we will miss them all the more.

All Americans today are thinking, as well, of the families of these men and women who have been given this sudden shock and grief. You're not alone. Our entire nation grieves with you. And those you loved will always have the respect and gratitude of this country.

The cause in which they died will continue. Mankind is led into the darkness beyond our world by the inspiration of discovery and the longing to understand. Our journey into space will go on.

In the skies today we saw destruction and tragedy. Yet farther than we can see there is comfort and hope. In the words of the prophet Isaiah, "Lift your eyes and look to the heavens. Who created all these? He who brings out the starry hosts one by one and calls them each by name. Because of His great power and mighty strength, not one of them is missing."

The same Creator who names the stars also knows the names of the seven souls we mourn today. The crew of the shuttle Columbia did not return safely to Earth; yet we can pray that all are safely home.

May God bless the grieving families, and may God continue to bless America.

The Vision to Find It

An American hero is somebody who gives of themselves without question or praise. An American hero, for example, would be somebody who would fight for our rights, our constitution, our safety, and our freedoms without question. This would be an easy answer to me right now – it would be the men and women who have and are fighting for all of this while we sit here and exercise our rights.

Cathey
Houston, TX

U.S. Representative Martin Frost –
paid tribute to Dr. Kalpana Chawla, a mission specialist, who was honored at the University of Texas-Arlington, her alma mater, after the loss of the Columbia space shuttle.

I join with my colleagues in expressing this body's deep grief over the loss of Columbia and her brave crew. I was privileged to attend the memorial for our seven astronauts in Houston yesterday. The deeply moving words in honor of the Columbia revealed how profoundly this tragedy has affected people in Texas and across our country.

And today in my District in North Texas, one of those astronauts, Dr. Kalpana Chawla, is being remembered at her alma mater, the University of Texas at Arlington.

K.C., as she was known by friends at UTA, was a true pioneer and a role model for young people on two continents. K.C. was the first Indian American to travel into space, and her achievements brought great pride to people in her home country of India and her adopted home in North Texas.

While aboard the Columbia, K.C. sent an e-mail to students in her hometown Karnal, India. She wrote: "The path from dreams to success does exist. May you have the vision to find it, the courage to get onto it, and the perseverance to follow it. Wishing you a great journey."

There can be no doubt that K.C. and the other astronauts aboard the Columbia had the vision and perseverance to follow their dreams. Those dreams led them into space on a mission of discovery that made them heroes.

As we reflect upon the lives of Dr. Chawla and her fellow crew members, we have a shared responsibility to forge ahead with their mission. After the House passes this worthy resolution honoring our fallen heroes, it will be our duty as Members of Congress to commit our government to a full investigation of the causes of this tragedy - and just as importantly, to recommit America to our mission exploring the frontiers of space.

How has the technology from the space program impacted your life? Share your story with us at -
www.ModernDayHeroes.com

Modern Day Pioneers

I believe an American hero is someone who can honor some elements or historical events of the past, with the humility and maturity to "agree to disagree" with other elements. Not only will (s)he honor history, but hone prowess and patriotism, with belief that America has yet to reach its destiny. The American hero helps to bridge this gap each day in what (s)he proactively thinks, says, and does; exemplified by acts of love, courage, self-sacrifice and accepting personal, family, social, work inconveniences -- ready and willing to serve; contributing to other people within our country, assisting others who dream to have such a country as ours; maintaining a commitment to contribute to the growth, humanity, dignity and greater good of America and its global co-existence with all other countries.

Jonnetta Chambers, M.A.
AchieveLifeSuccess.com
Rialto, CA

U.S. Senator Mike Enzi

Today, here in the Senate and the House, in Houston, TX, all across the country, and in places throughout the world, people of all faiths and from all walks of life will take a moment to remember the tragic loss of the crew of the Space Shuttle Columbia this past weekend [2003]. As we do, we will put aside our differences and come together as a family to remember those who were lost and the great cause for which they gave their lives.

For me, the story of this past weekend's events begins when I was growing up--a Boy Scout who was fascinated by rockets and rocketry. That interest continued to show itself as I became a young man who was fascinated by the two latest creations of the day--television and the start of our space program. As science worked to develop the tools we would need to explore outer space, television gave us all a front row seat so we would see what was happening.

Back then, the early successes in rocketry--mostly by Russia--fired our imaginations and steeled our will to win the race to reach the heavens. It was only natural for me and the people of Wyoming to feel so moved. After all, we were the products of the pioneer spirit. Our ancestors had left the comforts of the East behind and headed west looking for a new life and to explore what was then the new frontier. They were pioneers.

As television became a more common addition to our homes, it brought the next new frontier--space--into our very living rooms. Each day we could see the latest events of the day that were happening around the world beamed right into our living rooms. We watched in fascination as things that were happening miles and miles away were seen right in the comfort of our own homes. For me, the stars of the sky came in second place in importance only to the stars of the space program. Me and all of my friends, especially those who had been in the Scouts, wanted to be just like them.

I still remember the days when we would go to a local field and work on our own experiments in rocketry. Then, as we grew older, when a new flight was announced by NASA, we would grab the first chance we had to watch it as the miracle of television brought the wonders of space flight to our homes and our schools.

Competition was with the Russians. But now there is cooperation with the Russians in space and with the space station.

Our efforts to explore space and the continuing impact of seeing it all live on television made for a powerful pair as we heard the words of John F. Kennedy as he challenged the nation to land a man on the moon. His vision led us onward and upward. And it wasn't all that long afterwards that my wife and I--newlyweds--felt a personal stake in what we saw on the television before us. We sat spellbound as we watched Neil Armstrong take his one small step on the Moon that meant so much for all mankind.

Neil Armstrong was part of a long line of astronauts who braved the odds to do the impossible as, together as a nation, we reached for greatness. Over the years, there had been disappointments, failures and tragedies, but with each success we felt like we had a grip on the process and that the odds would be forever in our favor.

Somewhere along the way in the years that passed, we forgot that space is a cold, unfriendly place and that space flight brings with it great risks and dangers as well as great rewards. We forgot the lesson learned from the early days of the space program--that when we dream great dreams and achieve great successes, we are also courting great danger.

We think of the shuttle as an airplane. And we know how safe airplanes are. That danger was brought painfully home when we launched the Space Shuttle Challenger.

All at once and without warning, the reliable space machine we had come to trust and take for granted blew up and disintegrated before our eyes.

I remember that day so well because it was the day we were to send our first educator into space, Christa McAuliffe. In schools all over the country, children and their teachers watched excitedly as a school teacher prepared to make her voyage into space. When it ended in tragedy, a lot of fathers and mothers sat down that night with their children to talk about what they had seen at school that day. They got a lot of tough questions from little children with sad eyes who wondered why these things have to happen.

Mothers and fathers have no answers for those questions and they can only say that sometimes bad things happen to good people. They can only hug and hold and remind their little ones that there is a God and somehow He works all things for His good. Someday we may know what that good is, but for now, all we can do is trust and hope and pray.

Now we have felt that pain for a second time. The first brought us an awareness of the risks we take in exploring the unknown. It reminded us that despite the best of planning and preparation sometimes things happen that we could never have possibly prepared for. Now we watch these events unfold for a second time with a different sense--and from a different perspective. We remember the risks of space flight. But, as we mourn those who were lost, we renew our feeling of determination and our resolve to succeed no matter the odds or the obstacles to be overcome.

The crews of the Challenger and the Columbia--those modern day pioneers--will be forever linked in our minds, tied together by the same terrible helplessness we felt as we watched both tragedies unfold. Each time we searched for answers that we knew would never come. In the end, each time we found ourselves more determined than ever before to move ahead and to continue the exploration of space that must never end. And, in the end, that is the important lesson we will take with us. We may experience defeat, but we will never be defeated. In this and all we pursue in life, we will ultimately succeed as long as we hold true to our dreams and follow our star.

And the success is far-reaching. I have a heart repair that would not have been possible without the space program. Science moves on, stimulated by the unknown and represented by space.

When the crew of the Challenger died, President Reagan comforted the nation with the words that the crew that had slipped the surly bonds of Earth had reached out and touched the face of God. This past weekend, President Bush assured us that the ``God who names the stars also knows the names of the seven souls we mourn today.''

Then and now, both crews left us with our eyes gazing toward the skies and the heavens above, hopeful and prayerful that if they had to leave us, they had done so in pursuit of a better place as they returned, not to Earth, but to their home in God's holy heaven.

This night, and the next, and for many to come, when we go out on our back porch or sit in the backyard and look up at the stars, we will remember the Challenger and the Columbia and their valiant crews. The lights of the sky will remind us of their indomitable spirit and our pledge that as long as there are stars in the skies, we will never stop reaching out to them to explore, to dare and to dream in space and on Earth. That is our life, our legacy and our shared vision as Americans. It is what makes us unique, and it is why our nation will always be known as the land of the free and the home of the brave.

Intrepid Explorers

A hero is not necessarily a celebrity, though there is no reason a celebrity can't be a hero; too many Americans now confuse true heroism with celebrity hood. You'll never read about most of the real heroes in the newspaper or see them on television. They are the moms and dads who are raising their children to be honest, productive citizens. They are the firemen, the policemen, the salesmen, the repairmen and the thousands of others who allow our society to function and ensure this continues to be the greatest nation in the history of the world.

Rex Nelson
Little Rock, AR

Governor Bob Wise

This week, I was humbled by the request to join several local religious leaders in a ceremony memorializing the seven astronauts lost on the 8th of February [2003]. The words of these clergy and the beautiful music that accompanied the service were a wonderful tribute to the heroes we lost on the Columbia.

I heard many references to the NASA family during the immediate aftermath of the catastrophic loss of the shuttle. We lost seven members of the American family, and seven members of the human family. As a family, it is important that we come together to grieve and to celebrate the lives of these intrepid explorers.

Not one life of the seven was wasted. These lives, though cut tragically short, were overfull with accomplishment. They defended their countries, saved lives and advanced the cause of scientific progress, even before they left the earth for the final time. In this last mission, especially, they represented the best of peaceful cooperation and determined courage.

Tuesday, I joined the assembled religious leaders in expressing sympathy with the immediate families of the astronauts. I knew that nothing said or done could or should take away the pain of their loss; my only hope was that, in time, they would take some comfort in the knowledge that their loved ones were international heroes who gave their lives to the noblest of human endeavors.

They knew the risks, and they undertook their mission. They faced challenges, personal and professional, as we all do. The success they achieved was not the result of luck or privilege. They were endowed with the same brave spirit that lived in America's first settlers, and this spirit lives on in our memories of them.

Israel lost its first space traveler, and we send our condolences, as a nation, to the Israeli people. As the rest of the world poured out its support to us after the terrorist attacks of 2001, and, today, with the loss of our astronauts, we send our message of brotherhood and support to the people of Israel.

These seven came from across our country, from Israel and from India. They left the ground as individuals united in pursuit of knowledge. They will forever remain in our hearts, as well as our history books, heroes.

How would you define the term "American hero"? Let us know at -

www.ModernDayHeroes.com

Chapter 4

Standing Guard in a Foreign Land

September 11, *1998*

Modern day heroes walk among us everyday. They have chosen to fight for good, they have learned the value of sacrifice, and they have given beyond what could be expected. We celebrate their lives because they remind us of the potential we all possess.

Amanda Flaig
Cincinnati, Ohio

President William J. Clinton

Perhaps in all of history there has never been a greater foreshadow of the evil that was yet to come. The loss of American life at the embassies in Kenya and Tanzania has been attributed to the same man who would make his most formidable strike at the American way of life just three years and over three thousand lives later. The evil that is Usama (a.k.a Osama) bin Laden.

President Clinton remarks at a memorial service for the victims of the embassy bombings on September 11, 1998. The President spoke at 12:12 p.m. at the Washington National Cathedral. In his remarks, he referred to Bishop Ronald H. Haines and Dean Nathan Baxter, Washington National Cathedral; Jesse Jackson; Janet Langhart, wife of Secretary of Defense William S. Cohen; Prudence Bushnell, U.S. Ambassador to Kenya; and John E. Lange, U.S. Charge d'Affairs, Tanzania.

Bishop Haines, Dean Baxter, Reverend Jackson, clergy; Vice President and Mrs. Gore, Secretary Albright, Secretary Cohen, Janet, Secretary Shalala; to the Members of Congress; our military service; distinguished members of the diplomatic corps, especially those from Kenya and Tanzania. Most of all, to the members of the families, friends, and colleagues of the deceased; the survivors of the attacks; Ambassador Bushnell and Charge Lange; my fellow Americans.

Today we are gathered in a truly sacred and historic place to honor and to celebrate the lives of 12 Americans who perished in service to our nation--their goodness, their warmth, their humanity, and their sacrifice. The two sides of their lives; who they were in their labors, and who they were as husbands and wives, sons and daughters, friends and colleagues came together. For as they showed every day in their devotion to family and friends, their work was about bringing better lives to all.

They worked to create opportunity and hope, to fight poverty and disease, to bridge divides between peoples and nations, to promote tolerance and peace. They expressed both their patriotism and their humanity, as Adlai Stevenson so well put it, "In the tranquil and steady dedication of a lifetime."

In the book of Isaiah it is written that the Lord called out, "Whom shall I send, and who will go for us?" And Isaiah, the prophet, answered, "Here am I, Lord; send me." These Americans, generous, adventurous, brave souls, said, "Send me. Send me in service. Send me to build a better tomorrow." And on their journey they perished, together with proud sons and daughters of Kenya and Tanzania.

Some of the Kenyans and Tanzanians worked alongside our Americans at our embassies, making vital contributions. Others were simply, unfortunately, nearby, working or studying, providing for their loved ones, doing what they do and did every day. For those people, too, we mourn, we honor, we thank God for their lives.

All of them were taken too soon, leaving behind families, many including young children, and devoted friends and colleagues. No tribute from us can rouse them from a long night of mourning. That takes time and the mysterious workings of the heart. But surely some comfort comes with the memory of the happiness they brought, the difference they made, the goodness they left inside those whom they loved and touched.

Last month at Andrews Air Force Base, Hillary and I walked out into the hangar that day to meet the families and share with them the homecoming of their loved ones for the last time. There we saw a larger family, many standing and pressed together, people from the State and Defense Departments, from our military, from AID and the CDC. They, too, lost brothers and sisters. They, too, must be immensely proud of their friends, the traditions, the accomplishments, the life they shared.

All of us must stand together with our friends from Kenya and Tanzania and other peace loving nations--yes, in grief, but also in common commitment to carry on the cause of peace and freedom, to find those responsible and bring them to justice, not to rest as long as terrorists plot to take more innocent lives, and in the end, to convince people the world over that there is a better way of living than killing others for what you cannot have today. For our larger struggle, for hope over hatred and unity over division, is a just one. And with God's help, it will prevail. We owe to those who have given their lives in the service of America and it's ideal to continue that struggle most of all.

In their honor, let us commit to open our hearts with generosity and understanding; to treat others who are different with respect and kindness; to hold fast to our loved ones; and always to work for justice, tolerance, freedom, and peace.

May God be with their souls.

American Blood

A Hero Comes Home

A hero is not made, he's born.
His destiny awaits,
'Till fulfillment comes, this hero yearns,
To seek, to serve, to save.
With the courage of a lion,
He defends the cause at hand,
He will take his last breath trying
He may fall, yet he'll still stand.
A valiant soldier completes his task,
Though his tour has been cut short;
A much greater life awaits this man,
As he's greeted by our Lord.

This hero paid the greatest price,
He gave his all for his home land,
As we breathe the breath of freedom,
Let's thank God for this great man.
We will not take him for granted
By forgetting what's been done;
We will wave our flag in honor
For the victory he's won.
For service to his country,
The tenacity he's shown,
God's arms are open, welcoming,
A hero has come home.

Nina L. Toth
Export, PA

President William J. Clinton

In a world with germ warfare and nuclear arsenals so large they can destroy the world in an instant several times over, it is the terrorist we fear most. The most evil man the 21st century has known, Usama (a.k.a. Osama) bin Laden, first made his presence known to the average American during the years President Clinton was in the oval office. After the bombing of a U.S. –Saudi military facility in 1995 that killed 7, and after the fuel truck bomb at an American base in 1996 that killed 19 American soldiers while wounding over 515 others, and after the two American embassy bombings in 1998 that killed 291 people including 12 Americans, Usama bin Laden set his gaze of terror on yet another American military target, the U.S.S.

Cole. One can only ask why it took our nation so long to act with our new level of resolve.

President Clinton addressed the nation after the bombing of the U.S.S. Cole.

I have just been meeting with my national security team on today's tragic events in the Middle East, and I would like to make a brief statement.

First, as you know, an explosion claimed the lives of at least four sailors on one of our naval vessels, the U.S.S. Cole, this morning. Many were injured; a number are still missing. They were simply doing their duty. The ship was refueling in a port in Yemen while en route to the Persian Gulf. We're rushing medical assistance to the scene, and our prayers are with the families who have lost their loved ones or are still awaiting news.

If, as it now appears, this was an act of terrorism, it was a despicable and cowardly act. We will find out who was responsible and hold them accountable. If their intention was to deter us from our mission of promoting peace and security in the Middle East, they will fail, utterly.

I have directed the Department of Defense, the FBI and the State Department to send officials to Yemen to begin the investigation. Secretary Albright has spoken with President Salih of Yemen, and we expect to work closely with his government to that effect.

Our military forces and our embassies in the region have been on heightened state of alert for some time now. I have ordered our ships in the region to pull out of port, and our land forces to increase their security.

Tensions are extremely high today throughout the entire region, as all of you know. I strongly condemn the murder of Israeli soldiers in Ramallah today. While I understand the anguish Palestinians feel over the losses they have suffered, there can be no possible justification for mob violence. I call on both sides to undertake a cease-fire immediately, and immediately to condemn all acts of violence.

Finally, let me say this. The Israeli-Palestinian conflict is one of the greatest tragedies and most difficult problems of our time. But it can be solved. The progress of the last few years -- progress that brought Israel to the hope of a final peace with true security, and Palestinians to the hope of a sovereign state recognized by the entire world -- was not made through violence. It happened because both sides sat down together, negotiated, and slowly built up the trust that violence destroys.

Now is the time to stop the bloodshed, to restore calm, to return to dialogue, and ultimately to the negotiating table. The alternative to the peace process is now no longer merely hypothetical. It is unfolding today before our very eyes.

Now, I need to go back to work on this, and so I won't take questions right now. But the Department of Defense will offer a briefing today and will be able to answer the questions that are relevant to today's events.

Thank you.

How have the terrorist acts of Usama (a.k.a Osama) bin Laden impacted your life and family? Share your story with us at -

www.ModernDayHeroes.com

This Call to Duty

An American hero to me is someone who dies to self. What that means is that the individual puts the needs of the cause above their needs. Without regard for their personal safety they accomplish the mission objectives.

Mathew J. Falk
452 AMXS, 452AMW, 4th Air Force
Crew Chief

General Henry H. Shelton, USA
Chairman of the Joint Chiefs of Staff

Mr. President; distinguished members of Congress; Secretary Cohen; Secretary Danzig; families; friends and other distinguished guests; fellow members of our Armed Forces. Last week, we lost a part of America, a part of ourselves, and a part of our family.

But while the U.S.S. Cole belonged to the Cole and Navy families, they are also part of a much larger family. They are now and forever more, apart of the family of patriots that has made our nation the greatest country on earth. They are now with those patriots who gave of themselves for freedom, who gave of themselves for our way of life, and who freely answered our nation's call to duty. For our tomorrow, they gave their today.

For, all of us who have worn or who wear the uniform of our nation's fighting forces join you in feeling this loss. We will never forget those brave men and women who sailed into harm's way and who paid the ultimate sacrifice in the defense of freedom. And those who perpetrated this act of terror should also never forget that America's memory is long and our reach longer.

Today, we also remember that there are thousands of men and women at sea, just as there are soldiers, airmen, Marines and Coast Guardsmen on patrol and on watch, protecting America's interests. Americans who put service above self, and patriotism above profit.

At Arlington National Cemetery, there is a particular appropriate inscription. It reads: "Not for fame or reward, not lured by ambition or goaded by necessity, but in simple obedience to duty as they understood it, these men suffered all, sacrificed all, and died."

The men and women of the U.S.S. Cole, whom we honor today, truly understood this call to duty, this call to service and to America. May God bless them and keep them, and may God be with their families.

Standing Guard for Peace

An American hero is a young mother with five children who, at the outbreak of WWII, went to work at Redstone Arsenal packing Howitzer shells. She clawed her way out of what was left of the plant that exploded around her, and raised her children to be solid citizens while suffering post traumatic stress syndrome before it had a name. God bless that mother who was a WWII hero as surely as the soldiers who went to battle. She was a soldier who never received a Purple Heart, or a thank you for her sacrifice.

Nancy Mayes
Point Pleasant, WV

President William J. Clinton –
addressed those in attendance at the memorial service for the crew of the U.S.S. Cole in Norfolk, Virginia on October 18, 2000.

Secretary Cohen; Attorney General Reno; Secretary Danzig; General Shelton; distinguished Members of the Senate and House; Governor; Admiral Clark; Admiral Natter; Chaplain Black, Master Chief Herdt; Master Chief Hefty; the sailors of the U.S.S. Cole; the family members and friends; the Norfolk Naval community; my fellow Americans.

Today, we honor our finest young people; fallen soldiers who rose to freedom's challenge. We mourn their loss, celebrate their lives, offer the love and prayers of a grateful nation to their families.

For those of us who have to speak here, we are all mindful of the limits of our poor words to lift your spirits or warm your hearts. We know that God has given us the gift of reaching our middle years. And we now have to pray for your children, your husbands, your wives, your brothers, your sisters, who were taken so young. We know we will never know them as you did or remember them as you will; the first time you saw them in uniform, or the last time you said goodbye.

They all had their own stories and their own dreams. We Americans have learned something about each and every one of them over these last difficult days as their profiles, their lives, their loves, their service, have been given to us. For me, I learned a little more when I met with all the families this morning.

Some follow the family tradition of Navy service; others hoped to use their service to earn a college degree. One of them had even worked for me in the White House. Richard Costelow was a technology wizard who helped to update the White House communications system for this new century.

All these very different Americans, all with their different stories, their lifelines and love ties, answered the same call of service and found themselves on the U.S.S. Cole, headed for the Persian Gulf, where our forces are working to keep peace and stability in a region that could explode and disrupt the entire world.

Their tragic loss reminds us that even when America is not at war, the men and women of our military still risk their lives for peace. I am quite sure history will record in great detail our triumphs in battle, but I regret that no one will ever be able to write a full account of the wars we never fought, the losses we never suffered, the tears we never shed because men and women like those who were on the U.S.S. Cole were standing guard for peace. We should never, ever forget that.

Today, I ask all Americans just to take a moment to thank the men and women of our Armed Forces for a debt we can never repay, whose character and courage, more than even modern weapons, makes our military the strongest in the world. And in particular, I ask us to thank God today for the lives, the character and courage of the crew of the U.S.S. Cole, including the wounded and especially those we lost or are missing:

Hull Maintenance Technician Third Class Kenneth Eugene Clodfelter; Electronics Technician Chief Petty Officer First Class Richard Costelow; Mess Management Specialist Seaman Lakeina Monique Francis; Information Systems Technician Seaman Timothy Lee Gauna; Signalman Seaman Apprentice Cheron Louis Gunn; Seaman James Rodrick McDaniels; Engineman Second Class Mark Ian Nieto; Electronics Warfare Technician Third Class Ronald Scott

Owens; Seaman Apprentice Lakiba Nicole Palmer. Engine Fireman Joshua Langdon Parlett; Fireman Apprentice Patrick Howard Roy; Electronics Warfare Technician Second Class Kevin Shawn Rux; Mess Management Specialist Third Class Ronchester Managan Santiago; Operations Specialist Second Class Timothy Lamont Saunders; Fireman Gary Graham Swenchonis, Jr; Ensign Andrew Triplett; Seaman Apprentice Craig Bryan Wibberley.

In the names and faces of those we lost and mourn, the world sees our nation's greatest strength. People in uniform rooted in every race, creed, and region on the face of the earth; yet, bound together by a common commitment to freedom and a common pride in being American. That same spirit is living today as the crew of the U.S.S. Cole pulls together in a determined struggle to keep the determined warrior afloat.

The idea of common humanity and unity amidst diversity, so purely embodied by those we mourn today, must surely confound the minds of the hate-filled terrorists who killed them. They envy our strength without understanding the values that give us strength. For them, it is their way or no way. Their interpretation, twisted though it may be, of a beautiful religious tradition. Their political views, their racial and ethnic views. Their way or no way.

Such people can take innocent life. They have caused your tears and anguish, but they can never heal, or build harmony, or bring people together. That is work only free, law-abiding people can do. People like the sailors of the U.S.S. Cole.

To those who attacked them, we say: you will not find a safe harbor. We will find you, and justice will prevail. America will not stop standing guard for peace or freedom or stability in the Middle East and around the world.

But some way, someday, people must learn the lesson of the lives of those we mourn today, of how they worked together, of how they lived together, of how they reached across all the lines that divided them and embraced their common humanity and the common values of freedom and service.

Not far from here, there is a quiet place that honors those who gave their lives in service to our country. Adorning its entrance are words from a poem by Archibald Macleish; not only a tribute to the young we lost, but a summons to those of us left behind. Listen to them. The young no longer speak, but:

They have a silence that speaks for them at night.

They say, "We were young, remember us."

They say, "We have done what we could, but until it is finished, it is not done."

They say, "Our deaths are not ours; they are yours; they will mean what you make them."

They say, "Whether our lives and our deaths were for peace and a new hope, we cannot say; it is you who must say this."

They say, "We leave you our deaths. Give them their meaning."

The lives of the men and women we lost on the U.S.S. Cole meant so much to those who loved them, to all Americans, to the cause of freedom. They have given us their deaths. Let us give them their meaning. Their meaning of peace and freedom, of reconciliation and love, of service, endurance and hope. After all they have given us, we must give them their meaning.

I ask now that you join me in a moment of silence and prayer for the lost, the missing, and their grieving families.

[A moment of silence is observed.]

Amen. Thank you, and may God bless you all.

Do you have a family member in the military? Tell us why you are proud of them at -
www.ModernDayHeroes.com

Chapter 5

The Unthinkable Evil,
The Unforgettable Heroes

Flight 93

I feel a real hero is not a football or other sports star, nor an actor, a politician or other notable "famous" person. A real hero is just the "average Joe" that rarely ever sees any recognition for his efforts. A real hero is one who gives selflessly of his time, energy, and money for the good of others without ever asking for anything in return and when offered, turns it down. He or she is not looking for recognition or money, he is doing what he does out of his love for others. Whether he is a soldier carrying his wounded buddies off the battlefield or throwing himself in front of the bullet, or he is a woman giving of her meager food supply to help someone who has even less, that person is a hero in my eyes.

Young children, who instead of spending their time playing Nintendo, collect socks or other things for charity are heroes also. The man who jumps into a flooded creek to save someone is a hero. A fireman who runs into a burning building to save someone instead of running away is a hero. A policeman trying to save the public from criminals is a hero. Someone who stands for the unborn children to convince people to give them for adoption is a hero in my eyes. In short, I suppose, a hero to me is just an average person who thinks of others before his own safety and comfort without ever asking for anything in return.

Sherri Myers
Reviewer for Romancejunkies.com

U.S. Representative John Murtha

I doubt that any American will forget where they were and what they were doing the morning of Sept. 11, 2001. That morning, I met in the Capitol with House Minority Leader Dick Gephardt and then went to a meeting of the Defense Appropriation Subcommittee, which was working on the legislation that annually funds our nation's defense.

We were preparing to move money from a missile-defense program into counter-terrorism initiatives because several of us were convinced that terror in America was a much greater threat than a missile attack from abroad.

None of us realized just how imminent that threat was.

But as we were getting started, we learned of the twin towers of the World Trade Center being hit, and then I got a call from the Pentagon alerting us that a bomb had just gone off there. It turned out that it wasn't a bomb but another airplane crashing into the building. About that time, we saw people running outside, and the police told us we needed to evacuate because there was a plane that they thought might be heading for the Capitol.

That plane, it turns out, was United Airlines Flight 93.

While waiting outside the Capitol, we heard a sonic boom, which we thought was another explosion. We figured out later that this was the jet fighters that had been scrambled and sent toward Pennsylvania to possibly intercept Flight 93.

That action proved to be unnecessary because of the heroic actions of the people on board Flight 93.

The next morning, I drove home and toured the crash site in an old coalfield in Pennsylvania's 12th District.

Reporters seemed to be surprised when I started calling the passengers and crew "heroes." But it had been easy for me to reach the conclusion that these people were indeed heroes.

I'd heard separate media reports about cell phone calls in which passengers found out about the World Trade Center attacks. I'd heard first-hand reports of the erratic flight pattern of the plane just before it crashed and got the impression that the plane had started to break apart before the crash. That would indicate that a struggle had gone on in the cockpit that jarred the plane in the air as it traveled between Pittsburgh and Greensburg. That's when the air traffic controllers in Cleveland called for evacuation of the air traffic tower at the Johnstown airport.

Hearing these reports, I quickly came to the conclusion that the people on board had fought back.

They obviously realized that the plane they were on was going to kill a lot of people unless they intervened. And so, with courage we can only imagine, they developed and launched a plan to take back control of the plane.

The terrorists obviously miscalculated – the Americans were certainly not the soft cowards that the terrorists thought we'd be.

The passengers and crew of United Flight 93 are national heroes – they were the first Americans to give their lives in fighting back against terrorism here in America when they brought down this airplane in an abandoned coalfield in rural Pennsylvania.

It is fitting and proper that our nation takes time on September 11th this year to honor these heroes along with the thousands who died in the attacks at the World Trade Center and the Pentagon.

On September 11 this year, I recommit myself to work on reducing the threat of future terrorist attacks, and improving our ability to respond to such attacks. We must make further improvements in our intelligence operations, keep the terrorists on the run abroad, and develop better methods of detecting and responding to chemical, nuclear or biological attacks. I will also continue to work toward creating a national memorial at the Flight 93 crash site to honor these true heroes.

On September 11 this year, I encourage everyone to fly the American flag and to take time to reflect, not only on the great tragedy of that day, but also on the great triumph that took place in the skies over rural Pennsylvania.

Tuesday Morning

We stand here on the only island of freedom that is left in the whole world. There is no place left to flee to ... no place to escape to. We defend freedom here or it is gone. There is no place for us to run, only to make a stand.

President Ronald Reagan

Governor John G. Rowland –
addressed the Interreligious Prayer Service at the Cathedral of St. Joseph in Hartford, Connecticut.

How do you begin to speak of the unthinkable? Words can only begin to express the overwhelming loss we all feel today. Words cannot express the sorrow, the disbelief, and the grief we all share for the thousands impacted by Tuesday's tragedy. But our words, and our community of spirit, are ways we can give voice to our feelings – words that represent the fullness of our hearts – words that convey the grief we all share.

This was the most horrific event of our lifetime, and even of our parents' lifetime. The terrorists did not observe any of the laws of humanity. The goal of terrorism is to reduce our society, to instill fear and hatred.

We cannot let the desire for revenge become the overpowering emotion. If we allow hatred to take hold, then the terrorists will have won. When we respond to evil with pure anger, evil claims more victims of the spirit. The very concept of terrorism is to instill terror, to make us doubt what is in our souls because of what we see with our eyes.

Make no mistake -- the battle of good against evil is always being waged. If we allow our spirit to be forever tainted, if we allow our hearts to be forever hardened, then military might cannot reclaim what we have lost inside ourselves.

In the days and weeks ahead, we are going to hear so many remembrances, so many stories about the people who have perished, about their goodness, their families, about their lives, and the loved ones from whom they were taken.

Among the people killed in the plane crashes on Tuesday was Father Frank Grogan: my friend, my mentor, my religion teacher at Holy Cross High School in Waterbury. It was Father Frank who convinced me to volunteer at Southbury Training School and to organize my friends to work with the mentally retarded. It was Father Frank who convinced me to go on Catholic retreats to find my own spirituality.

Father Frank taught me about grace and service to others. He was one of the most sensitive men I have ever known. I know if Father Frank was with us here today -- in flesh as well as in spirit -- he would ask us to be persuaded by our better natures. If Father Frank had not been on that flight, he most likely would have been at a service like this one, urging us to carry on or helping us to understand.

If the World Trade Center is rebuilt, and these crimes against humanity are punished, and that's all that happens, then the terrorists will have achieved part of their objective. They will have dealt a spiritual blow to which we have not responded.

But if one result of this horrible tragedy is that each of us pledges to fight against evil, to stand in ways large and small against hatred and intolerance, and to live as a community, then the terrorists will not have won.

We are here today as a true community. There is something that binds us together that reaches far beyond religion – a commonality more powerful than the separations of race or geography or gender – and that is the innate goodness of human beings.

The true face of the human race is the face of this congregation. It is the face of the rescue workers, the firemen, the police officers, the everyday heroes who give blood, the iron workers and medical personnel. It is the face of the countless millions of people across this country and across the world who have offered their prayers, their tears, their help, and their spirit.

That is the spirit of America that must rise from this disaster. That is the best way to honor the friends, the families, and loved ones that have been lost. Then, the irony of these acts of cowardice will be that as a people, we became stronger, not weaker... that we became kinder, not harsher... and that we became more sensitive to each other, that we learned even more, to trust, to love, to honor, and to help. Then, we will have embraced God's lesson to love one another as God loves each of us.

We can honor those slain in New York and Washington by declaring that we will not be a people of the lowest common denominator. We can honor them by letting our anger be tempered into resolve, and by resolving to make our world a place where terrorism has no home, no haven, and no place to hide.

Today the fabric of our great country is being tested. In these most difficult times – with the heart of our nation bursting with sadness – we must ask God for the courage to carry on. We must ask God to bring strength and healing to the families of so many innocent lives lost.

In many ways, this tragedy has brought out the best within us all. The acts of kindness and understanding that seemed so far removed from American life just a short while ago have returned in abundance. This stain of violence on our lives is being washed away by the compassion and caring of our people.

On Tuesday morning, we all woke up and left home for our jobs or schools or places of worship. And when we all woke up that morning, we shared a common goal, the same goal our parents had, and their parents before them: a strong, safe future for all of our children. Today, we still share the same goal. And we are more resolved than ever to achieve it.

That is the best testimony, the best proof that no act of terrorism, no matter how horrific and senseless, can destroy the mighty power of Americans, united in spirit.

No act of terrorism can destroy God's law. Our destiny as a nation is to be kinder to each other, to love a little more, and to hate a little less.

To find out more information on the terrorist attacks of 9-11, visit our resource center at -
www.ModernDayHeroes.com

Terrorist Attacks

Is your hero an athlete who handles a ball well? Or an actor who is envied for his good looks and great talent? Or is it a successful business person who invested well and grew rich?

My heroes are neither actors, athletes, nor millionaires. They are ordinary people like small town folks who rally to help their neighbors. Some of my heroes are fragile, gray-haired grandmothers who spend many hours at a computer keyboard sending encouragement and love to sick children via the Internet. And some of my favorite heroes are gentle, loving mothers in cancer wards who rock their dying children as they cling to hope and pray for miracles.

Many of our nation's greatest heroes arose from the smoking ashes of the World Trade Center on September 11; and many heroes never did emerge from that smoldering rubble.

What makes a person a hero? Not superhuman strength or uncommon abilities. Heroes are ordinary people who express extraordinary, self-sacrificing love. Thank God for heroes!

Marsha Jordan
Harshaw, WI

U.S. Representative Brad Sherman

Yesterday we suffered the greatest loss of American life on American soil since our Civil War. I fear that we are reacting as if a few hundred Americans died at the hands of a small band of terrorists. I fear that we will just launch a dozen cruise missiles and call it a day like we did after our embassies were bombed in East Africa.

Let us wake up! There are probably 10,000 or more dead Americans. That is four times the number that died at Pearl Harbor.

I do not know whether Osama bin Laden is responsible, but I join the distinguished gentleman from California in demanding that Afghanistan extradite bin Laden to the United States because we do know that bin Laden killed Americans on the U.S.S. Cole and bombed our embassies in East Africa.

But let me go further. If the Taliban government refuses, we should go to war. It is a war we can win, as we won the war in Kosovo, chiefly with air power and with the support of local allies. The Northern Alliance of Afghanistan shelled Kabul last night. That alliance may have suffered the death or the severe wounding of its leader, General Masoud at the hands of bin Laden's assassins just 2 days ago. However, the Northern Alliance is intact, and if the Afghan Government does not surrender bin Laden by the end of this week, then the Northern Alliance should be the best armed rebel army in the world by the end of this month.

We can, with permission or with impunity, fly over the territory necessary in order to bomb the Taliban and resupply the Northern Alliance. A war against the Taliban government of Afghanistan will involve American casualties, but how many thousands of casualties will we suffer if we allow a foreign government to harbor and support well-organized, well-financed terrorist groups capable of mass murder.

This will be a war against the Taliban, but it is not a war against Islam. I join the prior speaker in saying we must respect Americans of all faiths.

September 11, 2001 is a day that will live in infamy. This may be the greatest loss of life on American soil since the Civil War.

Today's loss of life may approach or exceed the loss of life at Pearl Harbor. After Pearl Harbor some suggested appeasement, and withdrawal from Asia and the Pacific. Instead the greatest generation made the greatest sacrifices to win our greatest victory.

America must mobilize for a war against terrorism, not only against the criminals responsible for today's horrific events, but all terrorism.

This is not a war against Islam, or against Muslims. Our last three wars were waged to protect people who happen to be Muslim. We restored independence to the people of Kuwait and then engaged in two further wars in which we had no economic stake. In the mid-1990s, we protected the Bosnian Muslims from genocide. In 1999, we went to war against Serbia, a Christian country, to protect its Albanian Muslim minority from ethnic cleansing.

Today we suffered greater casualties than in all three of those wars combined.

There are some dancing in the streets of certain foreign cities who believe that the terrorists who killed thousands of American civilians have proven their strength by killing thousands of civilians. America has the power to kill civilians by the tens of thousands or the tens of millions. However America's great strength is that we do everything possible to avoid killing civilians, even those who dance today in delight.

For years, we have begged our friends to curtail investment and aid to countries which support terrorism. Now in this war for decency and civilization, we must have the full support of our allies. Those who claim to be friends of America can no longer do business as usual with countries which harbor terrorists.

We appreciate the statements of sympathy from the Taliban government in Afghanistan, but this is clearly insufficient. The Taliban government must turn over Osama bin Laden and his associates to the United States. If the Afghan government gives us excuses instead of giving us bin Laden, we must take harsh action. This would include providing arms and perhaps air cover to the forces in Northern Afghanistan and the legitimate government of that country. These forces have fought the Taliban to a standstill without our help. With very substantial American help these forces will march into Kabul.

We appreciate the statements of sympathy from chairman Arafat, but we must demand that he arrest terrorists in areas he controls.

We should not wait until we have identified the particular criminals responsible for today's tragedy, nor should we limit our response to one particular terrorist organization. Osama bin Laden may or may not be responsible for today's crimes, but he is responsible for the attack on the U.S.S. Cole and for the second worst terrorist attack against America, the bombing of our embassies in east Africa. We must demand bin Laden be turned over to the United States to be tried for those crimes.

Even if we totally destroy the organization responsible for today's crimes, other organizations will try to surpass today's evil.

We must root out all terrorist organizations. We must take harsh action against any country that harbors or supports terrorists.

We should seek U.N. approval for our action; but we must act even if the U.N. does not.

Election Day

An American hero is a man, woman, or child who loves America enough to see what is not right, and attempt to correct it. This often means sacrificing their life before the country realizes that the changes proposed are good and needed and benefit all.

Dr. Letitia S. Wright, D.C.
Rancho Cucamonga, CA

U.S. Representative Stephen F. Lynch

Today our thoughts and prayers are with the families affected by these horrible tragedies. These are vicious attacks by cowards upon innocent people.

Locally we now know that two flights, carrying 157 passengers and crew, from Boston, have crashed. Our prayers are with their families.

Today our country has been tested, and our actions will prove an historic truth: In times of adversity, the people of the United States demonstrate the ideals of our American democracy.

Well our democracy endures. In fact, today Margaret and I and tens of thousands of you exercised our most basic right, the right to vote. As today reminds us, we can never take these rights for granted. I am grateful for the voters' confidence in me.

Over the next few days our nation will join together to mourn our brothers and sisters who have died. We will hold close those who bear the scars of this tragedy. We will aggressively pursue the evil parties that have committed these crimes.

We will not be cowed, nor change our principles, but will continue to set an example for the world.

And by these actions we will show the true strength of America.

To Run to Ground
a Vicious Foe

An American hero is someone who doesn't care who gets the credit.

Katerina Tavoularis
Costa Mesa, CA

George J. Tenet –
Director of the Central Intelligence Agency
spoke to the CIA workforce on September 12, 2001 about the terrorist attacks from the day before. Here are excerpts of his remarks:

Good afternoon.

Yesterday, the entire American people—joined by men and women around the globe—recoiled in horror at the barbaric acts against our country.

In my hometown of New York, at the Pentagon, and in the skies over Pennsylvania, the bloody hand of evil struck again and again, stealing thousands of innocent lives.

As the devastating toll of terror comes into focus, we are sure to find among those who were lost friends, colleagues, and others we hold dear.

Our thoughts and prayers are with all the victims, with those searching and caring for them, and with those who mourn them.

I urge all of you to take the time to think of brothers and sisters that we, as Americans, have lost and to pray for those who survive them.

The images of fire and destruction are forever etched in our minds. And in our hearts, amid the numbing shock, there has been profound grief and renewed resolve.

As President Bush said last night, the search for the sponsors of these unspeakable acts has already begun. Our agency is among the leaders of that search.

The fight against those who use the weapon of terror to menace and murder is necessarily hard. The shield of fanaticism— wielded by those ready to forfeit their lives to achieve their twisted dreams—is not easily pierced.

But it has been pierced before, and it will be pierced again.

Though we did not stop the latest, terrible assaults, you—the men and women of CIA and our Intelligence Community—have done much to combat terrorism in the past.

Hundreds, if not thousands, of American lives have been saved by the brave men and women of our Counter-Terrorism Center, our Directorate of Operations, our analysts, our scientists, our support officers—all who work relentlessly every day against this difficult target.

I know that together, we will do even more in the future.

The response yesterday—from our Counter-Terrorism Center, the Ops Center, Global Support, our entire Security Staff, and many, many others—was absolutely magnificent. Today, I am—as I always have been—very, very proud of all the men and women in this organization.

The important thing for us now is to do our job. To run to ground a vicious foe—one without heart or pity. A foe who has killed Americans, but who hopes in vain to kill the ideals and values that define all of us as Americans.

The terrorists behind these atrocities—and those who give them shelter and support—must never know rest, ease, or comfort. The last word must not be theirs.

For the future must belong to the champions of freedom, not its enemies. That is our aim—today, tomorrow, always.

This is a time for us to come together. To bring all our talents to bear in a steely determination to do what we are called to do— protect our fellow citizens.

It is our turn again to step up to a challenge, and to meet it as we meet all challenges, with commitment and courage.

Put some spirit in your step, square your shoulders, focus your eyes...we have a job to do.

Many years ago, Winston Churchill—a giant of democracy—recalled his reaction on hearing the news of another surprise attack on America, this one at Pearl Harbor:

There were, he wrote, "many, not only in enemy countries [who] might discount the force of the United States. Some said they were soft, others that they would never be united. They would fool around at a distance. They would never come to grips. They would never stand blood-letting."

But, Churchill concluded, "I had studied the American Civil War, fought out to the last desperate inch. American blood flowed in my veins. I thought of a remark which Edward Grey had made to me more than thirty years before—that the United States is like 'a gigantic boiler. Once the fire is lighted under it, there is no limit to the power it can generate.'"

Indeed there is not.

I thank you all very, very much for your hard work. May God bless you all.

We Will Not Forget.
And We Will Act.

An American hero is anyone (adult or child) who goes to the assistance of another human being without conscience thought of the risks to their own life.

Laura Walters

Senator John Edwards
remarked on the terrorist attack on America. These remarks were given on September 12, 2001.

We each awoke yesterday to a much different world than the one we have to accept today.

On the most basic and important level, we have lost the lives of heroes and victims. We know that behind the devastating numbers are real Americans, with real families, with real accomplishments, with real hopes.

We also know - sadly - that we can never reclaim these lives.

We can only honor them and remember them, and in their names we can devote ourselves to taking every action to assure that no further Americans make these supreme sacrifices.

My scripture teaches us to "weep with them that weep, [to] be of the same mind one toward another."

I speak now to the families of those who have been taken.

We in this chamber cannot erase yesterday, although we wish we had a way to do that.

In the difficult days and years that will come, we will keep their lives and their names and their sacrifices in our hearts and we will translate our grief and anger into a determination to prevent this tragedy from being repeated.

I know that it is little solace for real loss, but it is an important commitment I truly believe they would each wish us to make.

We will not forget.

And we will act.

For 225 years now, America has been more than a nation-state; more than a set of borders, or a piece of land.

America is an idea – and that idea is freedom. Freedom of thought; freedom of movement; freedom to shape our lives and our society in the way we choose.

Yesterday morning, it wasn't just America that came under assault. It was the hopes and aspirations of freedom-loving peoples across this world.

Mr. President, there is a reason America does not bow down to terrorism; there is a reason we live by the rule of law – and not by the law of the jungle; there is a reason we will return to our homes and office buildings, and reclaim our skies and our pride; there is a reason we will marshal all our resources, all our resolve, and the awesome strength of our military to catch these death-mongers, to punish them, to make them pay for their ugly misdeeds:

Because we surrender our freedom to no one.

I commend President Bush for his leadership in this difficult time, and I urge all of my colleagues, on both sides of the aisle, to stand with him.

From time to time, from issue to issue, the votes in this chamber may be divided. But when it comes to defeating terrorism and hate, the United States Senate will not be divided.

Some have wondered, in the aftermath of this tragedy, whether our country will ever be the same again.

Of course, we need to make our airports safer – and we will.

We need to make our flights more secure, and their flight patterns more inviolate – and we will.

We need to do more to root our terrorism in the countries where it is tolerated, funded, and harbored – and we will.

But the strength of a nation is measured not in airport scanners or flight controls. It is measured in the grit and will of our people when it's needed the most.

By that standard, America is the strongest, toughest, most resilient nation on God's Earth.

Scripture also tells us that "whosoever will be great among you, let him be your minister; and whosoever will be chief among you, let him be your servant."

We glimpsed that greatness yesterday, in rescue efforts in New York City and at the Pentagon – with policemen and firemen, military personnel, and so many brave volunteers putting themselves in harm's way to save lives. Too many of them paid the ultimate price for their courage.

My Senate office was practically flooded with calls yesterday from concerned North Carolinians – people who wanted to give blood, to donate clothes and blankets, to open their hearts in this time of solidarity and need.

I am especially proud that a group of Marine medical personnel from Camp LeJeune in Jacksonville, North Carolina is preparing to leave for New York to assist in any way they can.

Today, we cannot help but think: how fragile is the safety and security we take for granted.

But throughout our history, we have weathered war and pestilence; we have met every kind of disaster, both natural and man-made; we have mastered every challenge and conquered every foe.

The spirit of America is strong. The power of freedom will overcome. And by reaffirming that freedom through strength, justice, and compassion, we will honor the memory of those now departed, and give renewed purpose to those who will now carry on.

In God We Trust

Of course I would say I think my husband is a hero, he serves in the Army as a pilot. In my eyes he is a hero, and every solider who chooses to serve, but sometimes I think the real heroes are the ones left behind.

The Military Wife.

We run households, we have babies, we take care of kids, and friends who need us. We do this with our heads held high; it's our way of serving our country. Our husbands need to know that everything is okay back home, so that they can function as soliders. This is just my opinion. I live in a military community and I see this day after day, and it is awesome. To see wives of all walks, pull together and do what has to be done.

> Mel
> Wife of a Soldier

U.S. Representative Zach Wamp

We know that fear is one of the most powerful forces in the world today. Yesterday, the lowest of the low, the dregs of our international community, used fear to carry out inhumane acts on all of humanity. Today, we claim the truth that one force is greater than fear. That is love.

Throughout the ages, love has conquered fear over and over again.

Our love for our fellow man will overcome fear of these outrageous criminals.

Our love of freedom will overcome our fear of tyranny.

Our love of country will overcome our fear of terrorism.

Our love of God will overcome our fear of Satan himself.

Our love of goodness will overcome our fear of evil.

Our love of peace will overcome our fear of war.

Today we stand together, our President, the United States Congress, and 270 million people, mourning those lost, comforting those left behind, praying for our nation at this dark hour.

Yesterday, our House Chaplain, Father Daniel Coughlin, prayed that "In God we trust," our nation's motto, but that today, may it be our strength.

Much of our character has been born from adversity. An even stronger America must rise from the ashes of these fiery crashes so that good does once again triumph over evil.

May the peace of God that passeth all understanding be with us now and forevermore.

The Flag at Half Staff

There is a special sadness that accompanies the death of a serviceman, for we're never quite good enough to them - - not really; we can't be, because what they gave us is beyond our powers to repay. And so, when a serviceman dies, it's a tear in the fabric, a break in the whole, and all we can do is remember.

President Ronald Reagan

Governor Mike Huckabee

Hello, this is Gov. Mike Huckabee with a comment from my corner of the Capitol. I would like to share with you a heartwarming story that occurred two days after the terrorist attacks on New York and Washington. There probably are dozens of similar stories across this state that illustrate just how strongly Arkansans and Americans have pulled together in the wake of this tragedy.

Every morning at Northwest Elementary School in El Dorado, two flags are raised as the student body looks on. The U.S. flag the school uses is one that flew over our nation's Capitol in Washington. The Arkansas flag at Northwest Elementary is one that flew over our state Capitol in Little Rock. The fifth-grade students who raise the flags were trained by Darrien Martin of the El Dorado Police Department. He's at the school each morning and each afternoon along with police officers Randall Conley and Eric Price to assist with traffic control and other duties. Officer Conley also has worked with the students, teaching them to stand silently with their hands over their hearts as the flags are raised.

On this particular Thursday morning, Officer Price stepped into the crosswalk and stood at attention as the U.S. flag was raised to half-staff. Suddenly, all of the traffic on what otherwise is a busy street stopped. For a few precious moments, the entire neighborhood was quiet as the flag went to the top of the pole and then came back down to rest at half-staff. Those who had been driving down College Avenue turned off their car engines and got out of their automobiles. These adults, who on a normal day would be racing to their next appointment, joined the students of Northwest Elementary in reciting the Pledge of Allegiance. Next, the school's music teacher stepped forward and began to sing "The Star-Spangled Banner." Everyone joined in on that beautiful September morning, just 48 hours removed from the horror of Sept. 11. As the children turned around and re-entered the building, there were many tears in the eyes of the adults standing by their vehicles on College Avenue.

I wasn't in El Dorado to witness this, but I was in Searcy that day and saw other displays of patriotism. At a 7 a.m. meeting with local business leaders, the Pledge of Allegiance was recited with what seemed to be a bit more resolve than usual. Later that morning, I spoke to the student body at Harding University. Harding attracts students from across the country and around the world. Standing in front of a huge American flag, I had the privilege of talking about the events of that memorable week. There wasn't a sound in the cavernous Benson Auditorium. It was the most attentive group of 5,000 people I had ever addressed. The highlight of the day, though, came during the afternoon when I visited with the students at Sidney Deener Elementary School. Their parents had dressed them in red, white and blue. Yes, they were young, but they could sense something had changed in our country.

To honor those who died in New York and Washington, it's important we not allow this sense of unity and patriotism to die. Display our nation's flag at your home and place of business. Continue to give blood to the Red Cross. Remain active in your church and civic organizations. Pray for our country's leaders and those in the armed forces. Contribute to the disaster relief funds. We've received many calls from those wishing to assist in the recovery efforts in New York. You can best assist by making a donation to the recently established New York State World Trade Center Relief Fund. The fund will be used for victim support and to help pay for the emergency response effort in lower Manhattan. Donations may be sent to the New York State World Trade Center Relief Fund at P.O. Box 5028 in Albany, N.Y., 12205. Those wishing to phone in a contribution can call 1-800-801-8092.

Gov. George Pataki of New York asked me to notify Arkansans this is the central collection point. He's urging contributors to go ahead and mail in their checks rather than trying to call since they expect phone lines to be flooded for several weeks. Gov. Pataki's office and the White House have asked us to discourage people from volunteering to assist in New York City. Frankly, they don't need additional volunteers at this time. Instead, they'll be needing billions of dollars for the recovery effort. Following our widespread tornado outbreaks in 1997 and 1999, and following our ice storms last December, New York was one of the states that came to the assistance of Arkansas. I hope Arkansans will respond at this time by giving generously to this fund. Let's all continue to pull together in this time of national crisis. The terrorists wanted to get the attention of Americans everywhere. They got our attention, and they'll rue the day. Until next week, this is Gov. Mike Huckabee.

How many U.S.A. flag designs have there been in American history since 1776? Find the answer at-
www.ModernDayHeroes.com

We Must Wage a War

True *American* heroes are a sublime blend of spirit and grit, with just a dash of pride nestled between integrity and commonsense. They are confident, caring, honest and humble...they are leaders *by* example who do unto others *better* than others have done unto them.

Michelle S. Stein
Washington, DC (via Lubbock, Texas!)

U.S. Congressman Brad Sherman –
gave his support for the use of United States Armed Forces against those responsible for recent attacks against the United States in the House of Representatives on September 14, 2001.

In certain foreign cities there were those who danced in the streets believing that the terrorists' ability to kill thousands of American civilians showed the terrorists' strength. America's strength is not our ability to kill civilians, but our great strength is that we do everything possible to avoid killing civilians.

We must remember that our conflict is not with Islam and not with Muslims. The last three military campaigns of the United States were to protect Muslim people in Bosnia, in Kosovo and in Kuwait.

For years we have urged our allies to join us in curtailing investments and aid to countries that support terrorism. Now we must insist that they join us in this effort. Those who claim to be America's friends can no longer do business as usual with countries that support terrorism, nor can we allow European bank secrecy laws to stand in our way of tracing the money that was spent on this horrendous action.

We must wage a war against all of the well-organized, well-financed terrorist groups who have dedicated themselves to killing Americans. Chief among this group is the one headed by Osama bin

Laden. He is probably responsible for the atrocities of September 11, and certainly responsible for the attack on the U.S.S. Cole in Yemen and the attack on our embassies in East Africa. As long as the Taliban government in Afghanistan harbors Osama bin Laden, he will be working every day to top the evil of September 11.

It is easy to blame our intelligence agencies for what happened, but as long as we have allowed Osama bin Laden and others to sit there in safety, launching attack after attack against America, some of those attacks will be successful. We must demand that the Taliban government hand Osama bin Laden and his henchmen over to us now and stop harboring terrorists. If they refuse, then we must initiate hostilities. We will prevail by aligning ourselves with the Northern Alliance. Hostilities with the Taliban may involve American casualties, but failure to act will involve thousands and tens of thousands of American casualties.

The Pain of Injury

An American hero is an ordinary person who rises up to accomplish extraordinary things.

Scott Sheldon
Costa Mesa, CA

George J. Tenet
Director for the Central Intelligence Agency

The following message from Director of Central Intelligence George J. Tenet was read by a senior CIA official on September 14, 2001 at a ceremony at CIA Headquarters marking the National Day of Prayer and Remembrance:

Today, Americans of every background and every faith are joining together across our great, grieving country to remember the brothers and sisters taken from us this week by the vile, vicious hand of terrorism.

Thousands of families — among them our friends, colleagues, and neighbors — are struggling with the sorrow of loss, the pain of injury, and the ache of uncertainty.

Millions more, though, stand with them and with all the victims of these atrocities. For in this noble nation — bloodied but most assuredly unbowed — good has answered evil.

Good in the heroism of rescuers, relief workers, and in every American who has stepped forward to offer every kind of care and comfort. You are firmly and honorably among them.

But the men and women of the Central Intelligence Agency — along with our partners throughout the government — have an additional, decisive task.

To us belongs the mission of unmasking the authors and sponsors of this evil. Those who on a seemingly ordinary Tuesday attacked decency itself. Those who have defiled every standard of humanity.

The road ahead will be neither short nor easy. Yet it is one we must take without hesitation. Indeed, we have already taken the first steps, as a nation and as an agency.

Part of our response can be seen around you. The task forces, the heightened tempo of our global operations, the surge in support and security.

But there is a crucial part that cannot be seen. The determination that is cut into our hearts, the resolve that is burned into our minds.

Ours is a shared commitment to a single goal: To do what we can—to do what we must—against the sort of unspeakable horror that has now invaded and shattered so many, many lives.

Those we remember deserve no less. May our prayers be with them, and may God bless you all.

A Foundation of Our Democracy

The world enjoys many types of modern day heroes. They are in our military, in our police, in our schools, and even in our homes.

Ever since the horrific attacks on our freedom on September 11, 2001, our nations Firefighters have become respected and revered heroes. The 343 members of the Fire Department of New York were, are, and always will be heroes in every sense of the word.

For the past 27 years I have been a firefighter, and I have seen many acts of heroism around our country. For the most part, firefighters function in the background of life, for they do not desire fanfare or kudos. Firefighters receive attention in the aftermath of earthquakes, wild land fires, and devastating campaign fires. And then they instantly become heroes for a period of time. But then the memories of their courageous activities fade away. I would like the citizens of the USA to know, no matter which part of the US, in cities large and small, in career or volunteer fire departments the firefighters are always there for you - 24 hours a day 365 days a year. So the next time you see a fire engine drive by, please wave "hello" and thank you.

James M. Ellis
Costa Mesa Fire Department
Fire Chief

U.S. Representative Jay Inslee –
addressed the firefighter's in Edmonds, WA on September 15, 2001.

Tuesday was not the first day in American history that firefighters have rushed toward danger - not away from it - selflessly placing themselves in harm's way while the world seemed to crumble all around.

American firefighters, Washington firefighters, Edmonds firefighters have been placing their lives on the line for their fellow human beings as long as the community has been around and it is fitting that the sacrifices that have been made should be memorialized.

To our fallen firefighters -- and to those among you who serve today: on behalf of our community, I say, you have our respect, you have our gratitude and we are forever in your debt.

We will mourn our dead.

We will pray for their families.

We will find the perpetrators and their supporters and exact justice.

We will not be stopped by any government that attempts to harbor terrorists.

But we will do more than this.

We will deprive terrorists of even the temporary success of robbing us of what they really want - our confidence.

We will keep our American spirit shining.

We will not allow hatred to infect our communities and we will stand up against those who attempt to harass or intimidate people of any particular faith or ancestry in this time of threat. We are all Americans.

We are confident that our children will be safe in schools, and we will tell them so.

And we are confident that we will maintain that dynamic energy of our economy which has marked our national history.

We will not pull into economic isolation.

My friends, this is a time to stand together, and stand with the President of our nation with unyielding action against those who participated in, or supported the terrorists who killed so many of our fellow citizens.

Many have asked me what it is they can do to aid in this effort. Here are a few suggestions:

1. Donate Blood.
2. Demonstrate Commitment to America's Financial Institutions.

We can deny the perpetrators of this act their certain hope that they can damage our economy as they have destroyed the lives of many of our citizens. We should have confidence in our economy and our financial institutions.

If hundreds of firefighters can risk their lives by entering the burning World Trade Center buildings, we can help prevent a possible market downturn.

3.   Display the American Flag.

The House of Representatives passed a resolution encouraging all Americans to display the flag.

4.   Vote.

Voting is a foundation of our democracy, and our democracy has come under attack this week. To show a great demonstration in the strength of our democratic system, vote this Tuesday, September 18th.

As the days go on, I hope you and yours can find peace in the confidence that America will weather this challenge as we have so many times in the past. I hope you will give me your thoughts and wisdom on this subject as time goes on.

Unconquerable Qualities of America

A hero is someone who goes beyond what is expected just because a job needs to be done. They deserve to be admired for their achievements although they have the qualities in their lives that enable them to work silently behind the scenes and allow others to take the credit.

They want the best for others.

Michael B. Collier
Costa Mesa, CA

U.S. Representative Luis Gutierrez –
remarked for the Laborers International Convention on September 16, 2001.

I want to thank my good friend General-President Terry O'Sullivan and Secretary-Treasurer Armand Sabitoni for the very kind and generous invitation to join you at your national convention.

I have been proud to have a close association with many members of your union for a long time. I am intimately familiar with the vital work that you do and I am very proud to consider myself a friend, ally and partner with the leaders and members of the Laborers Union. I want to say a special hello to Terry Healy and all of my friends and constituents from Chicago and the 4th Congressional District of Illinois.

I apologize for not joining you in person. As you may know, because of the extraordinary events of the past week, Congress stayed in session much later than expected and travel has been difficult. I look forward to seeing as many of you in person as possible as soon as I can.

I speak to you today in a vastly changed America from the world we were contemplating when Terry O'Sullivan and I first spoke about the possibility of me addressing the laborers.

Obviously, it goes without saying that this is an incredibly difficult time for every American and for every person who values freedom and respects the law across our globe. I know that there may still be some members of your union missing in New York. My thoughts and prayers are with the families of your missing brethren and with the families of every victim of this tragedy.

I also know that many of your members are in New York right now helping day and night with rescue and recovery efforts. I salute and thank them.

This tragedy has reminded us of the most invincible and unconquerable qualities of America. That is this: in the midst of tragedy, we always produce heroes. In the midst of long nights of despair, we always move toward a morning of hope. Your workers are among the thousands and thousands of Americans who are giving us hope for the future at a time when the present is filled with sadness.

I also know that members of your union helped to build the World Trade Center. And I know that members of your union will help to rebuild it. And I know that the members of the Laborers Union – and all members of organized labor – will stand together with all Americans and we rebuild not only those twin towers in New York but our national spirit, and resolve and commitment.

I look forward to working with your union – and every labor union member across America – as we show the world just how united we are and how quickly we will recover. We'll do it together and we will set an example for the world of how people can come together and overcome difficulty and meet the toughest challenges.

When Terry O'Sullivan and I spoke about the topic of my remarks today, we agreed that I would spend a few moments talking about immigration. And in the wake of our tragedy, I cannot think of a more important or timely topic.

Because those of us who believe that honoring the hard work that immigrants do should be a top priority for our nation know that we will be facing some new challenges.

Because there will be people who want to hold America's immigrant community responsible for the tragedy that has occurred.

There will be those who make no distinction between the millions of workers and their families who come to our nation only because they want to sweat and toil and contribute, and the handful of cowards who came here only to wage war.

Let me be clear: the people involved in the terrorist attacks on September 11 were not immigrants. They were criminals.

And no supporter of immigrants wants criminals to benefit in any way from any legislation designed to help the real, hard-working immigrants who help to make America – and your union – great.

We all need to remember that immigrants were not immune to the suffering that occurred on Tuesday and continues today. Immigrants lost their lives and lost family members. Like every resident of our nation, immigrants saw their lives changed and dreams delayed on Tuesday. Like every other resident of our nation, immigrants are outraged at this cowardly act, determined to defend America, committed to rebuilding.

No matter their nationality, I have heard repeatedly from the immigrant community again and again this week – we're with America. We're flying flags. We're grieving for the victims and their families. We're helping to build a better future.

So I believe all of us must stand up to those who say that immigrants or immigration policy is responsible for this tragedy and encourage people to simply look around at all of the immigrants – from Mexico to Poland to Korea to Ireland – who are part of the solution, not part of the problem.

Because I think when we look at the real immigrant population in America, only one word comes to mind.

And that word is work.

All across America today, immigrants are doing among our nation's hardest work. They are working the longest hours, often at the toughest jobs.

And nobody knows this fact better than the Laborers Union. I know that you have more immigrants among your members than any building trade union.

And I know that your leaders and your members understand better than anyone that the future of the American labor union movement depends on successfully reaching out to immigrants from every nation and making them a welcome and thriving and respected part of our workforce.

If you doubt the importance of immigrants to America's labor force, I invite you simply to think about America today.

Think about the fruit that you ate this morning.

Think about the people who are cleaning your room at the hotel.

Think about those who sometimes care for your children, or work in our hospitals, or serve your food and bus your tables in the restaurants at this convention.

And imagine who would be doing those jobs without immigrant labor to America?

The facts and figures about our immigrant population are clear.

In both New York and Illinois, immigrants pay nearly one billion dollars per year in taxes. California's fruit industry – a ten-billion dollar industry – is almost entirely dependent on immigrant labor.

And all across America, forward-looking labor unions are strengthening themselves – increasing their membership, improving their bargaining position, reaching out to new industries and trades – by including more immigrants.

When you organize new workers, you open new doors for all of your members. By being on the cutting edge of America's new and changing labor force, you improve the quality of life for every laborer.

The growing, emerging voices of America's immigrant community makes it easier for all of us to fight for the priorities and needs of working men and women.

To take steps to make our workplaces safer and make OSHA enforce sensible worker safety rules.

To protect the rights of labor union members to go on strike and have their strike respected.

To guarantee prevailing wage laws and to make sure every worker in America earns a living wage for their hard work.

To stop discrimination of any kind in the workplace.

These are the important goals of the Laborers Union and making immigrants a strong, thriving, growing part of your union help everyone to reach those goals.

So let me just say a few words quickly about how we get there – how we help every American worker benefit from immigrant workers.

To reach that goal, we need to make it easier for immigrants to become full, participating members of American life. And to do that, we need to help those workers who are here without documentation to legalize their status.

Now let me be clear who I am talking about.

First, I am talking about law-abiding residents of our nation. People who have respected the laws of our nation once they have come here and represent no threat of any kind.

Second, I am talking about people who have demonstrated their ability and desire to work.

I think our nation needs to take action immediately to legalize these people.

We accept their labor. We take their taxes. We depend on their contributions. It is time that in return we give them the respect they deserve.

I am the co-sponsor of HR 500, a bill that will allow longtime residents to adjust their status. I am the co-chairman of a Democratic task force crafting a legalization bill that we hope to move forward and pass during this session of Congress.

I need you support. I need the Laborers union and all union members to stand up and say, "It's time every working person in this country is treated fairly and justly and with decency."

I will fight for that goal. I will fight for the rights that immigrants have earned by working at the hardest jobs for the longest hours. I will help immigrants to reach the American dream that they desire.

But I can only do it with your help.

Together, we will reach that goal.

I want to thank once again my friends Terry O'Sullivan and Terry Healy for their day-today leadership and their very kind invitation to be with you today.

**Nominate a candidate for our Modern Day Hero® Award at -
www.ModernDayHeroes.com**
Additional information regarding this award found at the end of this book.

Enemies of Freedom

Like wisps of smoke on a windy day; fame, physical beauty, fortune, and power; all are transient and, ultimately, illusive. Notoriety is for now, but that which endures is heroic material. American heroes must not only illuminate and exemplify the great timeless virtues; they must be rooted in the rich tradition that is America: the Spirit of '76 -- the Grand Experiment in Human Freedom. Equality, Liberty, Tolerance, Individual Rights, E Pluribus Unum: these are beacons and anchors that guide us and stabilize us through the tumultuous storms of history. Our American heroes must serve as the Captains of the great ship of state.

> Monty Warner
> Morgantown, WV

President George W. Bush –
addressed a Joint Session of Congress and the American people on September 21, 2001.

Mr. Speaker, Mr. President Pro Tempore, members of Congress, and fellow Americans:

In the normal course of events, Presidents come to this chamber to report on the state of the Union. Tonight, no such report is needed. It has already been delivered by the American people.

We have seen it in the courage of passengers, who rushed terrorists to save others on the ground -- passengers like an exceptional man named Todd Beamer. And would you please help me to welcome his wife, Lisa Beamer, here tonight. [Applause.]

We have seen the state of our Union in the endurance of rescuers, working past exhaustion. We have seen the unfurling of flags, the lighting of candles, the giving of blood, the saying of prayers -- in English, Hebrew, and Arabic. We have seen the decency of a loving and giving people who have made the grief of strangers their own.

My fellow citizens, for the last nine days, the entire world has seen for itself the state of our Union -- and it is strong. [Applause.]

Tonight we are a country awakened to danger and called to defend freedom. Our grief has turned to anger, and anger to resolution. Whether we bring our enemies to justice, or bring justice to our enemies, justice will be done. [Applause.]

I thank the Congress for its leadership at such an important time. All of America was touched on the evening of the tragedy to see Republicans and Democrats joined together on the steps of this Capitol, singing "God Bless America." And you did more than sing; you acted, by delivering $40 billion to rebuild our communities and meet the needs of our military.

Speaker Hastert, Minority Leader Gephardt, Majority Leader Daschle and Senator Lott, I thank you for your friendship, for your leadership and for your service to our country. [Applause.]

And on behalf of the American people, I thank the world for its outpouring of support. America will never forget the sounds of our National Anthem playing at Buckingham Palace, on the streets of Paris, and at Berlin's Brandenburg Gate.

We will not forget South Korean children gathering to pray outside our embassy in Seoul, or the prayers of sympathy offered at a mosque in Cairo. We will not forget moments of silence and days of mourning in Australia and Africa and Latin America.

Nor will we forget the citizens of 80 other nations who died with our own: dozens of Pakistanis; more than 130 Israelis; more than 250 citizens of India; men and women from El Salvador, Iran, Mexico and Japan; and hundreds of British citizens. America has no truer friend than Great Britain. [Applause.] Once again, we are joined together in a great cause -- so honored the British Prime Minister has crossed an ocean to show his unity of purpose with America. Thank you for coming, friend. [Applause.]

On September the 11th, enemies of freedom committed an act of war against our country. Americans have known wars -- but for the past 136 years, they have been wars on foreign soil, except for one Sunday in 1941. Americans have known the casualties of war -- but not at the center of a great city on a peaceful morning. Americans have known surprise attacks -- but never before on thousands of civilians. All of this was brought upon us in a single day -- and night fell on a different world, a world where freedom itself is under attack.

Americans have many questions tonight. Americans are asking: Who attacked our country? The evidence we have gathered all points to a collection of loosely affiliated terrorist organizations known as al Qaeda. They are the same murderers indicted for bombing American embassies in Tanzania and Kenya, and responsible for bombing the U.S.S. Cole.

Al Qaeda is to terror what the mafia is to crime. But its goal is not making money; its goal is remaking the world -- and imposing its radical beliefs on people everywhere.

The terrorists practice a fringe form of Islamic extremism that has been rejected by Muslim scholars and the vast majority of Muslim clerics -- a fringe movement that perverts the peaceful teachings of Islam. The terrorists' directive commands them to kill Christians and Jews, to kill all Americans, and make no distinction among military and civilians, including women and children.

This group and its leader -- a person named Osama bin Laden -- are linked to many other organizations in different countries, including the Egyptian Islamic Jihad and the Islamic Movement of Uzbekistan. There are thousands of these terrorists in more than 60 countries. They are recruited from their own nations and neighborhoods and brought to camps in places like Afghanistan, where they are trained in the tactics of terror. They are sent back to their homes or sent to hide in countries around the world to plot evil and destruction.

The leadership of al Qaeda has great influence in Afghanistan and supports the Taliban regime in controlling most of that country. In Afghanistan, we see al Qaeda's vision for the world.

Afghanistan's people have been brutalized -- many are starving and many have fled. Women are not allowed to attend school. You can be jailed for owning a television. Religion can be practiced only as their leaders dictate. A man can be jailed in Afghanistan if his beard is not long enough.

The United States respects the people of Afghanistan -- after all, we are currently its largest source of humanitarian aid -- but we condemn the Taliban regime. [Applause.] It is not only repressing its own people, it is threatening people everywhere by sponsoring and sheltering and supplying terrorists. By aiding and abetting murder, the Taliban regime is committing murder.

And tonight, the United States of America makes the following demands on the Taliban: Deliver to United States authorities all the leaders of al Qaeda who hide in your land. [Applause.] Release all foreign nationals, including American citizens, you have unjustly imprisoned. Protect foreign journalists, diplomats and aid workers in your country. Close immediately and permanently every terrorist training camp in Afghanistan, and hand over every terrorist, and every person in their support structure, to appropriate authorities. [Applause.] Give the United States full access to terrorist training camps, so we can make sure they are no longer operating.

These demands are not open to negotiation or discussion. [Applause.] The Taliban must act, and act immediately. They will hand over the terrorists, or they will share in their fate.

I also want to speak tonight directly to Muslims throughout the world. We respect your faith. It's practiced freely by many millions of Americans, and by millions more in countries that America counts as friends. Its teachings are good and peaceful, and those who commit evil in the name of Allah blaspheme the name of Allah. [Applause.] The terrorists are traitors to their own faith, trying, in effect, to hijack Islam itself. The enemy of America is not our many Muslim friends; it is not our many Arab friends. Our enemy is a radical network of terrorists, and every government that supports them. [Applause.]

Our war on terror begins with al Qaeda, but it does not end there. It will not end until every terrorist group of global reach has been found, stopped and defeated. [Applause.]

Americans are asking, why do they hate us? They hate what we see right here in this chamber -- a democratically elected government. Their leaders are self-appointed. They hate our freedoms -- our freedom of religion, our freedom of speech, our freedom to vote and assemble and disagree with each other.

They want to overthrow existing governments in many Muslim countries, such as Egypt, Saudi Arabia, and Jordan. They want to drive Israel out of the Middle East. They want to drive Christians and Jews out of vast regions of Asia and Africa.

These terrorists kill not merely to end lives, but to disrupt and end a way of life. With every atrocity, they hope that America grows fearful, retreating from the world and forsaking our friends. They stand against us, because we stand in their way.

We are not deceived by their pretenses to piety. We have seen their kind before. They are the heirs of all the murderous ideologies of the 20th century. By sacrificing human life to serve their radical visions -- by abandoning every value except the will to power -- they follow in the path of fascism, and Nazism, and totalitarianism. And they will follow that path all the way, to where it ends: in history's unmarked grave of discarded lies. [Applause.]

Americans are asking: How will we fight and win this war? We will direct every resource at our command -- every means of diplomacy, every tool of intelligence, every instrument of law enforcement, every financial influence, and every necessary weapon of war -- to the disruption and to the defeat of the global terror network.

This war will not be like the war against Iraq a decade ago, with a decisive liberation of territory and a swift conclusion. It will not look like the air war above Kosovo two years ago, where no ground troops were used and not a single American was lost in combat.

Our response involves far more than instant retaliation and isolated strikes. Americans should not expect one battle, but a lengthy campaign, unlike any other we have ever seen. It may include dramatic strikes, visible on TV, and covert operations, secret even in success. We will starve terrorists of funding, turn them one against another, drive them from place to place, until there is no refuge or no rest. And we will pursue nations that provide aid or safe haven to terrorism. Every nation, in every region, now has a decision to make. Either you are with us, or you are with the terrorists. [Applause.] From this day forward, any nation that continues to harbor or support terrorism will be regarded by the United States as a hostile regime.

Our nation has been put on notice: We are not immune from attack. We will take defensive measures against terrorism to protect Americans. Today, dozens of federal departments and agencies, as well as state and local governments, have responsibilities affecting homeland security. These efforts must be coordinated at the highest level. So tonight I announce the creation of a Cabinet-level position reporting directly to me -- the Office of Homeland Security.

And tonight I also announce a distinguished American to lead this effort, to strengthen American security: a military Veteran, an effective governor, a true patriot, a trusted friend -- Pennsylvania's Tom Ridge. [Applause.] He will lead, oversee and coordinate a comprehensive national strategy to safeguard our country against terrorism, and respond to any attacks that may come.

These measures are essential. But the only way to defeat terrorism as a threat to our way of life is to stop it, eliminate it, and destroy it where it grows. [Applause.]

Many will be involved in this effort, from FBI agents to intelligence operatives to the reservists we have called to active duty. All deserve our thanks, and all have our prayers. And tonight, a few miles from the damaged Pentagon, I have a message for our military: Be ready. I've called the Armed Forces to alert, and there is a reason. The hour is coming when America will act, and you will make us proud. [Applause.]

This is not, however, just America's fight. And what is at stake is not just America's freedom. This is the world's fight. This is civilization's fight. This is the fight of all who believe in progress and pluralism, tolerance and freedom.

We ask every nation to join us. We will ask, and we will need, the help of police forces, intelligence services, and banking systems around the world. The United States is grateful that many nations and many international organizations have already responded -- with sympathy and with support. Nations from Latin America, to Asia, to Africa, to Europe, to the Islamic world. Perhaps the NATO Charter reflects best the attitude of the world: An attack on one is an attack on all.

The civilized world is rallying to America's side. They understand that if this terror goes unpunished, their own cities, their own citizens may be next. Terror, unanswered, can not only bring down buildings, it can threaten the stability of legitimate governments. And you know what -- we're not going to allow it. [Applause.]

Americans are asking: What is expected of us? I ask you to live your lives, and hug your children. I know many citizens have fears tonight, and I ask you to be calm and resolute, even in the face of a continuing threat.

I ask you to uphold the values of America, and remember why so many have come here. We are in a fight for our principles, and our first responsibility is to live by them. No one should be singled out for unfair treatment or unkind words because of their ethnic background or religious faith. [Applause.]

I ask you to continue to support the victims of this tragedy with your contributions. Those who want to give can go to a central source of information, libertyunites.org, to find the names of groups providing direct help in New York, Pennsylvania, and Virginia.

The thousands of FBI agents who are now at work in this investigation may need your cooperation, and I ask you to give it.

I ask for your patience, with the delays and inconveniences that may accompany tighter security; and for your patience in what will be a long struggle.

I ask your continued participation and confidence in the American economy. Terrorists attacked a symbol of American prosperity. They did not touch its source. America is successful because of the hard work, and creativity, and enterprise of our people. These were the true strengths of our economy before September 11th, and they are our strengths today. [Applause.]

And, finally, please continue praying for the victims of terror and their families, for those in uniform, and for our great country. Prayer has comforted us in sorrow, and will help strengthen us for the journey ahead.

Tonight I thank my fellow Americans for what you have already done and for what you will do. And ladies and gentlemen of the Congress, I thank you, their representatives, for what you have already done and for what we will do together.

Tonight, we face new and sudden national challenges. We will come together to improve air safety, to dramatically expand the number of air marshals on domestic flights, and take new measures to prevent hijacking. We will come together to promote stability and keep our airlines flying, with direct assistance during this emergency. [Applause.]

We will come together to give law enforcement the additional tools it needs to track down terror here at home. [Applause.] We will come together to strengthen our intelligence capabilities to know the plans of terrorists before they act, and find them before they strike. [Applause.]

We will come together to take active steps that strengthen America's economy, and put our people back to work.

Tonight we welcome two leaders who embody the extraordinary spirit of all New Yorkers: Governor George Pataki, and Mayor Rudolph Giuliani. [Applause.] As a symbol of America's resolve, my administration will work with Congress, and these two leaders, to show the world that we will rebuild New York City. [Applause.]

After all that has just passed -- all the lives taken, and all the possibilities and hopes that died with them -- it is natural to wonder if America's future is one of fear. Some speak of an age of terror. I know there are struggles ahead, and dangers to face. But this country will define our times, not be defined by them. As long as the United States of America is determined and strong, this will not be an age of terror; this will be an age of liberty, here and across the world. [Applause.]

Great harm has been done to us. We have suffered great loss. And in our grief and anger we have found our mission and our moment. Freedom and fear are at war. The advance of human freedom -- the great achievement of our time, and the great hope of every time -- now depends on us. Our nation -- this generation -- will lift a dark threat of violence from our people and our future. We will rally the world to this cause by our efforts, by our courage. We will not tire, we will not falter, and we will not fail. [Applause.]

It is my hope that in the months and years ahead, life will return almost to normal. We'll go back to our lives and routines, and that is good. Even grief recedes with time and grace. But our resolve must not pass. Each of us will remember what happened that day, and to whom it happened. We'll remember the moment the news came -- where we were and what we were doing. Some will remember an image of a fire, or a story of rescue. Some will carry memories of a face and a voice gone forever.

And I will carry this: It is the police shield of a man named George Howard, who died at the World Trade Center trying to save others. It was given to me by his mom, Arlene, as a proud memorial to her son. This is my reminder of lives that ended, and a task that does not end. [Applause.]

I will not forget this wound to our country or those who inflicted it. I will not yield; I will not rest; I will not relent in waging this struggle for freedom and security for the American people.

The course of this conflict is not known, yet its outcome is certain. Freedom and fear, justice and cruelty, have always been at war, and we know that God is not neutral between them. [Applause.]

Fellow citizens, we'll meet violence with patient justice -- assured of the rightness of our cause, and confident of the victories to come. In all that lies before us, may God grant us wisdom, and may He watch over the United States of America.

Thank you. [Applause.]

Chapter 6

American Resolve

An Unpayable Debt of Honor and Gratitude – The First Casualty of the War on Terror

Americans who commit to protecting our borders, both near and afar, will probably have no real idea of how what they do will impact the future of our country.

Michele Ryan
Business Owner

George J. Tenet
Director of the Central Intelligence Agency
These are the remarks by George J. Tenet at the funeral of Johnny Micheal Spann at Arlington National Cemetery on December 10, 2001.

Here today, in American soil, we lay to lasting rest an American hero. United in loss and in sorrow, we are united, as well, in our reverence for the timeless virtues upon which Mike Spann shaped his life—virtues for which he ultimately gave his life.

Dignity. Decency. Bravery. Liberty.

From his earliest days, Mike not only knew what was right, he worked to do what was right. At home and school in Alabama. As a United States Marine. As an officer of the Central Intelligence Agency. And as the head of his own, young family.

And it was in the quest for right that Mike at his country's call went to Afghanistan. To that place of danger and terror, he sought to bring justice and freedom. And to our nation—which he held so close to his heart—he sought to bring a still greater measure of strength and security.

For Mike understood that it is not enough simply to dream of a better, safer world. He understood that it has to be built—with passion and dedication, in the face of obstacles, in the face of evil.

Those who took him from us will be neither deeply mourned nor long remembered. But Mike Spann will be forever part of the treasured legacy of free peoples everywhere—as we each owe him an immense, unpayable debt of honor and gratitude.

His example is our inspiration. His sacrifice is our strength.

For the men and women of the Central Intelligence Agency, he remains the rigorous and resolute colleague. The professional who took great pride in his difficult and demanding work. The patriot who knew that information saves lives, and that its collection is a risk worth taking.

May God bless Mike Spann—an American of courage— and may God bless those who love and miss him, and all who carry on the noble work that he began.

Keep informed on the War on Terror with valuable information provided in our e-newsletter. Sign up at – www.ModernDayHeroes.com

America's Character Will Prevail

I would consider a hero to be someone who is there for someone: a friend, relative, or even a stranger. They may need at smile, a hug, words of encouragement, or even just a hello. So many people forget or get so busy to go "out" of their way to do the little things. These things can always make someone's day & sometimes without the "hero" knowing. Thanks to all those that try to make this world a nice place to live in!

Amy Diamond
Fountain Valley, CA

U.S. Representative Ellen Tauscher

On September 11, we were all in horror as we witnessed events that we never expected to encounter. We knew that the threat of terror existed, but it was similar to the threat of an earthquake. It was out there, but you didn't think about it on your way to work.

Our nation has endured the bombing of the World Trade Center in 1993 along with the tragic events involved in the destruction of the Alfred P. Murrah Federal Building in Oklahoma City in 1995. Though both were difficult ordeals, neither prepared us for these cataclysmic events. Nothing could have.

For most of us, the tragic losses of life in New York, Washington, Pennsylvania, and in some of our neighbors' own families is still quite a shock. For me, it was like seeing my past crumble and watching America's innocence crumble with it.

I grew up across the river in New Jersey and watched the World Trade Center towers being built as I walked back and forth to high school every day.

After I graduated from college I was unable to find a job teaching. I thought of the towers that I had watched gradually rising from lower Manhattan, and they seemed almost like a welcome mat that New York had laid out. They promised the success that comes with hard work and a lot of determination. They were the closest physical testament my generation had to the American dream and were a potent symbol of America's financial strength.

So, I went to New York and headed to Wall Street. For the first year and a half I lived at home, taking the train in and out of the World Trade Center every day.

Soon I was working at the New York Stock Exchange only a block and a half from the Twin Towers, trading stocks amid the flying ticker tape and shouts of "sell, sell, sell" and "buy, buy, buy."

Since being elected to Congress, I spend more time thinking about national security than the NASDAQ. As a member of the House Armed Services Committee, I work with and personally know many of the men and women who serve our country around the world and at the Pentagon.

But one doesn't need a physical or emotional connection with the World Trade Center, Pentagon, or the heroes aboard United Airlines Flight 93 to be deeply impacted by these tragic events. Families are grieving, and the world is grieving with them.

As we grieve, gone are the labels we use for ourselves - Congresswoman, firefighter, business executive, mother. We are all Americans.

We are proud of what the World Trade Center, Pentagon, and passengers on the United flight symbolize -- our free-market system, the strongest economy and military in the world, and the indomitable American spirit.

Sadly, the things that make America wonderful made the World Trade Center and the Pentagon targets. But after two weeks of endless questions from our children and ourselves, one thing remains unquestioned. Our American character.

We are a strong and resilient people. Our diversity is our strength. We do not shrink from the threat of terror. Lawless thugs do not intimidate us. We have never been defeated in protecting our home territory. Adversity has never stopped us.

And we will prevail.

Our State's Most Pressing Needs Will Never be Solved by Government

To me, an American hero is an individual who strives to be better mentally, physically, and spiritually than he or she has been in past and then works to help others develop that same drive. My American heroes see within themselves and within others the best that they can be and invest their time, talents, and resources in turning those visions into reality. An American hero is one who works to make heroes out of others.

Dane Parker
Costa Mesa, CA

Governor Mike Huckabee

Hello, this is Gov. Mike Huckabee with a comment from my corner of the Capitol. The terrorist attacks of Sept. 11, the war in Afghanistan that followed those attacks, the anthrax scares, and other events of recent weeks have led us to appreciate this Christmas season more than ever. Being close to home has taken on a new meaning for millions of Americans. Family is more important. For many, the religious aspect of life has an added significance. Tradition is more meaningful. Christmas combines religious beliefs, family, home, and tradition. The most special Christmas memories are those of watching the faces of children and grandchildren light up on Christmas morning as they come into a room to open their gifts.

The economic downturn has forced Americans to simplify their holiday plans. The downturn isn't good, but the trend toward a simpler Christmas celebration is a positive thing. I hope you've resisted the temptation to become trapped in the harried Christmas mindset. Christmas is meant to be a celebration. Why turn it into a period filled with stress and anxiety? Why not instead use this as a time of quiet reflection on the many ways God has blessed our state and nation? Why not thank God for those blessings by helping make life more pleasant for our fellow Arkansans? The Christmas seasons I've enjoyed most were the ones when I focused on the true meaning of the day -- a child born in a stable in Bethlehem who gave us everything and expects us to give something in return.

We come in daily contact with people who need a smile, a hug or an act of kindness. The other members of our family need to know what we enjoy about them rather than constantly hearing about the traits that annoy us. We need to praise children for their achievements rather than reminding them of their failures. We should compliment our co-workers for the efforts others in the office never notice. That stranger out in the parking lot could use a smile rather than a cold, nervous glance. This is, after all, Arkansas. We're supposed to be a place known for smiles.

Let's never forget those less fortunate than ourselves. For every Christmas gift you bought, there was an Arkansas child needing a new coat. For every hour you spent in the mall, there was a lonely senior citizen praying someone would stop by for a visit or simply call on the phone. For every Christmas card you sent, there was a parent wishing someone would take the time to teach him to read to his children. In this period of government budget cuts, we should realize anew we rely too much on government to solve problems. Government can hand out checks, but it's not good at offering love, compassion, and companionship. That must come from people working individually and through churches and civic organizations. If I've learned one thing in more than five years as governor, it's that our state's most pressing needs never will be solved by government.

I'm not saying you shouldn't enjoy receiving Christmas gifts and shopping for others. To the contrary, our country needs you to spend money this holiday season to boost the economy. But keep your perspective. Those gifts will be broken or thrown away 20 years from now. On the other hand, the gifts you give to improve the lives of others always will be remembered. One of the saddest bumper stickers I've ever seen read, "He who has the most toys wins." You know, I've never attended a funeral in which the speakers extolled the material accumulation of the deceased. If you look back, you'll find the Christmas seasons you enjoyed the least were the ones when you were caught up in the frenzy of the season. Remember those long waits to find a parking spot at the mall? Remember worrying about whether the meal you were cooking would turn out looking like those pictured in Gourmet magazine? Remember worrying about if you had the right sheets on the bed in the guest room and the right towels displayed in the bathroom? Remember fretting you had left someone off your Christmas card list? I hope you haven't been overwhelmed while trying to make your home resemble the places shown on the Martha Stewart Christmas special. Christmas should never be another of life's hassles we must endure. Decorating a tree shouldn't be work. It should be a fun way to spend an afternoon with the family. Buying gifts shouldn't be a headache. It should be a way to show loved ones they're an important part of our lives. Christmas cards aren't an added expense. They're a way to keep in touch with friends.

Model this holiday season after the simple ones. Think back to the relatives who came over for dinner and the cousins with whom you played in the yard. Think back to the beautiful Christmas Eve church services you've attended. Light a candle. Say a prayer. Hug a child. Drop some money in that Salvation Army bucket. Send a note to someone in the armed services you know who is spending this Christmas away from home. After the roaring economy of the 1990s, perhaps the horrible tragedies of Sept. 11 reminded us of the things that are truly important in life. From the Huckabee family to yours, merry Christmas.

Chapter 7

Lest We Forget

Lessons of September 11ᵗʰ

In my estimation, not only is an American hero the firefighter who runs into a burning building or the police officer facing down a gunman, but an American hero is also the everyday man. The teacher who goes into school everyday and without adequate tools manages to teach the children and impart a sense of pride in learning. Or the parent, who works 2 jobs, is on the PTA but still makes it to their children's ballgames. Or the caregiver who gives of them self unconditionally for the comfort of the patient; they are not selfish, nor are they seeking affirmation. An American hero thinks of others before themselves. An American hero thinks of the good of the community as a whole.

Mary Lewellen
Kirkland, WA

U.S. Senator John Edwards

America's war on terrorism has just begun. The military campaign in Afghanistan has been a tremendous success, but the effort to stamp out terrorist cells will require a sustained commitment by the United States and our allies.

I recently returned from a seven-day, six-nation trip to central Asia, including Afghanistan, as part of the first group of senators to visit the country since the war began.

The bipartisan delegation had three basic goals: first, to encourage and support the men and women who are serving our country in the military; second, to talk to the military and intelligence officers on the ground to see how the operation is going; and third, to meet members of Afghanistan's new government and other key leaders in the region.

The experience offered valuable lessons for our continuing effort to fight terrorism.

Above all, we saw the extraordinary commitment and sacrifice of our young men and women serving overseas. The troops we met in Afghanistan and aboard the U.S.S. Theodore Roosevelt in the Arabian Sea are operating under very difficult conditions. We saw firsthand the freezing temperatures, the crude accommodations, and the strains of living in a remote and dangerous place.

Despite these difficult conditions, our troops are full of pride and enthusiasm. They do their work with professionalism and a commitment to their country. I wish everyone could see what a fine job they are doing. They make me very proud to be an American.

We also learned that leaders throughout the region are very supportive of the United States' efforts. I went to central Asia expecting to find a measure of resentment of the U.S. among the leaders of these nations. Instead, Chairman Hamid Karzai in Afghanistan, Pakistani President Pervez Musharraf, Turkish Prime Minister Bulent Ecevit, and others expressed a strong commitment to our common battle against terrorism.

At the same time, we also saw that the war against terrorism is far from over. From the news at home, it is easy to get the impression that the battle is basically finished, and we are now just cleaning up. There is no question the war has achieved major victories, breaking down the Taliban and disrupting al Qaeda in Afghanistan. However, much remains to be done.

Osama bin Laden and other terrorist leaders remain at large. Afghanistan remains a dangerous place. (Our delegation was flown in under cover of darkness and had to avoid restricted areas littered with land mines.) Our troops are still very much in harm's way. It also is becoming clear that the struggle against terrorism cannot be confined to Afghanistan and will have to expand to other parts of the world.

The visit confirmed that our fate as Americans is tied to the fate of people living on the other side of the globe. Before September 11, Americans could reasonably believe that things that happened in Afghanistan or Pakistan could never directly impact their own lives, their safety, and the security of their families. After the attacks on America, we know that if we ignore faraway problems, we do so at our own peril.

Osama bin Laden is no criminal mastermind. He is a common thug who was able to thrive in an environment of political despotism, religious extremism, and economic instability. Although I am confident we will get bin Laden and the leaders of al Qaeda, there are many more terrorists ready to take their places if we let them.

We can no longer allow breeding grounds for terrorism to exist like in pre-war Afghanistan. We will have to remain engaged, not only in Afghanistan, but also in the entire region. Having seen these countries firsthand, I know this will be no easy task. We are going to have to be involved on many levels and in many different areas, including economic development, education, and law enforcement.

Our commitment to this part of the world is not an act of charity. It is an investment in our own security. American leadership and engagement — designed to spread freedom and stability — are the best weapons in the fight against terrorism.

United We Stand

An American hero, whether he is Bill Gates, Sen. John McCain or President Abraham Lincoln, is a person who has made the lives of many citizens better.

Charlee Smith
Templeton, CA

U.S. Congressman Todd Platts

One year ago today, the lives of all Americans were forever changed. For the terrorists, the story of the September 11 attacks is one of immense hate, a hatred for the principles of freedom, liberty, and equality for which our great nation stands. For Americans, however, the story of September 11 is a story of immense love, a love of country, a love for human life.

Firefighters, police officers, and everyday citizens were heroic in rescuing victims of the attacks, and later in recovering the remains so as to properly honor those lost. Countless other citizens volunteered to assist and encouraged relief workers. Across the country, flags waved, hands were clasped in historic unity, and voices joined in prayer and in patriotic song.

In response to the attacks, America has been made stronger. Americans better appreciate the sacrifices that police officers, firefighters, and emergency personnel make every day to ensure our safety. And we certainly have a much deeper admiration for the courageous devotion to duty of our servicemen and women, our men and women in uniform, who fight to defend our precious freedoms throughout the world.

President Bush so profoundly captured the enduring spirit of America when he stated last year, "We will not tire. We will not falter. We will not fail. United we stand."

God bless those who lost loved ones in the attacks of September 11 and those who gave their lives seeking to save the lives of others, and certainly God bless the United States of America.

A Change of Priorities

An American hero is someone who is selfless and noble. They stand for what is right at any cost, even if it leads to their persecution or death.

Rosanne Rex
Nampa, ID

U.S. Representative F. James Sensenbrenner, Jr.

Since September 11 last year, life has taken on new meaning. For some, that day's devastation has caused them to become more cynical, changed by the events of a few hours. For others, each day since then has taken on more significance as they realize what it means when people say that you can't take life for granted. But for all of us the memories of that day will live on as we not only think about the people trapped in the World Trade Center, the Pentagon and the hijacked planes, but also remember their loved ones who were helpless to prevent the tragedies. As the President said in his proclamation earlier this month, "Those whom we lost last September 11 will forever hold a cherished place in our hearts and in the history of our nation. As we mark the first anniversary of that tragic day, we remember their sacrifice; and we commit ourselves to honoring their memory by pursuing peace and justice in the world and security at home."

Life after September 11 took on new meaning for members of Congress too. We reacted by changing our priorities and began work on legislation to respond to that day's horrific events. One of the first things we did was pass legislation authorizing the use of U.S. Armed Forces against those responsible for the attacks. Since then, Congress passed numerous bills dealing with the issues that are widely believed to have allowed the events of September 11 to occur. They include: strengthening airline security and our nation's borders, restructuring the Immigration and Naturalization Service to make it a more efficient agency, and passing the Patriot Act to improve information sharing between enforcement at intelligence communities. More recently, the House passed legislation to create a new Department of Homeland Security in response to the President's request for a flexible, effective department with a singular mission of protecting our nation. Financially, we have also passed legislation to provide the Department of Defense with the resources it will need to address the new challenges that now face the nation.

Many individuals have changed their priorities too. Spurred by our war against terrorism and the words of the administration and various law enforcement agencies, Americans have begun to pay more attention to their surroundings and take better note of anything that appears out of the ordinary, particularly in airports. Gone are the days when one can easily dismiss peoples' errant behavior as harmless without making sure that that is indeed the case. As we learned, the price to pay for not checking can be awfully steep.

After the events of that Tuesday, life in Washington, DC, returned to some semblance of normalcy. Yet, a year later, although life appears the same as always, there is a difference. Certainly, Congress is in the middle of its appropriations debates as it almost always is this time of year, and Republicans and Democrats are embroiled in many of the same arguments that typically take place around now. However, there is now an underlying sense of wariness, in our nation that didn't exist before, but this is good, as it shows that we have learned from last year's events. It demonstrates that as a nation, we have- grown. September 11, 2001 wasn't that long ago, but America has lived a lifetime in the year since that fateful day.

Safer Today Than Ever Before

American heroes are:

Mothers and fathers who quietly and effectively instill in their children ideals and virtues which enable them to lead productive and beneficial lives in the widest sense of those words, and to assist them to establish their own similar families.

Lafe Parkin
Husband and Father

U.S. Representative Mario Diaz -Balart

By mid-morning two years ago, the World Trade Center towers were rubble, the Pentagon was smoldering, and there was a crater in the Pennsylvania countryside. We had been attacked.

For weeks afterward, we were filled with shock, rage, and anguish. Most of all, we felt vulnerable.

As time passes, the images and sounds of September 11 become increasingly distant. The tears we cried on that terrible day have long dried, and it becomes easier to dismiss the horror.

I, for one, hope we NEVER forget.

On the two-year anniversary of that terrible day in which nearly 3,000 people died, we recall those horrific images. We remember those who tragically died. But we also remember what makes this country so great, and that we must do everything we can to ensure our survival.

As more hearings and reports are done to see where we were under-prepared and how we can remedy that, we must always remember that the intelligence community, former administration, and current administration are not the enemy. Nineteen terrorists, as part of a vast world-wide terrorism network, were the enemy. And terrorists continue to threaten the United States and the rest of the world.

In recognizing this enemy, we must diligently continue to improve our nation's security. Already, in remarkably swift and bipartisan fashion, Congress has enacted several extremely successful measures that make us more secure today.

Last fall, Congress created the Department of Homeland Security. This new Cabinet-level department merged and streamlined 22 existing federal agencies to better combat terrorism. As the largest reorganization of the federal government since 1940, this was a massive and historic undertaking, but it was vitally important to breakdown the bureaucracy that allowed the attacks to happen. Now the different agencies involved in providing national security are better coordinated and able to share crucial information.

Congress drastically improved airport safety by authorizing air marshals on passenger flights, arming select pilots, and allowing the Transportation Security Administration to manage airport security screeners. Since these measures were enacted, possible scares have been averted, and terrorism has been removed from the skies.

In authorizing the use of force in Afghanistan and Iraq, we were able to eliminate al Qaeda's terrorist training grounds and remove a terrorist regime. Congress has also authorized funds to help rebuild these countries so that people in those countries can taste the sweetness of freedom and fight against the terrorists who hate it.

Congress has also taken steps to protect the public against chemical and biological warfare. In July, the U.S. House of Representatives passed Project BioShield legislation, which seeks to enhance research, development, procurement, and use of biomedical countermeasures. Congress continues to consider other measures to protect us against chemical and biological warfare.

Six weeks after September 11, Congress passed the controversial Patriot Act. Due mainly to misinformation about the Patriot Act, several people are concerned that they may lose their civil liberties because of it. However, in a poll conducted on July 31 by Fox News, only four percent claimed that the Patriot Act affected their civil liberties. Instead, the Patriot Act has given authorities the means to capture and neutralize alleged terrorist cells in Buffalo, Detroit, Seattle and Portland while protecting our citizens. In fact, criminal charges have been brought against 255 individuals, and 132 of those have been convicted or pleaded guilty.

Most importantly, there have been no more terrorist attacks at home.

September 11 reminds us of many things, including the fact that we live in a dangerous world. Congress is committed to continue fighting terrorism and securing our freedom.

For more information and updates on the Patriot Act, visit us at –

www.ModernDayHeroes.com

Real Heroes

Extraordinary times bread extraordinary people, and that is simply the story of America. America is a country that has created and nurtured heroes. Our modern day heroes are not much different than those who blazed the trail to write our Constitution and braved the wilderness of our great country. While the challenges are different, and far more complex, today's heroes still have to make extraordinary sacrifices in the face of extraordinary public pressure to conform and to not be different.

My modern day heroes are the families who are making sacrifices to allow mothers to be at home and raise their children to be tomorrow's heroes. My modern day heroes are the men and women who go to work each day and, whether as a waitress who doesn't cheat the restaurant owner, or the CEO who insists an ethical culture in his or her organization. My modern day heroes are the people who are leaders in our nation's capitol, our state houses, and local council chambers. They are people of character who are brave enough to govern by the principals so clearly outlined in our constitution, rather than by whim of what feels good at the moment or by popular pubic opinion polls.

Heroes of the past, today, and the future, are the people of character who live each day practicing the core ethical values of being honest, treating others with respect, doing what they are supposed to do, following the rules, being kind, and doing their share to make their community better.

Vickie Talley
Talley and Associates, Inc.
President

Governor Tom Vilsack

Our thoughts today turn to the victims who died last September 11th in the planes, at the Pentagon, and in the fallen towers of the World Trade Center. They were the first casualties of a war on terrorism that has changed the world in a dramatic fashion in just the past 12 months.

Our thoughts also turn to the families and friends of the victims who live with the memories of that terrible day.

Today, we also remember the heroes of September 11th – the firefighters, police officers and other emergency personnel who went into harm's way without hesitation. Some of the New York firefighters who rushed into the burning towers were not even officially on duty that day, and others had just finished working an overnight shift. Hundreds of them died. We remember the heroic passengers of United Flight 93, who rose up against the hijackers, and crashed their plane into a Pennsylvania field. They sacrificed their own lives to keep that plane from reaching its target and bringing death to others.

Today we honor the men and women in our armed forces, serving to defend freedom and fight terror in Afghanistan and around the world. We honor the members of the National Guard who guard our airports and other facilities to keep America safe from attack. Now, many Iowa National Guard members are playing an increasing role in the war on terror as more of our troops are called to active duty.

The defining moment of September 11th has become the individual and collective acts of those heroic people. September 11th gave Americans a new meaning of the word "hero." Too often in our culture, we think of powerful, wealthy, famous people as heroes, even if they've never done anything heroic. September 11th showed stories of real heroes, who sacrificed for others and committed their lives to something bigger than themselves.

Real heroes are the people who go to work in those caring and protection professions and who put themselves at risk every day to keep the rest of us healthy and safe. Real heroes, everyday heroes, are the people who make a difference every day in the lives of the people around them. In Iowa today, let us commemorate the memory of September 11th by honoring the everyday heroes in our neighborhoods and hometowns.

On September 11th, terrorists struck at symbols of American economic strength and military might, but they could not destroy the American spirit of heroism and service. Today as we remember the victims, we can also take comfort in knowing that America's everyday heroes are more committed than ever to making our state, our nation, and our world a better place.

3,000 Innocent Americans Did Not Die in Vain

My father James T. Clark was a hero to me, and not just because of the sacrifices that he made for my brothers and me growing up in Chicago. He was taught the lessons of sacrifice and honor on a battlefield in Korea.

When he was diagnosed with cancer, he didn't flinch. He had faced death before. During his last months of life, I learned valuable lessons in strength, pride, and dignity. It is because of his example in war and peace I serve in the military today.

The Silver Star Medal is awarded to: Sergeant James Clark, Infantry Company F, 7th Infantry Regiment, 3d Infantry Division, United States Army. During the early morning hours of 15 June 1953, in the vicinity of Chat-Kol Korea, Company F, Sgt. Clark, a squad leader, had the mission of counterattacking and regaining control of positions overrun by the enemy in earlier action. The enemy, detecting the position of his squad, laid in heavy artillery and mortar fire, inflicting friendly casualties and forcing the squad to temporarily seek cover. Sgt. Clark, with complete disregard for his personal safety, searched the area for wounded. Upon finding one man seriously wounded, he quickly administered first aid and carried him to safety. He then returned to the impact area and formed a defensive perimeter from which he directed intense and accurate fire forcing the enemy to retreat with numerous casualties. Sgt Clark's outstanding gallantry and devotion to duty reflect great credit upon himself and the military service.

Jeffrey Clark
US Navy, Lieutenant

[It should be noted that the Department of the Navy, via the Secretary of the Navy, awarded the Navy and Marine Corps Commendation Medal to Jeffery Clark of the US Navy. Lieutenant Jeffery Clark credits his father's example of integrity, strength, and honor for his own success and honors.]

Meritorious service as ship's nurse while assigned to the U.S.S. John F Kennedy (CV 67) from March 2002 to March 2004. Lieutenant Clark consistently performed his demanding duties in an exemplary and highly professional manner. He was instrumental in providing outstanding emergency care in an austere and remote environment aboard John F Kennedy during Operation Enduring Freedom.

His outstanding treatment of Man-Down situations, including the life-saving treatment of a coalition sailor who required multiple blood transfusions, prompted praise from the Battle Group Commander and resulted in his co-authoring of an article in a peer reviewed journal. As Medical Training Team Leader, He trained over 2000 of the ship's crew in Cardio Pulmonary Resuscitation, wound treatment, and stretcher bearing techniques resulting in an overall score of 93% and two consecutive Blue M awards for medical readiness. Lieutenant Clark's exceptional professionalism, distinctive accomplishments, and dedication to duty reflected credit upon himself and were in keeping with the highest traditions of the United States Naval Service.

U.S. Senator Mark Pryor

Two years have past since the tragedy of September 11th 2001, but the visions of smoke rising out of the World Trade Center and the Pentagon, and the pain and terror on the faces of those who lost family members, friends and colleagues remain vivid in our minds. Within seconds, America realized that it was not invincible.

More than a thousand of miles away from Manhattan's ground zero, the Pentagon, and the field in Shanksville, Pennsylvania, Arkansans felt the vibrations of this tragedy. Families in Batesville, Pine Bluff, Jonesboro, and throughout the state learned about the deaths of friends and family members. Just a few months later, thousands of families would celebrate Thanksgiving and Christmas without the moms, dads, sons, and daughters who had been deployed in the fight against terrorism. Soldiers began to guard the Little Rock National Airport and Arkansas Nuclear One. And we all began to care for our neighbors a little bit more. On September 11, 2001, life for Americans changed forever.

September 11th is made bearable only by the true heroism displayed on that day and everyday thereafter. We will never forget the selfless acts demonstrated by our firefighters who ran into burning buildings; police officers who went the extra mile to help the frightened and frail; EMT, doctors and nurses who cared for the injured; and everyday individuals who raised money for the victims of this tragedy.

Along with these heroes, we have hundreds of thousands of servicemen and women who continue to risk life and limb in places such as Afghanistan, Turkey, and Iraq in the name of democracy and all it embodies. They put themselves in harm's way not for personal aggrandizement or advancement, but for immense love of country, liberty, and family. I ask all Arkansans to join me with continued support for our men and women in uniform.

I ask also that Arkansans pray for the families who lost their loved ones in the tragic terrorist attacks. The healing process is a long and difficult road, and these families need our support and compassion.

Finally, we must ensure that the more than 3,000 innocent Americans did not die in vain on September 11th. We must continue taking those steps necessary to protect our homeland. This means ensuring that our first responders have the tools they need to confront terrorism at home. It means ensuring that our servicemen and women have cutting-edge equipment, training, and technology they need to complete their mission. It means working together by placing our safety and our children's safety above politics.

Americans have endured great hardship and heartbreak as a result of the terrorist attacks, but this has not broken our faith, courage, and an unshakable commitment to freedom, democracy and each other. Today, we remember the tragedy of September 11th, and we honor its victims. We will never forget them.

**What is your definition of an American hero?
Share it with us at-
www.ModernDayHeroes.com**

The Heroes That Were Found

Heroes to me are those who get up everyday, work for their living, and pay their taxes. Taking responsibility for their actions, they educate themselves and their children, and make themselves an asset to this great nation versus a welfare waif. They live within their means, enjoy life, and share with others without being asked. Heroes are those who take the time to understand we are a republic and stand upon that principal while improving everything about them.

Heroes are the mothers or fathers who work hard all day and then run home to coach a little league ball team. Heroes are the Boy and Girl Scouts that go clean up litter from the roadways. Heroes are the volunteers at the hospital who sit and listen with the old and frail. Heroes are the folks who still get their hands dirty in construction. Heroes don't have to charge into a burning building or take on an armed criminal but they do. Heroes are those who are not afraid to stand up for what's right and stomp what's wrong. Heroes understand the bill of rights and the constitutional freedoms we strive to preserve and vote to do so. Heroes are respectful of traditions, faith, and are courteous to all they encounter.

Hero is, in my humble opinion, the short term for - American.

> Caylen Perry
> Panhandle, TX

U.S. Representative Sue Wilkins Myrick

On Friday, September 6 of this year, a special Joint Session of the United States Congress gathered in New York City to remember the terrorist attacks of September 11, 2001. This special session reminded us of the lives that were lost and the heroes that were found all across this country on that terrible day. I am honored to have taken part in this unique session.

We convened at Federal Hall, where the first Congress met over two centuries ago, and a few blocks from where the World Trade Center towers once stood, proud and tall.

Mr. Speaker, we met to remember the thousands of lives that ended so abruptly that day. We prayed for the families of those that were lost. We prayed for the families who had to say goodbye before they were ready. The wound that America suffered on that day will always be remembered.

We also expressed our most sincere thanks to the firefighters, police officers, emergency personnel, and all others who risked and gave their lives on that day. These brave men and women, along with their peers across the country, risk their lives every day to protect those around them. Expressing our thanks to them is a long overdue action.

Finally, Mr. Speaker, we recommit ourselves to eradicating terrorism from the world and to making sure that those responsible for this horrible attack on America are brought to justice. American soldiers are now stationed across the globe, helping to create a world where those who live in freedom can also live free of the fear of terrorism. America and the world owe these soldiers a debt of gratitude.

I am proud to have joined Congress on September 6, to remember the lives that were lost and to show those who would harm America that we will not forget, but we will overcome.

Every Generation of Americans Must Prove Itself

All the warriors protecting our way of life are our modern day heroes.

I get a chill every time I hear of our fighters in Afghanistan. Taking nothing away from those in Iraq and other places, these guys next door are doing the dirtiest work in the most extreme parts of the world.

Frank Welch
USCG-ret.

U.S. Representative Tom Udall –
released the following statement in observance of the second anniversary of the September 11 terrorist attacks:

Today is the commemoration of both incalculable loss and limitless courage, of enduring sorrow, and indomitable spirit.

Today, we embrace all that we have retained as a nation in the past two years – our strength, our sense of purpose, our unity, and our veneration of the principles and freedom and justice – for today, the hearts of Americans are beckoned at once by sorrow and resolve, and we should call the heed of both.

Much has been said about how September 11 changed America forever because it demonstrated our vulnerability. But I believe a more profound change came about because that day demonstrated the true nature, and the true measure, of our strength as a nation. That strength comes not from our size or our wealth, but from our courage. There is hope in the memory of September 11 because we learned just how enduring and expansive is the bravery of free people.

It is vital that we continue to honor the victims of the attacks and stay true to its lessons. On that day, two years ago, we saw not just an unprovoked attack on innocent lives. We saw one of the finest examples of selflessness and service our nation has ever seen. Nearly 400 police, firefighters, and emergency rescue personnel were among the 3,000 victims that day simply because, without hesitation or doubt, they answered their call to duty.

The spirit of service runs deep in New Mexico. I believe that is why the attacks of September 11 resonated so intensely in our state. Immediately after the attacks, I was proud to see the outpouring of support from New Mexico and across the country as countless Americans donated blood or raised money for the families of victims.

Every generation of Americans must prove itself. Two years ago today, this generation was tested. There is much we have done to combat the evil of terrorism, but there is far more that we still must do. The only fitting tribute to those who were lost or injured on September 11 is the assurance that we have done everything in our power to prevent such horror from touching our shores again.

Nominate a candidate for our Modern Day Hero® Award.
More details at the end of this book or at –
www.ModernDayHeroes.com

Freedom Isn't Free

While all nations have their respective heroes, an American hero is different in that he personifies the uniqueness of the American nation herself. The American hero, like the country he represents, is comforted by the warm embrace of tradition, yet is unafraid to forge his own path. He is brimming with compassion for the less fortunate, yet believes that individuals should have the freedom to fail. He is content to mind his own business, yet moved to action at the sight of injustice. Ultimately, the American hero is committed to the idea of liberty because he recognizes its inherent virtue and understands that it is liberty that affords every American the opportunity to be heroic.

James D. Pidd, II
High School Teacher

Governor Mike Rounds

In the two years between September 11, 2001 and today, South Dakota and South Dakotans have changed.

Two years and one day ago, many of us "took for granted" that we would never have the terrorist carnage that had been in the news for many years from far off lands. It was only pictures and sounds on the evening news from places half way around the world, right?

Two years and one day ago, many of us "took for granted" our firemen and policemen and the dangerous work they do. Those jobs were just other people's jobs, right?

Two years and one day ago, many of us "took for granted" the every day safety we and many previous generations enjoyed. We felt comfortable in our daily lives... so comfortable; perhaps we didn't realize just how comfortable we were.

But one day later than two years and one day ago, all that changed.

9-11 changed South Dakota and changed South Dakotans. We don't "take" any of those things "for granted" any more.

I think the War in Iraq has had a similar effect. Over 1,600 of our own South Dakota men and women have been involved in one way or another.

In understanding their mission to a foreign land, we have again and much more often about the precious freedoms that we enjoy here in South Dakota and have sometimes "taken for granted."

In the same way that our appreciations for our firemen and policemen have increased tremendously, I think ALL South Dakotans have realized all over again the importance of what our soldiers do for us.

We have realized all over again that...

It is the soldier, not the preacher, who has given us freedom of religion.

It is the soldier, not the reporter, who has given us freedom of the press.

It is the soldier, not the writer, who has given us freedom of speech.

It is the soldier, not the campus organizer, who has given us the freedom to assemble.

It is the soldier, not the lawyer, who has given us the right to a fair trial.

AND, It is the soldier, not the politician, who has given us the right to vote.

Without the soldier protecting, guarding and cherishing our freedoms, we too could have easily become the victims of dictators throughout nation's history.

So, as we celebrate freedom tonight, let us also be grateful and thankful to all of America's soldiers of the last 200 years who have given us the freedoms we enjoy today.

I am going to end by sharing a message with you.

Last Monday, one of my staff in the Governor's office got an e-mail from one of the National Guardsmen in the 200th Engineer Company of Pierre, Chamberlain, Mobridge and Lemmon. They are currently in Iraq.

I'd like to read part of this young soldier's message to you---

After joking about the weather and the mortar attacks, he wrote this at the end of his e-mail--

"The task that we have taken on as Americans is a huge one to say the very least. The various facets of this operation are simply mind boggling.

When one considers just for a moment some of the major categories that have to be addressed and put back online; banking and commerce, province and local fire and police protection, water and power districts, agriculture, education, defense, and a government to direct and fund all the categories.

Civilian and military personnel are working on all of these areas and making positive strides on all fronts. You will not read or hear of all the good things that are happening. The follies and the casualties make the headlines.

We are a very fortunate people-- let us share our freedom and liberty with those less fortunate. I hope and pray that we have the fortitude and heart to follow thru with this operation called 'Enduring Freedom'."

I don't know this young man, but I am certainly proud to be living in the state where he is from.

He knows that we already have "enduring freedom" here in the United States and South Dakota.

But, He also cares about the other "less fortunate" people of the world enough that he wants them to have "enduring freedom" too.

We should be and we are very proud and very grateful for this young man and for all of the men and women who serve in our National Guard and our armed services.

Because they are making so many sacrifices for us and the future generations, I hope that they know they already have our "enduring" love and gratitude for what they are doing for us.

Thank you and God bless America.

Chapter 8

In Defense
of America

Peace is Best Achieved from a Position of Strength

Lest we forget our heroes!
Be ever vigilant!

Solon Owens
Eugene, OR

U.S. Representative Martin Frost

I rise in support of this bipartisan resolution. It provides the best opportunity for a peaceful resolution by giving the President the discretion to use force if Iraq does not permit full and comprehensive inspections of all sites that could be used to develop biological, chemical or nuclear weapons.

I hope, as do the American people, that the President will use this discretion wisely, and that Saddam Hussein will understand that the community of nations will not permit him to develop and maintain weapons of mass destruction.

Today's vote is a difficult one. Many House members have worn their country's uniform in time of war, and have seen the horrors of battle first-hand. And we all understand the sacrifices that we may be asking our brave young men and women to make in the months to come. As Democratic Caucus Chairman, I have presided over numerous meetings on this subject recently. I have listened carefully to my colleagues and to policy experts who have followed Saddam Hussein's activities over the years. In the end, I have come to the conclusion that the course set out in this resolution is the wisest path for our nation.

The resolution makes clear that our first preference is for the President to work through the United Nations to obtain multilateral support for a tough regime of weapons inspections. It requires the President to report back to Congress and to consult with us on an ongoing basis. But in the end, it gives the President the authority to commit U.S. troops if all diplomatic efforts fail.

Giving the President this discretion is highly appropriate. In so doing, we make clear to Saddam Hussein that it is in his interest to permit the inspectors full and unfettered access now. Should he fail to do so, he will face the full might of the United States military - the strongest and finest fighting force in the world today.

No one wants war. We all want peace. And peace is best achieved from a position of strength. So I want to personally recognize the work of our Democratic Leader, Dick Gephardt, in narrowing and improving the resolution originally offered by the administration. We vote today on a better, more focused approach because of the hours he spent negotiating with the White House over the final product.

And I want to say a word about the role of the Minority in our system of government. Some suggest that the Minority's role is to automatically oppose everything sought by the President. I disagree. The Minority can play a constructive role by working to improve a Presidential proposal, and thereby helping achieve a national consensus. That is particularly true in matters of foreign policy. So I urge all my colleagues, regardless of how you voted on the Spratt or Lee substitutes, to join Democrats and Republicans in voting for this bipartisan resolution.

This bipartisan resolution will send the strong, clear signal that America is committed to ending the threat that Saddam Hussein poses to the world, through diplomacy if he will allow it, but through military action if he refuses.

Evil Will Not Stand

Heroes never think of themselves as heroes, it seems. Perhaps because they know that a reward on earth may detract from rewards waiting in Heaven.

We know, and can honor them by quiet respect, joy, love, and by teaching their ways and deeds to younger generations... and never letting them grow old alone, forgotten in their quiet stoicism.

Heather Leigh
Ft. Myers, FL

U.S. Senator Mike Enzi

On Monday, March 17, the attention of the world was focused on Washington, DC and the White House. The President was about to speak to the nation about Saddam Hussein and the refusal of the Government of Iraq to live up to its signed agreements and the resolutions of the United Nations to eliminate their stock of weapons of mass destruction. In the 15 or so minutes that followed, our President made clear his determination to take action and resolve the situation in Iraq. He said he was going to end forever the evil presence of a dictator in Iraq who had done nothing during his reign but abuse his power as he pursued his dreams of glory and increased power and prestige, while showing little regard for the health and welfare of his own people.

As the President spoke with passion and conviction on the need to rid the world of Hussein's dictatorship, he cut through the rhetoric and the misleading positions and promises that had been so often heard during the past few years. He made it clear that this was an ultimatum of more than words--action was sure to follow if his words were left unheeded. He did everything he could to make it abundantly clear to Saddam Hussein and the people of the world that such evil would not be allowed to stand. He stated a final deadline.

Soon after he spoke, the movement of our troops intensified as an international coalition took up their positions surrounding Iraq as we all waited for Saddam Hussein's response. There could be only one acceptable response to the President's message. Saddam had to leave Iraq, relinquish his power, and take his sons and family with him. Anything less would be unacceptable.

Now we have our answer. A deadline has been set which has come and gone. In response, our troops are now advancing into Iraq and heading for its capital of Baghdad. A series of events that began years ago with our defense of Kuwait will now end where it must-- with the removal of Saddam Hussein and an end to his brutal dictatorship.

As our troops head further into Iraq, they will be heading into unknown dangers and trouble that cannot be accurately predicted, though they have been trained and will be prepared for it.

Will Saddam Hussein try to use chemical weapons to prolong his hold on power? What has he hidden from the team of inspectors that he may now want to unleash? These and so many other questions will be in the minds of our troops as they come closer and closer to Iraq's capital city. The rewards that will come with our success will be great. But, as we know from our past experiences, the sacrifices that may lie ahead may be equally as great.

War is a very dangerous business, and Wyoming is no stranger to the kind of sacrifice it sometimes requires from those who serve in our military. Down through the years, the people of Wyoming have always answered the call to protect and preserve the peace and answer the threat of any enemy of our nation, wherever it has led them. Many paid the ultimate price.

In 1991, when Saddam Hussein decided to attack Kuwait and drain that country of its supplies and resources, our Armed Forces were there to respond to the cry for help that came from Kuwait.

Joining in as part of that effort was one of Wyoming's own, Manuel Davila. Manuel was a brave young man, a father, and a nice guy who had a kind word for everyone he met. He was the kind of person you would want on your side if there were tough times ahead. There were tough times on the horizon as this battle began and we were fortunate to have brave men and women like Manuel on our side.

I watched Manuel grow up because he came from my home town. He loved his life, and he loved Wyoming. But he loved freedom more. When he was called on to bring the freedoms he loved to people he had never met, he did not hesitate. He traded his beloved blue skies and mountaintops of Wyoming for the flat dessert and skies darkened by Saddam Hussein's desperate attempts to delay the end of his occupation by setting every oil well he could on fire. He traded the sweet smell of Wyoming's clean mountain air for the use of a gas mask and the threat of exposure to the Iraqi war machine's stock of gas and chemical weapons.

Sadly, he was one who didn't come home from that war. But he did leave behind a legacy of standing up for what you believe in, keeping your word, and never allowing evil to win by failing to act or by doing so little in response it was as if you did nothing at all.

Then came September 11, and another round of attacks by a madman fueled by hatred and a mad desire for power. Once again we looked to our sons and daughters to respond and to end the threat of terrorism once and for all. The bravest and best of Wyoming and many other states were soon on the front lines, ready to put their training into action. As they did, one of the first lost was Jonn J. Edmunds, a young man from Cheyenne, who was killed as our nation took action against those who supported and planned the terrorist attacks of that terrible day.

Now, as we stand here together in prayerful support of our armed forces, I have no doubt that Manuel and Jonn and all the others who have served so bravely in our military over the years would be proud of their comrades and their liberation of Iraq which is finally at hand.

Soon Iraq will be welcomed back into the family of nations and the rights so cherished by our nation, and our people will be part of the daily routine in Iraq, too. By our actions we are showing the world that the rights with which we are endowed by our Creator, the rights to life, liberty, and the pursuit of happiness, which are a part of our own Declaration of Independence, were intended to be claimed not just by the people of our own nation. They are to be rightfully claimed by people all over the world as well.

As we wait for today's news from Iraq, we are fully aware of the seriousness of the challenge that lies before us, its difficulty and its magnitude. For the first time since I was a young boy, we are facing an enemy who is faceless and nameless and may have operatives who sympathize with him who may strike us on our own soil. With the exception of Pearl Harbor, we have never faced that kind of a threat in our lives. September 11 changed that and we must now all be more vigilant for in a very real sense we are all part of the war effort, just as we were in the days of World War II.

As the effort to remove the tyranny of Saddam Hussein continues, the fate of both our nations hangs in the balance. The degree of our success in what we set out to do and the aftermath as we work to bring a lasting peace to Iraq will speak volumes to the world about our ability to walk our talk.

When this war is over and Iraq is free, we will have sent a message to all those who would deny their people the basic rights of human existence. The world will no longer tolerate their abuse of power and their refusal to acknowledge or respond to the needs of their people. We will also have ended the regime of a dictator and eliminated his stock of weapons of mass destruction. We will have taken a strong, decisive action which will help to increase the security of our nation and the world.

Ronald Reagan once said that "Some people live an entire lifetime and wonder if they have ever made a difference in the world. The marines don't have that problem."

Neither does the Army, the Navy, the Air Force, the Coast Guard, or the Merchant Marine. Through their brave and courageous actions on behalf of the people of Iraq, they will do for that country what they did for the people of Kuwait. They will give them their country and their lives back. They will give them the chance to dream again about a better future for their children. They will give those who live under oppression around the world a real reason to hope that someday things will be better for them in their own country.

We all know what brave, remarkable people our soldiers are. They don't see any limits to what they can do because they will never quit until the job is done, and the war is won. We owe them each a debt we will never be able to repay. We can never forget that it is because of them, and not us, that the rights enumerated in our Constitution are guaranteed. Whether it is freedom of religion, the press, or freedom of speech, it has always been the efforts of our soldiers that have provided us with a platform from which to speak, and the ability to exercise these and all our rights. Even those who have spoken out against their efforts have our soldiers to thank for their right to do.

Tonight, when we spend those last few minutes tucking our children into bed, I hope we all take a moment to comfort our children and our grandchildren, and to assure them that things will be all right someday soon. Make sure they know they can sleep peacefully tonight and in the nights to come, because the brave men and women of this nation, our sons and daughters, and perhaps their own sisters and brothers, are ever vigilant, on guard and have taken a stand on our behalf. We can take a great deal of pride in them all.

As a member of the Senate, I have always been very proud of the way we come together whenever we are faced by a threat, or forced to use our nation's military to answer an attack or address a wrong. As our young men and women head into battle, I know I won't be the only one who will bow his head to pray.

May God bless and protect the men and women of our armed forces. May He watch over the Iraqi people and keep them safe from harm as we fight to liberate their country and bring them freedom and peace, a just peace that will recognize their rights and ensure that they have food, medicine, and the essentials of life that have been denied them for too long. May our victory be swift, so their wait for relief will not be long. And may all our loved ones return home safely, and in peace.

The Citizen-Soldier

A hero, to me, is the state of mind to recognize what is right and the courage to do it no matter what the personal consequences. In this sense, the definition of heroism has not changed. It is as ancient as mankind itself. Only the circumstances have changed to alter our interpretation of heroic acts.

Those people who are the weft and woof of the fabric of our society are no less heroes than the ones who charge into burning buildings to save other people. If circumstances present themselves, the one who umpires at the Little League baseball game today will be the one risking his or her life for others tomorrow, and the one who is taking the time to help an elderly person load their groceries in the car today will be the one taking a bullet for a brother-in-arms tomorrow.

This giving of oneself for the benefit of others is a uniquely American attribute, and it defines us a nation. It is the God-given glue which binds us together, and, because of which, no evil force on this planet can tear us apart.

Mr. El Roy Ray
Katy, TX

U.S. Representative Stephen F. Lynch

General Zukauskas, Lieutenant Colonels Becker and Walsh, distinguished guests and to the men and women of the Eleven Seventy-Third and your friends and family, good afternoon.

It's with tremendous pride that I stand before you today as you prepare to join tens of thousands of your brother and sister citizen-soldiers who already answered the call to duty.

Aristotle was one of the first to write about the various kinds of courage shown by mankind. He was searching for the greatest type of courage. He considered the courage of a parent trying to save a child from a wild beast or the courage of a mercenary who is paid to fight. In the end, he determined that the single greatest form of courage was that of the citizen-soldier, who puts down the tools of his trade, leaves his family, and goes to war to defend his nation and his way of life.

And that's what each of you did when you answered the call. For that, you have my thanks, my respect, and my admiration.

You serve in a battalion with a proud history and more than 50 years of service to our country. Some were called on to defend our nation during the Gulf War. Some of you will be in harm's way for the first time in your lives. But all of you will be serving the most noble of causes — protecting the safety and security of all Americans.

I want every one of you and your families to know, war is not inevitable. The men who represent you in Washington, Senators Kennedy and Kerry and Congressman Delahunt and I, are doing everything in our power to ensure that war is the absolute last resort, that every diplomatic measure is exhausted before a single shot is fired. That's why hundreds of UN weapons inspectors are on the ground in Iraq right now, we are giving Saddam Hussein the opportunity to avoid war by terminating his weapons programs immediately. If he fails to do so voluntarily, Saddam knows that the world is ready to use military force to disarm his regime.

Each one of you will be a reminder that America will not back down from aggression or intimidation or threats to our security. My great hope is the sight of you standing shoulder to shoulder with those tens of thousands of men and women in uniform already in the Middle East will convince Saddam Hussein that his only viable option is to comply with the resolutions of the UN and disarm. As George Washington said at the dawn of the American Revolution, "To be prepared for war is one of the most effective means of preserving peace."

Every one of you is being asked to make an extraordinary sacrifice, to leave your family, your career, and your community behind, and none of you backed down from your duty. Your service in the coming months will help to prevent an oppressive regime from acquiring weapons of mass destruction, whether we are forced to go to war or not.

You have given your parents, your friends, your husbands and wives, your children, and your nation every reason to be proud of what you're doing.

I'd like to leave you with a thought by Robert F. Kennedy: "It is from numberless diverse acts of courage and belief that human history is shaped. Each time a man stands up for an ideal, or acts to improve the lots of others, or strikes out against injustice, he sends a tiny ripple of hope...which can sweep down the mightiest walls of oppression and resistance."

Please watch out for one another and for yourselves as you embark on your mission. Thank you for all that you've done and all that you're going to do for every one of us.

May God watch over the men and women of the Eleven Seventy-Third and these United States of America.

Have a story of courage? Share it with us at –
www.ModernDayHeroes.com

The Call of Duty

An American hero is an American who knows the difference between right and wrong, and chooses to do the right at all times.

Kyle Rex
Sweet, ID

U.S. Senator Herb Kohl

Last night the conflict the U.S. had worked hard to avoid, finally began. As we all watched from the safety of our living rooms, our men and women in uniform answered the call of duty and began to carry out the orders of their Commander in Chief. They set their own fears aside to carry out their mission and prepare for an extended and dangerous conflict. While we wait anxiously on the home front, we can only imagine the courage and resolve of our soldiers overseas.

While this conflict has left many in our country divided, everyone can come together to support our troops and hope and pray for their safe and rapid return. Americans have had a vigorous debate on the issue, but now that the decision has been made, we all join behind our soldiers, sailors, Marines, and airmen, as well as their families.

Over the last couple of months, I have had the privilege of meeting many of our citizen soldiers as they mobilized for war. These brave men and women were plucked from their everyday lives as mothers and fathers. They were taken from their jobs in offices and factory floors. They set their suits and ties aside to don the uniform of our armed services.

Citizen soldiers are the backbone of our military. Pentagon planning has put critical capabilities in our reserve component. Capabilities required every time the United States engages in a major military endeavor. Our reservists move the arms and ammo our forces depend on. They refuel our combat aircraft and guide them to safe landings. They build and repair airfields and military bases in lightening speed. The reserve component is always ready and prepared to join their brothers and sisters on active duty and provide seamless service.

These men and women often labor and train in relative anonymity during times of peace. It is in only times of conflict that communities discover how many of their friends and neighbors serve their country quietly year in and year out. In times of crisis, they are notable by their absence at scout meetings, in church pews, and parent teacher conferences.

The State of Wisconsin has had over 2,200 men and women called up for service in the National Guard and an additional 1,357 mobilized from the Reserves. Wisconsin has more people mobilized now than at any time since the Berlin Crisis. These men and women have been stationed all over the country, and all over the world. They come from throughout Wisconsin. In a state that does not have any large military bases, we are proud of the soldiers we send to protect our national security.

The men and women I met with in Beloit, Wisconsin, of the 1158th Transportation Company, proudly headed off leaving behind spouses and children, families and friends. These soldiers had very little time to put their affairs in order before being ordered into harms way, but there were no complaints, no grumbling. The families I met were concerned about the future, but ready to deal with the personal and financial difficulties. Many of them will have to deal with reduced income in addition to not having mom or dad around. They will struggle to make car and house payments, while anxiously watching the television for news on the war. Some families will have to spend the next few months linked only by e-mail and a few furtive phone calls.

A military family is a special kind of family that deserves our respect and admiration. I was struck to see young children bravely saying good bye to their parents without knowing what the future would bring. These youngsters did not ask for this war and do not understand it, but they too, are making sacrifices for our security.

Our soldiers are ready and willing to do their duty. They understand, better than anyone else, that freedom is not free. They are ready to pay that price today and every day. Members of the military everywhere understand that our way of life has been protected by past generations who were willing to give their lives. Today's soldiers stand ready to join those who came before them in putting their lives on the line for liberty.

When you talk to these soldiers you cannot help but feel proud of our country and our people. Our soldiers represent the best of the American people and American ideals. They are regular folks who are willing to take on extraordinary tasks when they hear the trumpet call of duty. They are a humble group who do not seem like heroes, but quietly, in their own way, they serve with distinction in times of crisis. They come from places like Medford, Rhinelander, La Crosse, and Spooner. They are police officers, construction workers, and computer technicians. They are our friends and family.

These soldiers and their families are making immense sacrifices for our security and the freedom of the Iraqi people. As they work to bring the freedoms we cherish to the people of Iraq, they face serious danger. They know that perhaps some of them will not come back. But they believe their mission is worth the risk. While many of us will talk about patriotism and service today, no words can do justice to the burden they have chosen to bear. My heart, my prayers, and my deepest gratitude go out to them during this difficult time.

The Greatest Generation

I believe that true American heroes are the common people who come to possess the characteristics of courage, strength, integrity, and charity. They seek to enhance the best qualities of the human family through consistent sacrifice and service to family, friends, and neighbors with no thought of personal gain. I am extremely fortunate to have had parents, grandparents, teachers and friends who have become my heroes.

Richard T. Rex
Sweet, ID

U.S. Senator Elizabeth Dole

To date, nearly 40,000 men and women from North Carolina's military bases have been deployed for duty in Operation Iraqi Freedom.

Last month, as a new member of the Senate Armed Services Committee, I visited three of our military installations in North Carolina. I have always had the greatest respect and admiration for the brave men and women who dedicate their lives to defending our freedoms. It was particularly important to me to visit our armed forces personnel at this critical moment in our history and to tell them how much I appreciate what they do for us, for our country, every day.

At Seymour Johnson Air Force Base, at Cherry Point Marine Corps Air Station, and at Fort Bragg, I was moved by the dedication, the commitment, the patriotism of the members of our Armed Forces and their families. They make me proud and thankful to be an American.

In a recent interview, my husband, Bob, was asked about his service in World War II – about being a part of "the Greatest Generation." He responded that it's the men and women of our military today who are the greatest generation. I agree with him completely. We have the best equipped, most capable, most courageous military force in the world.

I remember my first day, 12 years ago, as president of the American Red Cross, walking into my new office to find a letter from Colin Powell, then Chairman of the Joint Chiefs of Staff. One of the oldest Red Cross assistance programs, the Armed Forces Emergency Services, was in jeopardy due to a lack of donor interest. I promised Colin Powell right then and there that we would do whatever it took to preserve that program for our men and women in uniform – and we did.

Many people do not realize that wherever our military goes, the Red Cross goes with them to provide support and services, delivering approximately 4,000 emergency messages a day to our military men and women. On that first day on my job, during the Persian Gulf War, our thoughts and prayers were with the Red Cross and our armed forces.

Shortly after the war ended, I traveled to the Persian Gulf to thank the Red Crossers for their work and to deliver humanitarian aid to Kuwait. Even now, I can clearly recall the horror of Saddam Hussein's occupation of that country, oil fields burning, a hospital where scores of children had died because doctors and nurses fled the country to escape the horrors of Saddam Hussein and his forces. I put a call out, right then and there, for doctors and nurses to come to Kuwait through the American Red Cross sponsorship and about 50 American medical personnel responded immediately.

Saddam Hussein is a very dangerous man who continues to pose a threat to the region's stability, to his own people, and to the American people through his sponsorship of terror. Right now, he's passing weapons of mass destruction to Iraqi troops – weapons he claimed not to have. He would gladly pass these weapons to terrorists to use against America.

President Bush exhausted every option before resorting to military force. In his speeches and in Secretary of State Powell's recent speeches to the United Nations, both delivered powerful indictments of Saddam Hussein's reign of terror and his failure to meet the demands of the United Nations.

It's time to free the people of Iraq from Saddam Hussein's terror, to remove his weapons of mass destruction, to help Iraq establish democracy.

The liberation of Iraq will be the beginning, not the end, of our commitment to the people of Iraq. America will supply humanitarian relief, bring economic sanctions to a close, and work for the establishment of democracy and the long-term recovery of Iraq's economy.

I have the highest confidence in our Armed Forces, and I know they will complete the mission they are called to accomplish. As we go forward, my thoughts and prayers will constantly be with our Commander in Chief, with these men and women and their families, with the Iraqi people, and with all those on the front lines of this war.

May God bless them all, and may God bless this great land of the free and home of the brave – America.

**Share with us your definition of an "American hero" at –
www.ModernDayHeroes.com**

United Pride

American heroes understand, appreciate and fulfill their duty to God, country, and family. They stand firm in times of difficulty, honor commitments, and uphold strong personal beliefs and convictions. They are heroes every day by honorably accomplishing noble deeds, nobly done.

John M. W. Moorlach, C.P.A., CFP®
County of Orange
Treasurer-Tax Collector

U.S. Representative Ron Kind

I rise today in support of this resolution commending our brave men and women of the armed services. I wish them Godspeed and a quick and decisive victory so they can return home soon and safe.

America is the greatest democracy the world has ever known, and our most cherished liberty is the right to speak freely. As we raise the banner of democracy in Iraq, we must ensure people across this great land continue to have the freedom to talk about what's happening in our world. Freedom is what our soldiers have gallantly fought to protect since the Revolutionary War, and that's what our brave men and women are fighting to protect today.

In addition, we must start to think forward to the rebuilding effort following this conflict. I believe it is important that we engage the UN as soon as possible and start work on a resolution that structures the reconstruction and interim governance of Iraq under the auspices of the UN. We have the opportunity to unite the United Nations behind an effective, sustained commitment to rebuilding Iraq, including support for democracy and respect for human rights. Healing the rift in our international relations is important for our national security and maintaining our leadership in the world.

At this time though, with military action to disarm Saddam Hussein just underway, my thoughts and prayers are with the men and women in our military, as well as their families. Over 2,200 members of the Wisconsin Air and Army National Guard are serving on active duty. Our appreciation also goes out to their families and their employers for their support and sacrifice during these challenging times.

I want to particularly express my appreciation to the members and families of the Wisconsin Army National Guards' 229th Engineer Company out of Prairie du Chien and Platteville under the command of Captain Robert Pruitt, the 829th Engineer Detachment out of Richland Center under the command of Captain Kurt GeilfU.S.S., and the 1158th Transportation Company with members from Tomah and Black River Falls under the leadership of First Lieutenant Jason Stebbins, and Army Reserve's 652nd Engineer Company out of Ellsworth under the command of Captain Dean Kasparek. These units have been activated and deployed overseas.

I also want to thank Major General Al Wilkening, the Wisconsin Adjunct General and Lieutenant Colonel Tim Donovan of the Wisconsin Army National Guard, along with Colonel Mike Staszak, Commander of Fort McCoy Army Reserve Total Force Training Center, and his staff in western Wisconsin. The people of western Wisconsin are proud of their service and the service of all the men and women of our armed services during this important time in our nation's history.

As our military effort continues, I, and other members of Congress will work to ensure that our service men and women have all the resources necessary to fulfill their mission. Again, my thoughts and prayers are with those serving our country, as well as their families. America is firmly behind our troops and we're all hoping to see them home safe, secure and soon.

May God continue to bless the United States of America.

The Men and Women We Honor

A hero is a person who embodies the ideals and standards of a free society. A hero is someone who serves their community putting the needs of others before themselves. A hero is a mentor to youth. A hero stands strong for convictions, even under the direst of circumstance. A hero is someone who puts his or her life in jeopardy so that others may know the true taste of freedom. Heroes rarely intentionally think of themselves and are always thinking of others.

Mike Scheafer
City of Costa Mesa
City Councilmember

U.S. Representative Steny Hoyer

Our sixteenth President, Abraham Lincoln, once remarked, "while all contribute of their substance, the soldier puts his life at stake and often yields it up in his country's cause."

Today, we honor the bravery and sacrifice of our nation's armed forces who are putting their lives at stake half a world a way. And we say, "Your cause is noble and just. You are disarming a dangerous despot and ending his ruthless regime. You are liberating a proud people, who have toiled under the boot of Saddam Hussein and his henchmen for far too long. And you are strengthening the security of our nation, as well as the nations of the Middle East and the nations of the world."

All the world is now witnessing in the streets of Baghdad what we have known all along, your mission was never one of conquest. Your mission was the defeat of a tyrant, the liberation of

Iraq, and the expansion of universal values - freedom, democracy, basic human rights, and the rule of law.

We continue to pray for a quick conclusion to this war and for your safe return. And we say a special prayer for the American servicemen and women who have made the ultimate sacrifice. To their families and loved ones, please know that a grateful nation mourns your loss and shares your pain. Further, to the Americans who, like Pfc. Jessica Lynch, fell into enemy hands during this conflict and to those who are listed as missing, we offer this determined pledge, "We will not relent, we will not rest until you are safely returned to the country that you call home, a home for the brave, the brave like you."

Nearly forty years ago, President Kennedy said: "A nation reveals itself not only by the men it produces but also by the men it honors, the men it remembers."

Today, of course, we also note the vast contributions, bravery, and patriotism of our servicewomen. But President Kennedy's point endures. Our brave servicemen and women are a testament to history's eternal truth, freedom is not free; as well as its unforgiving lesson, the price that must be paid for freedom is always great.

This generation of Americans, and future generations, are indeed blessed that when freedom's call came, the finest, most professional, most skilled military in the history of the world answered. We will continue to be the land of the free as long as we are the home of the brave. May God continue to bless our country and our cause.

The Ultimate Sacrifice

In an age where pop culture and a cynical main stream media rule, the term "hero" has been mis-defined and cheapened to the point where it is almost meaningless. Be that as it may, a hero is a person who is willing to make the ultimate sacrifice by putting his life on the line unselfishly for others or standing up for their righteous convictions no matter how unpopular or dangerous to themselves.

Randy Rydjeski
History Teacher

U.S. Senator Mark Pryor

I come to the floor today to pay tribute to our men and women in uniform serving at home and abroad and honor their service to this nation.

Our servicemen and women have risen to the call in the fight against terrorism, they have risen to the call to ensure peace and stability in the world, and they have risen to the call to provide humanitarian aid to those in need.

I want to acknowledge the ultimate sacrifice of two our servicemen, who fell in the line of duty:

Hospital Corpsman Michael Vann Johnson, Jr., a 25-year old Navy medic serving in the 3rd Battalion of the 5th Marine Expeditionary Force. Michael was from Little Rock where his mother still lives. I talked with her, and I can tell you that she is also a soldier in her own right, bearing the burden of losing her child so that freedom might take root in Iraq.

Lance Corporal Thomas Blair, a 24 year-old Marine, whose father Al Blair resides in Gravette, Arkansas. Thomas Blair was among eight North Carolina-based Marines who disappeared during fighting on the outskirts of Nasiriyah, Iraq on March 23rd. He was confirmed as killed in the line of duty on March 24th.

I pray for their families and honor them as brave and selfless men who put [their] lives on the line to make the world safer for others.

I also honor the service of Lance Corporal James "Jason" Smedley of the U.S. Marine Corps. Jason was wounded in combat and, by the grace of God, will be returned to us. When not fighting for his country, Jason served in the office of Senator Lincoln assisting Arkansans. Thank you, Jason.

Mr. President, military service is not a job, it's a calling. It takes a special person to pledge to serve their country – risking life and limb in doing so. It takes courage, commitment and a true sense of self to be prepared to deploy and fight for America.

In talking to my kids about our responsibility to support our troops, I often talk about defending freedom and the principles of freedom. Freedom can be a big word for a child, but I am amazed about their understanding of the unique freedoms that we enjoy and why it's worth defending.

I often think about the children of our military men and women. I think about the boys and girls whose fathers and mothers are far from home or working long hours here in the United States. I want them to know that I appreciate the sacrifices that they are making, that I admire their valor in keeping their spirits up, and that their parents are doing a job that epitomizes the best of human character.

As a United States Senator and member of the Armed Services Committee, I stand ready to work with my colleagues and the President to provide any and all support possible to ensure the success of our military forces conducting these operations.

Mr. President, our nation is a nation of diverse views, ideologies, and opinions. We might not all agree on how or why we arrived at this point; nonetheless, we must come together as a country and support those servicemen and women who are currently risking life and limb.

As we stand here today, over 300,000 United States Military personnel, including a number of Arkansans, are forward deployed in Iraq, Kuwait, Afghanistan, Turkey, and the waters and skies all around the world and at bases around the country.

Mr. President, they put themselves in harm's way not for personal aggrandizement or advancement, but for immense love of country, liberty, and family. If they can hear me today, I say be assured, for the American people are behind you.

When appearing before the Senate Armed Services Committee a few weeks ago, General John Keane, Vice Chief of Staff for the United States Army, testified to the courage of our military personnel. He said when asked what their greatest challenge was, his division commanders replied, "Keeping our soldiers from being too brave."

We owe these men and women overseas and at home not only our gratitude, but also our very existence as the only country on Earth committed to promoting and spreading the ideals of democracy. Our military has kept us safe for over 200 years. We cannot thank them enough.

Just as we should thank our military overseas and at home, we should thank our first responders that protect our hometowns. Firefighters, police, and health care personnel risk their lives and sacrifice precious time with their families every day to keep us safe from those who would try to do us harm. Their commitment and contributions to national security and homeland security should not be forgotten.

Mr. President, I urge all Americans to pray for our troops, their families, and our President as we defend our nation and the world from those that seek to do us harm.

Patriotism and Love of Country

An American hero is one who is willing to sacrifice for God, family, and country to provide a better life for the next generation. Be it in a war zone or in an office high above a city, America is guarded by these loving people determined on keeping our dreams alive.

Robert Joslin
Pasadena, MD

U.S. Senator Mike DeWine

Shortly before Congress adjourned for the Easter recess, I came here to the Senate Floor and had a chance to speak briefly about the magnificent service that our armed forces are performing in Iraq. The hard-working men and women in all branches of our military, those who are serving in Iraq and those who are helping to support them, they are all doing an absolutely tremendous job. We are so proud of our service men and women and so grateful for their service and dedication to our country.

Since Operation Iraqi Freedom began forty days ago, we have watched on television and read in the newspapers about our troops' countless acts of bravery, strength, and leadership. We have seen our service men and women take control of Baghdad, driving out Saddam Hussein, and freeing the Iraqi people from his oppressive regime. And, we have rejoiced as the many statues of Saddam, and all that they represent, have toppled

But, at the same time, Mr. President, while there certainly are many reasons to rejoice, and there is clearly much to be thankful for, I also am reminded of something Dwight D. Eisenhower said nearly 60 years ago in a speech following the defeat of Nazi Germany in June 1945. General Eisenhower said that there are certain things that military honors and battlefield victories cannot hide. As he so eloquently said, Mr. President:

> "[Military] honors cannot hide . . . the crosses marking the resting places of the dead. They cannot soothe the anguish of the widow, or the orphan, whose husband or father will not return."

Sadly, Mr. President, there are many sons, husbands, and fathers who will not be returning home from Iraq. Our hearts go out to the families of those who have lost their lives. We pray for them. We pray for those who have been injured. We pray for those who are recovering. And, we think about them -- we think about them every day.

President John F. Kennedy once said that "a nation reveals itself not only by the men it produces, but also by the men it honors [and] remembers." And so today, Mr. President, I would like to honor and remember three valiant men from my home state of Ohio-- three brave men who gave the ultimate sacrifice to protect us and to protect our children and our grandchildren and the Iraqi people -- three brave men who serve as true examples of what defines patriotism and love of country.

Today, Mr. President, I would like to honor and remember the lives and sacrifices of Army Private Brandon Sloan, Army First Sergeant Robert Dowdy, and Marine Private First Class Christian Gurtner, all of whom upheld with strength and conviction what General Douglas MacArthur called the soldier's code, a code of "Duty, Honor, Country."

Mr. President, I did not have the privilege of knowing these men. I did, however, have the honor of attending their funerals and meeting their families and friends and hearing from them about the lives of these men and about their dreams and their hopes and their aspirations. I am grateful. I am grateful to have had that opportunity, and thank their families for allowing me to attend those services. I learned a great deal about these three Ohioans.

And though, Mr. President, I am here on the Senate Floor today to pay tribute to these men, I know that my words will fall short. My words will fall short because really, it is their families and friends and the men and women with whom they served, many still in Iraq right now, who knew them best. They are the people who could give the most adequate tribute.

But, at the same time, Mr. President, I do feel it is very important for my colleagues here in the Senate and for the American people to know what I have learned about these three fine men, because each of them, in his own way, has revealed the strength and greatness of our nation.

PVT Brandon Sloan was born in Cleveland, OH, on October 7, 1983, to the Rev. Tandy Sloan and Kimberly Sloan. Brandon was special. Rev. Walter Thornhill, the pastor at Brandon's church in Cleveland, remembered him as "a gentle person with a goodness of spirit."

He was a loving and caring person, with a strong faith in God. He radiated joy because of that faith, and his joy spread to everyone around him, especially to his younger sister, Brittney, and to his friends and to the community. His friends described Brandon as "a big guy, happy-go-lucky and loyal to a fault." His friend, Tony Tucker, said that Brandon was a "kind, sweet person . . . a cool person to be around." That was his faith shining through.

It wasn't surprising that Brandon was a popular and friendly student at Bedford High School in Bedford Heights, OH. He was a gifted athlete, who proved to be a talented football player, working hard on the field to earn a position as defensive lineman for the Bedford High Bearcats. Storeowners recalled how pleasant and personable Brandon was when he would stop by their stores after football practice in high school. He was a nice young man, who was respectful and considerate of others. Again, that was his faith shining through.

Brandon's faith in God, and the warmth that radiated from him because of it, extended to his love of country. When he turned 18 years-old, he enlisted in the United States Army. His service in the Army began with great promise. He became a logistics specialist and was assigned to Fort Bliss, TX. In January 2003, he was sent to Kuwait with the 507th Maintenance Company. But, after just one year of service, at the age of 19, Brandon was killed in action when the 507th was ambushed by Iraqi troops near Al Nasiriyah. He was killed while defending the nation he was so proud to serve and protect.

Mr. President, Brandon Sloan *wanted* to be a soldier. He was proud to be a soldier. His father, Reverend Sloan, recalled how

Brandon just exuded pride at his boot camp graduation. He wanted to protect his country, to protect us and our children and our grandchildren. His faith in God and his commitment to serving America is what made Brandon Sloan a very special person. He is a role model for us all.

I know that he will be greatly missed by his friends and his family. He leaves behind to cherish his memory his father, his mother, his sister, and his grandmothers, Dr. Rementa Pippen and Luberta Sloan. My prayers are with all of them.

1SG Robert Dowdy also was from Cleveland and also served and died with the 507th Maintenance Company, where he was the highest-ranking enlisted soldier.

Robert was born on August 21, 1964. He attended Cleveland South High School and before graduating in 1982, he lettered in five sports. After high school, Robert followed his older brother Jack, a former Marine, into the military, and his service carried him to bases in South Korea and across the United States.

Even when far away from home, however, he always kept close to Cleveland, and followed his beloved Cleveland Indians whenever and wherever he could, and, I might add, when they were having good seasons or bad seasons. One of Robert's other passions was distance running. He was an avid runner with a level of perseverance and commitment that permeated everything he did. His friends said that in a race, he always would cross the finish line in high spirits.

Robert also liked to take time to enjoy all things in life, including the little things. He was a devoted son, husband, and father. And, he loved doing small things for his family, like teaching his mother how to drive. His family was everything to him. His family was his life, his passion, his whole world.

Robert married his high school sweetheart, Kathy, and they were blessed by the birth of their daughter, Kristy. Their marriage was one of balance. Robert never made a decision without consulting Kathy.

They were equals.

They were partners.

They were best friends.

Robert had great respect for his wife and loved her and Kristy with all of his heart.

Robert's bravery as a soldier was something he passed on to his daughter, Kristy. At the young age of 14, she had the courage and the strength to design the program cover for her father's funeral. She created an enduring and heart-felt tribute not only for her father, but also for other Americans who have dedicated their lives to protecting us. For the program cover, she took a picture of her father and placed in the background additional pictures of policemen and firefighters saving lives on September 11th. I think we can be sure that Robert would have been so proud of his daughter, Kristy, as we know he always was.

Mr. President, 1SG Robert Dowdy not only was an inspiration to his family, but also to his fellow troops. He led by example. He led by his actions, not just by his words. As a First Sergeant, he was a leader. He was strong, yet compassionate. He truly loved those under his command, and they knew it. He touched their hearts. He loved them, and they loved him back.

MSG John Hite, who eulogized Robert at his funeral, relayed a story of a young soldier who was clearly touched by Robert's life and leadership. Master Sergeant Hite spoke of a big, strapping 6 foot, 4 inch, 250 lb. soldier, who came up to him the day before First Sergeant Dowdy's burial and told him about the love and admiration he had for Robert. As they talked, they were standing by a bouquet of flowers adorned with a tiny replica of Robert's machine gun, helmet, and combat boots. Before long, as this big, strong, tough Army soldier spoke of his love and admiration for First Sergeant Dowdy, his eyes swelled with tears. He looked at those combat boots and simply said, "No one will ever fill them...."

Robert Dowdy loyally served his country for 18 years and was only 18 months from retirement when he deployed for Iraq, a deployment he *volunteered* for so that another soldier could stay at home with his family. This act defines who Robert Dowdy was, and no one who knew him was surprised that he would offer to help a fellow soldier in this selfless way.

As his brother Jack said that "[Robert] was a very patriotic and very loyal man who loved his country. . . . He just wanted to serve his country to the best of his ability before he retired." 1SG Robert Dowdy did serve his country, and he served it loyally, heroically, and honorably.

In the end, Mr. President, he ran a good race. And, as St. Paul wrote in his second Epistle to Timothy (4:1-8): "He finished the course; he kept the faith. "

Robert Dowdy is survived by his wife, Kathy; his daughter, Kristy; his brothers, Jack Jr. and Jim; his sisters, Roxane and Anita; and his parents, Jack and Irene Dowdy. My heart goes out to them all.

PFC Christian Daniel Gurtner was born on June 23, 1983. He grew up in Ohio City, OH, and graduated from Van Wert High School in Van Wert, OH. He joined the Marines last year after graduating and was assigned to the 3rd Light Armored Reconnaissance Battalion, based out of Twentynine Palms, CA. He was deployed to Kuwait in February.

Christian's friends described him as respectful, motivated, and hard-charging. He was proud of what he was doing and was committed to the Marines. As his friends described, he was so excited about being in the Marines and was so honored to serve.

He frequently signed letters back home with the Marine Corps motto "Semper Fidelis." In February, one of the last times Christian spoke to his family, he told his mother that he was ready to do whatever was needed to protect our nation. He told her that he was "good to go."

And, in a letter he wrote home, a letter that his mother received just days ago and portions of which were printed in yesterday's *Washington Post*, Christian wrote of how he missed and loved his family, but that he was fighting so we all "can sleep better at night because there is less terrorism in the world." In typical fashion, he closed this letter with "Semper Fi."

Christian was a faithful, hard-working, and well-loved member of the Ohio City community. He loved to laugh, and, as his friend Alicia Sterling said, "He had this smile, and you knew when you saw that smile [that] you were going to get into trouble!"

Christian loved to have fun, and he loved to watch sports. He followed both the Atlanta Braves and The Ohio State University football team. He also enjoyed bowling and spent many evenings at the bowling alley with friends. To celebrate this, his friends brought to his funeral a bowling pin signed by his teammates. It was a touching gesture, and one of love and admiration for their friend and fellow teammate.

When he joined the Marines, Christian found a cause in which he believed deeply and a vehicle through which he could pursue his beliefs. He served our country well and fought valiantly to preserve the security of this nation and bring freedom to the Iraqi people. Christian Gurtner passed away on April 2, 2003. As CWO Suzanne Handshoe so fittingly said upon his death, "We lost a brother. As Marines, we honor our own."

Mr. President, Christian Gurtner was good-natured. He was loyal. He was true to his family and friends. And, he was just a decent, loving, kind-hearted young man, who died fighting for a cause he strongly believed in.

At his funeral, Christian's mother picked a very special song to be played in her much-loved son's honor -- a song called "Forever Young." When I heard that song, I was reminded of a poem that was sent to me shortly after my wife and I lost our daughter ten years ago. Our daughter was about Christian's age. It was sent to me by a dear friend of mine, Jock McKernan, who had lost his son, who was also about Christian's age. It was a poem that was written during World War I, by a man named Laurence Binyon. And, here is a stanza from that poem:

"They shall grow not old, as we that are left grow old; age shall not weary them, nor the years condemn. At the going down of the sun and in the morning, we will remember them."

And we, too, will remember you, Christian.

PFC Christian Gurtner is survived by an infant daughter; his mother, Eldonna, and his stepfather, Gary Wagonrod; and his grandmothers, Sally Mae Gurtner and Dorothy Wagonrod. They have been and will remain in my thoughts and prayers.

Mr. President, Brandon Sloan, Robert Dowdy, and Christian Gurtner demonstrated great nobility both in their lives and in their deaths. They revealed all that is good and strong about our nation, a nation they gave their lives for to defend and protect. Each of these men was an amazing individual, whose families and friends loved them dearly. My heart aches at their loss, but after learning more about these three remarkable men, I am even more proud to say that I am an American, that I come from a country and a state that could produce such admirable individuals, men who, indeed, upheld the code of Duty, Honor, Country.

Though they were but three of the several hundred thousand women and men who serve this country in the military, they represented the courage and the selflessness of them all. My wife Fran and I extend our most heartfelt sympathy and prayers to the families of Brandon Sloan, Robert Dowdy, and Christian Gurtner. To their parents, I must say that you raised incredible sons. We will never forget them.

As President Ronald Reagan said of the troops who perished at Normandy in World War II, "We will always remember. We will always be proud."

Americas' Armed Forces

An American hero is someone who follows their convictions whole-heartedly but is capable of re-evaluating them without fear or shame.

Kevin McCullough
Newport Beach, CA

U.S. Senator Dianne Feinstein

I rise today to honor the 24 young American men who have died in the conflict in Iraq. I would like to pay particular tribute, however, to the six men from my home state of California, and to talk briefly about each of them.

To date, these young men account for one fourth of all the Americans that have made the ultimate sacrifice. At the same, nearly 120,000 men and women now stationed in the Middle East, many of them in harm's way, are either from California or were stationed there before being deployed.

It is often said that California receives too much from the federal government - too much of the appropriations pie. But when you consider our population is 35 million and you remember that, on average, Californians pay more in federal taxes than they receive in federal programs, this is simply not the case. And Californians are playing a very prominent role in liberating the Iraqi people from the tyranny of Saddam Hussein.

Of the six Californians that have died so far, two were not yet citizens, while one was a direct descendant of the second and sixth presidents of the United States.

Together, they embody the depth and breadth of America's armed forces - men and women from all walks of life, willing to give their lives to defend our freedoms.

The first four I would like to honor: Corporals Jorge Gonzalez, Randal Kent Rosaker, and Jorge Garibay, and Sergeant Michael Bitz - were killed on March 23rd, in heavy fighting outside the town of Nasiriya.

Two were fathers with infant children that they never met, a third a son who followed his father into the military.

Twenty year old Corporal Jorge Gonzalez was part of the 1st Battalion of the 2nd Marine Expeditionary Brigade. He grew up in Rialto, with his parents, Rosa and Mario, and five siblings. He was an avid soccer player and a graduate of El Monte High School.

His last visit home was at Christmas. There, his younger sister Nancy, who was never affectionate with her brother, hugged and kissed him before he left. "I knew I had to do that," she said.

He also left behind his wife Jazty and their three week old baby boy, Alonso, who he never knew. He had hoped to retire from the Marines in a year and become a policeman.

Before leaving he told his anxious mother, "Don't worry, mom. If I die a Marine, I'll die honored."

Marine Sargeant Michael Bitz, a part of the 2nd Assault Amphibious Battalion, 2nd Marine Division, was just 31 years old. He grew up in Port Hueneme.

He loved being a marine so much, he reenlisted last fall. He loved his wife Janina so much that they had just renewed their vows. When he left for the Gulf, they were expecting twins, Caleb and Taylor, who are now a month old. They also have a two-year-old son, Joshua, and a 7 year-old son, Christian, from an earlier marriage.

In his last phone call to his mother Donna, Sargeant Bitz was able to tell her that he loved her, and in his last letter he said that he was her warrior. In classic Marine-style, he always called her "ma'am."

Corporal Randal Kent Rosacker was also a member of the 2nd Marine Expeditionary Brigade. He was a rough-and-tumble athlete who loved the outdoors, and ever since he was a boy, he knew he wanted to follow his father, Rod, into the military.

Corporal Rosacker grew up in San Diego, the son of Navy man. He played football, baseball, and wrestled for the Serra High School Conquistadors. His wrestling coach, Steve Stone, recalled when Randal broke his hand senior year, just before an important game.

"Well, we heard some thudding on the wall in the lockeroom," he said. "We walk in, and Randy had broken off his cast. He said, 'Coach, tape it up. I'm ready to go.'"

His former baseball coach, Chris Herrin, said that Rosacker's teammates could always count on him. "He was the kind of guy who you would want fighting for your country," Herrin said.

His grandmother, Patricia, said her grandson died doing something he loved, serving America. "He believed in what he was doing," she said. He was just 21 years old.

Born in Jalisco, Mexico, Corporal Jorge Garibay played football at Newport Harbor High School, in Costa Mesa. He, too, was just 21 years old.

One of his teachers, Janis Toman, described him as a hard worker who frequently returned to the high school campus in full uniform, to encourage students to do their best.

Ms. Toman received a letter from Corporal Garibay just a few hours before learning of his death, as she packed him a care package. "He wrote of simple things that we take for granted but make soldiers happy," she said. "Things like moving from a small tent to a bigger one."

"I want to defend the country I plan to become a citizen of," he wrote to her. He also left a tape recording before his deployment for his beloved uncle Urbano, whom he regarded as a surrogate father.

In the tape he said, "I'm being called to represent and serve my country. I don't know if I'll return, and I want you to know that I love you and how much I appreciate the support and love you have given me over the years."

Lance Corporal Jose Gutierrez was the first American killed in combat. He was struck by enemy fire while fighting alongside fellow Marines near the southern Iraqi port city of Umm al Qasr. He was 22 years old.

Corporal Gutierrez arrived in the United States when he was a 16 year-old orphan, having left poverty-stricken circumstances in Guatemala City and a country racked by a brutal civil war.

He traveled over 2,000 miles by foot, north through Mexico, in search of a better life here in the United States.

Like so many immigrants, his past was soon eclipsed by his new life as an American. He was taken in by the Mosquera family, of

Lomita, California. Nora and Max Mosquera had begun helping immigrant foster children when their own children had grown.

"He joined the Marines to pay back a little of what he'd gotten from the U.S.," Max Mosquera said. "For him it was a question of honor."

A tall and quiet young man who enjoyed soccer and chess, Jose learned English quickly and had plans to study architecture.

"He was such a good kid," remembered Robert Nobles, a physical education teacher at North High in Torrance, where Corporal Gutierrez graduated in 2000.

I have been told that news of his death has resonated throughout Guatemala. Every major newspaper, radio and TV station carried his story. He has been portrayed as a brave and selfless young man, which he most certainly was.

Navy Lieutenant Thomas Mullen Adams grew up in comfort, in the suburb of La Mesa, as a member of a family that traces its roots directly to John Adams, one of America's most important Founding Fathers.

He graduated from Grossmont High School in 1993 and the United States Naval Academy in 1997.

He received flight training in Pensacola, Florida, and inherited his love of flying from his father, John, an architect who helped design the Aerospace Museum in San Diego.

Promoted to lieutenant in the year 2000, Adams won two National Defense Service Medals, three Sea Service Deployment Ribbons and other awards.

"He's one of these amazingly clean-cut, all-American kids," his aunt, Elizabeth Hansen, told the *San Diego Union Tribune* newspaper. "He's the kind of kid that if you had a very special daughter, you would hope that she would snag him. He was just amazingly bright, funny, and kind."

In October of 2002, Lieutenant Adams was assigned as an exchange officer with the British Royal Navy's 849 Squadron, now on the aircraft carrier Ark Royal.

An avid soccer fan who had volunteered to go to Japan with the carrier Kitty Hawk in time for the World Cup finals last summer, he joined a local team near his base in Helston, England.

Lieutenant Adams' family said that he particularly enjoyed his time with the Royal Navy for two reasons: every ship had a pub on board, and he was allowed a weekly 20-minute phone call home. He died with the Royal Navy, when the helicopter he was flying in collided with another helicopter over the Persian Gulf. He was just 27 years old.

We all wish for a quick resolution to this war, to limit casualties, military and civilian, American, allied and Iraqi.

We wish that American and coalition forces will be able to liberate the people of Iraq soon, and that our men and women will be able to return home to their families.

Until then, however, they remain in our thoughts and our prayers, along with those that have already fallen.

All Americans owe an enormous, an almost incalculable, debt to these young men who were willing to sacrifice their own futures for the future of this country they so clearly loved, so that we, as a people, might be safe and free. Their sacrifices must never be forgotten.

Defeating Tyranny

An American hero is a man, woman, or child who loves America enough to see what is not right and attempt to correct it. This often means sacrificing their life before the country realizes that the changes proposed are good and needed and will benefit all.

> Dr. Letitia S. Wright, D.C.
> The Wright Place TV Show
> Rancho Cucamonga, CA

U.S. Representative Martin Frost –
spoke at the Dallas Baptist University's annual Memorial Day service and gave the following remarks.

Thank you, Dr. Cook. Good afternoon. It's a privilege to be here, especially to speak at an institution neighboring the Dallas-Ft.-Worth National Cemetery where Memorial Day is an everyday event.

Memorial Day is the time when our grateful nation pauses to remember the service and the sacrifice of those who have fought and died for all of us in battle. This year we should all be especially reflective.

Since last Memorial Day, 181 American service members have died in support of military operations in combat zones - 30 in the war against terrorism in Operation Enduring Freedom in Afghanistan and 151 in Operation Iraqi Freedom. Today Americans gather across the nation to honor them and all the men and women who have made the ultimate sacrifice for the freedoms that make the United States of America the greatest nation in the history of the world.

Throughout history, citizens have honored their fallen heroes. They have reflected on their character, their courage and their commitment. And, they have recognized what we recognize today – that freedom is not free.

The truth is, freedom is extraordinarily expensive. Just ask the soldiers, sailors, airmen, Marines, and Coasties who pay its bill. Or their parents, their spouses, and children who mortgage their lives every time our men and women in uniform prepare for battle.

All of them, and all of us, felt this lesson yet again in the war against Saddam Hussein. The brave men and women of our armed forces distinguished themselves by answering the call to defend liberty.

In Iraq, they confronted a tyrannical regime that ruled through terror. And, as they have many times before, American troops defended freedom by defeating tyranny and liberating a deeply oppressed people.

Here at home, our troops' families made sacrifices of their own. Children were born during their parent's deployment. Others went to school shaken to the core, telling teachers and friends, "My daddy is in the war." One spouse had full responsibility for childcare, housework, repair, and financial matters. And parents worried and prayed every day for their children's safe return.

Now that the war has ended, the nation has celebrated the safe return of our POWs and we continue to pray that the troops who still face hostilities will return home safely. But we cannot forget those brave Americans who were not so lucky, those Americans who will never enjoy a homecoming. The have made the ultimate sacrifice for America and for each and every one of us, and we will always remember and honor them.

As we reflect on their sacrifice today, it is appropriate for us all to remember that the strength of America lies in two underlying principles governing our use of force: (1) we are slow to anger and generally only act when directly provoked, and (2) during the past century, there has been a basic morality in our use of force – we have acted out of the best motives rather than out of a selfish desire for territorial conquest.

In World War I and World War II, there were attacks on our territory and our shipping. In World War II, we fought terrible dictatorships that threatened our very way of life. In Korea, there was a clear attack on an ally. In Vietnam, we determined that it was in our national interest to confront the spread of Communism. In Bosnia and Kosovo, we intervened for the best of motives, to bring order and stability to a very troubled part of the world. In Afghanistan, we pursued a regime that was providing sanctuary for Al Queda fighters who had launched the attacks of September 11th.

In the first war against Iraq, we responded to their attack on Kuwait. And we fought Iraq this year because we believed that they presented a threat to the stability of the Middle East.

In each of these wars American troops died fighting for our national interest, something we all can take pride in.

I have supported each of the military actions that have occurred during my 25 years in Congress; the two Iraq wars, Kosovo, Bosnia, and Operation Enduring Freedom in Afghanistan.

However, there is a limit on the use of force abroad. I do not believe force should be used against every regime we don't happen to like in the world. American lives and treasure are too precious to fight every dictator in the 21st century.

We are the greatest nation on the face of the Earth with the best armed forces ever developed in history. However, simply being the best, the biggest, and the baddest is not enough. In order to achieve the objectives of our national policy, we need the cooperation and support of our allies. Going it entirely alone and paying the entire cost of a military operation solely with American blood is not in the best interest of our country or its people. It was right for us to attempt to work through the United Nations in building support for our war against Saddam Hussein, and we need to continue to pursue international cooperation as we rebuild that war-torn country.

It is not enough for America to be feared because of our military might. American is great because we have earned the respect of the world through our commitment to freedom and Democracy. Our brave young men and women who have died for our nation have established us as a great moral power as well as a great military power. We are the ones who wear the white hats on the world stage. And now as we once again demonstrate that awesome military power, we must never forget our great tradition as warriors slow to anger but with a terrible swift sword once aroused.

We and the world face a terrible challenge with the emergence of Islamic fanaticism. We will never retreat from that challenge and we will ultimately prevail, as we did in Iraq, but we must use force wisely and with restraint. Syria, Iran, Iraq, and others may be terrible regimes but neither world opinion nor opinion in the United States will always support a foreign policy solely based on the use of the sword. I support a strong military and a strong America, but I also take seriously my responsibility not to unnecessarily sacrifice American lives, our national treasure.

And that brings us back to the significance of today's ceremony. We are here today to honor the men and women who have given their lives to make our nation great. And we should never forget them. All you have to do is open today's *Dallas Morning News* or the most recent edition of *Army Times* to see the pictures and read the names of the brave young people who died in Operation Iraqi Freedom. We owe them and the fallen of all our previous wars an enormous debt of gratitude. They are the ones who made us the great nation that we are today. As John F. Kennedy said, "A nation reveals itself not only by the men it produces but also by the men it honors, the men it remembers."

The role of those who fell in Iraq reminds us of some unfinished business in Congress. Ten of those who gave their lives were not yet citizens but willing to fight for our nation. Last year, long before our successful campaign in Iraq, I introduced legislation to recognize the contribution of our foreign born troops who are not yet citizens. According to the Department of Defense, the number of legal permanent residents serving on active duty has risen to 37,401 or about 3 percent of our military. Immigrants have fought in every American conflict and their military service reflects the strong strain of patriotism among generations who've chosen to come to America. And the patriotism of today's large Hispanic immigrant communities is particularly strong. For all of those reasons, I've been working for the last year to pass legislation to help remedy the obstacles these brave soldiers face on their path to citizenship. My legislation shortens the time they must serve in the military to qualify for priority in obtaining citizenship and waives fees and bureaucratic impediments for prompt processing of their applications. It is the least we can do for men and women who are willing to die for a country where they do not yet have the right to vote.

Now I want to make sure no one here thinks that I'm a regular reader of Dear Abby . . . but I did see a column recently that I saved for significant days like Memorial Day. She reprinted a poem written by a high school Junior ROTC cadet that has a special message.

I watched the flag pass by one day
It fluttered in the breeze
A young marine saluted it
And then he stood at ease.

I looked at him in uniform
So young, so tall, so proud,
With hair cut square and eyes alert
He stands out in a crowd.

I thought how many men like him
Had fallen thru the years
How many died on foreign soil
How many mothers' tears

How many pilots' planes shot down
How many died at sea
How many foxholes were soldier's graves
No, freedom is not free

I heard the sound of taps one night
When everything was still
I listened to the bugler play
And felt a sudden chill

I wondered just how many times
That taps had meant amen
When a flag had draped a coffin
Of a brother or a friend.

I thought of all the children
Of the mothers and the wives
Of fathers sons and husbands
With interrupted lives

I thought about a graveyard
At the bottom of the sea
Of unmarked graves in Arlington
No, freedom is not free

We honor those today that have paid the price for our freedom. The statue of Liberty reigns as the symbol of freedom across the world...But right here in Texas the Alamo stands as the ultimate symbol of sacrifice and heroism. As we leave today, I hope you will all remember the eloquence of William Barret Travis as he inspired a young 16-year old defender at the Alamo, saying, "Wherever you go, whatever you do, remember that freedom rests finally on those willing to die for it."

Today remember those who have died for us, but also remember as well the troops still patrolling the streets of Baghdad, Tikrit, and Mosul...or still searching for Osama Bin Laden in the hostile mountains of Afghanistan and Pakistan. They are in harms way. Pray for them...they are fighting for your way of life...

God bless them all and those who love them. God bless America and those who keep her strong.

The question of all questions, if called upon to do so, would you enlist in the military to fight for America and her freedom? Tell us at –
www.ModernDayHeroes.com

Support the Troops

Heroes are not born; they're made.

Amy Smith
Belmont Shore, CA

U.S. Representative Ron Kind

I rise today in support of this resolution honoring our brave men and women of the armed services. Their duty and sacrifice in Iraq and Afghanistan are appreciated by all Americans.

New challenges facing our nation demand increased vigilance on the part of our armed services. With these increased demands, the role of the National Guard and reserve forces is critical in providing the total force necessary to ensure our security. Over the past year, I have had the opportunity to meet with many National Guard and Reserve members from Western Wisconsin who have been called up for service Operation Enduring Freedom in Afghanistan and Operation Iraqi Freedom in Iraq.

Over 2,300 members of the Wisconsin Air and Army National Guard are serving on active duty. The people of Western Wisconsin are proud of their service and the service of all the men and women of our armed forces during this important time in our nation's history.

We still have much to do in terms of peacekeeping and rebuilding in Iraq and Afghanistan. In this effort, it is important that we engage our allies to share responsibility and pursue an effective, sustained commitment peace and stability in the region. If we can do this right, we will not have to again, sometime down the road, send our military forces over to fight.

In addition, we recognize today all of the 'round-the-clock' work put in by the military personnel and DOD civilian employees at military mobilization platforms around our nation. In Western Wisconsin, I represent Fort McCoy, one of the Army Reserves' power projection platforms. Ft. McCoy has been continuously processing and training mobilized members of the National Guard and Reserve for the past six months. Their efforts have been key in getting our forces ready for combat.

It is also important that we recognize the support and sacrifice of the families and employers of our troops. They are the backbone of our fighting forces, and we appreciate their commitment during these challenging times.

The American people and the congress of the United States stand behind our armed service members and those that support them. As our military effort continues, I, and other members of Congress, will continue to work to ensure that our service men and women have all the resources necessary to fulfill their mission.

My thoughts and prayers are with those serving our country overseas, as well as their families. America is firmly behind our troops, and we're all hoping to see them home safe, secure and soon.

May God continue to bless the United States of America.

Terrorism Must be Torn Out by its Roots

An American hero:

One who isn't afraid to stand up for ethics, integrity, honesty -- even if it means taking risks. And even more so, one who not only follows those principles, but works with others to achieve these goals.

Shel Horowitz
www.principledprofits.com
Hadley, MA

U.S. Senator Elizabeth Dole

Thousands of young men and women from bases in my home state of North Carolina are currently fighting the War on Terror in Iraq. We are forging a process of peace, and in doing so, we are moving toward turning control of the government and society back to the Iraqi people.

With the major battles over in Iraq, our nation is helping to rebuild schools and hospitals, water supply systems, and roadways. Part of the President's supplemental request is being designated for the continuation of these efforts. The stabilization of Iraq depends on providing the Iraqi people basic services as well as humanitarian relief. And the safety of our men and women in uniform depends on the stabilization of Iraq.

Our forces are on the offensive and continue to capture key figures in Saddam Hussein's evil regime, so that they may be brought to justice. The vast majority of the President's request will go directly to American troops-giving them the pay, the equipment, and other resources necessary to fight the War on Terror. We must ensure that these funds are available to allow them to complete their mission and return home safely.

Recently a proud grandmother met with my 102-year-old mother in Salisbury, North Carolina. This grandmother forwarded to me a letter from her grandson, Christopher Shawn Jensen, who is currently stationed in Baghdad. I would like to read to you what a soldier on the front lines has to say to this grandmother:

"I was invited to meet with a local Iraqi who works the engineering for our building's electricity...He graduated from the Baghdad University in engineering and showed me his class picture (from 1979). We talked about what it was like then and the difference now. You could see the suffering in his eyes as he talked about the years of terror the people lived with while Saddam was in power. I felt the same emotions of sadness for these people when I first rolled up here from Kuwait, to see their cheering faces of relief...many a soldier's eyes were filled with tears that day...I pray that we finish the job we started."

At the end of the letter to his grandmother, Shawn made a request to his friends and family. "I have started the ball rolling for several ideas," he writes, "to help in the effort to free Iraqis and also to help to make this a safer place for liberty and freedom." I know many of you have big hearts and want to help, you just don't know how. Here are some things you can help with. I have written to the Editor of the *Wilmington Star* newspaper. The children in Iraq learn on the dirty floors in their schools. They need approximately 200,000 desks for their schools. I am trying to build support for a program where the American citizen can buy support for the Iraqi children." And, Mr. President, let me add, my husband, Bob Dole, has already committed to Shawn's effort.

Shawn's letter continues, "We are also collecting money from the soldiers here and we are going to buy back weapons from the populous of Iraq. We are using the little money we earn in a combat zone to start this program. The regular citizens have all kinds of weapons like grenades, bombs, and rockets...things regular citizens don't need. We are asking American citizens to match funds that we are collecting for this cause. My father can be contacted for this via phone or a web-site that has been started."

Shawn Jensen understands, Mr. President, what freedom means to the people of Iraq, indeed he is seeing it firsthand. He is so committed to making Iraq a safe place for his fellow soldiers to complete their mission, and for the Iraqi people to live in a free and orderly society, that he and his fellow soldiers are making these tremendous sacrifices.

My friend, Secretary of State Colin Powell, described last week his visit to Iraq in the most poignant terms. He said, "Anyone who doubts the wisdom of President Bush's course in Iraq should stand, as I did, by the side of the mass grave in Iraq's north. That terrible site holds the remains of 5,000 innocent men, women and children who were gassed to death by Saddam Hussein's criminal regime."

Recently, in testimony before the Armed Services Committee, on which I serve, Ambassador Paul Bremer outlined a clear and well-defined course of action in Iraq. As he noted, there will be bumps along the way, but it is critical for us to stay the course. As he has said so poignantly, "Gone are Saddam Hussein's torture chambers," he wrote. "Gone are his mass killings and rape rooms. And gone is his threat to America and the international community." Mr. President, as we go forward, it is this that we should keep in mind.

Today in Iraq, streets are lined with shops selling newspapers and books representing varied opinions. Already, 160 newspapers have sprung up in Iraq; schools and universities are open; parents are forming PTAs; 95 percent of health clinics are open, and Iraq is on the way to a democratic government. Eighty-five percent of towns now have city councils! And a Constitution will soon be written, followed next year by elections which will provide legitimacy and credibility to the government and millions of dollars of humanitarian aid are going to the Iraqi people to make sure they have food, water, and shelter.

Iraqis are also being trained to maintain peace and order in their own country. Thousands of members of the Iraqi police force will be trained over the next several months in Eastern Europe. And the area around Saddam's hometown of Tikrit, one of the most dangerous sections in Iraq, is currently being patrolled by the Iraqi army. These measures are part of the larger goal of turning over the security of Iraq to the Iraqis.

Certainly, the operation there is proving to be a dangerous and more grinding conflict than some expected. The President addressed this fact candidly and resolutely in his recent address to the nation. While Saddam Hussein was building palaces, the infrastructure was deteriorating terribly, more than we realized. Adequate resources for the proper reconstruction are essential to providing security and allowing our troops to leave as soon as possible.

Eliminating terror is more than removing the leaders of an evil regime from power. Terrorism must be torn out by its roots, ensuring that there is no toehold for its sponsors to re-establish their violent ways. The bottom line: we can fight them there, or we can fight them here.

The President's call for a Supplemental Spending bill for operations in Iraq has spawned the most recent round of debate over the War on Terror. For those who have criticized the cost of the war, understand that inaction would be much more devastating. Just look at the September 11th attacks...one study has pegged the cost to the economy at well over $2 trillion dollars! And a Brookings Institution study estimates that a biological terrorist attack against a major U.S city would cost our economy $750 billion dollars!

There are other critics who have accused the military of being slow in their progress. But consider these numbers I heard recently from Defense Secretary Donald Rumsfeld. It took three years after World War II to establish an independent central bank in Germany; it was established in Iraq in two months. Police in Germany were established after 14 months; in Iraq, two months. A new currency in Germany took three years; it took two and a half months in Iraq. The Cabinet in Germany was created after 14 months; Iraq has a Cabinet today – after just four months!

We cannot afford not to do what is necessary to win the war against terror and secure our homeland. The funding for the war is necessary and significant, but it is temporary. And, the cost of fighting this war is well below the cost of previous conflicts.

And more than words... more than negotiations... the President's significant spending request sends an unmistakable signal to the sponsors of terror, to the liberated Iraqi citizens, and to the world, that the United States of America is staying the course. Attacks on U.S. troops and other targets in Iraq are aimed at undermining freedom and democracy, but these attacks will not cause us to shy away from our commitment. Failure to follow through in our mission would leave a lethal void, a void that would rapidly be filled by terror and its supporters. President Bush has said, "Liberty is not America's gift to the world, it is God's gift to mankind."

I believe that God's gift to all of his children is liberty, and also justice and equality, tolerance and opportunity. These belong to all people, no matter where they live. Let us remember the steadfast resolve of Shawn Jensen in that letter to his grandmother. He is a witness to a country being transformed from a reign of terror to a beacon of hope. Let us, like him, commit to the stabilization of Iraq diminishing the threat to our troops and ensuring greater stability and peace in the Middle East.

Have a letter from a family member fighting for America that you would like to share with the rest of us?
Share your letter with us at –
www.ModernDayHeroes.com

He was a Good Man

For me, heroes fall into 3 categories:

1) There are those who respond to a critical situation; it could be an accident, a condition of war, or some natural disaster. In all cases they rise above normal expectations and perform some great act that makes a significant difference in the life or lives of someone else.
H.E.R.O.
(Have Emergency React Outstandingly)

2) These are those who are placed in a situation where they are called upon to endure some major challenge for long periods of time with seemingly no end in sight. Favorite examples are parents of children born with Down's Syndrome or other birth conditions NOT normal; or close family or relatives of someone injured who willingly care for those who are forced to live the rest of their lives with some sort of handicap.
H.E.R.O.E.S.
(Helpers Effectively Reaching Out Eternally Somehow)

3) Those who overcome great odds to find, fulfill, and leave a legacy of their life's work. Examples are legion, outnumbered only by those WHO DO NOT!
H.E.R.O.E.S
(Humans Everywhere Reaching Objectives Eventually Supreme)

> Lowell Rex
> Camarillo, CA

U.S. Senator Mike DeWine

At a wreath-laying ceremony at Arlington National Cemetery on this day, Veterans Day, nearly two decades ago in 1985, President Ronald Reagan spoke about the responsibility we, the living, have in remembering those who have died for us on the field of battle. At that ceremony, President Reagan said this:

"There is a special sadness that accompanies the death of a serviceman [or woman], for we're never quite good enough to them -- not really; we can't be, because what they gave us is beyond our powers to repay. And so, when a service [member] dies, it's a tear in the fabric, a break in the whole, and all we can do is remember."

Mr. President, today I come again to the Floor of the United States Senate to remember an Ohio serviceman who gave his life to protect us, to protect our families, and to help liberate the Iraqi people. Army Private First Class Marlin Tyrone Rockhold, who proudly served with the 3rd Battalion, 7th Infantry Regiment of the 3rd Mechanized Infantry Division, was killed on May 8, 2003, by a sniper in Baghdad.

He was 23 years old.

Marlin Rockhold, "Rocko" to his family and friends -- was born in Hamilton, Ohio, on July 1, 1979. He attended school in Butler County and graduated from Hamilton High School in 1998, where he was a well-liked student and member of the Hamilton Big Blue football squad. As his grandmother, Eileen Henderson, described, "Marlin just about always had a smile. He was a person you just had to like."

Though a "kidder" growing up, Marlin also had a quiet, determined, serious side. After graduation, he set out to realize a dream, a dream he had since childhood. Marlin Rockhold's dream, Mr. President, was to join the military. From the time he was a little boy, he wanted to become a soldier. He wanted to see the world. He wanted to see a life outside of Hamilton. He wanted to serve the country he so dearly loved.

And so, on March 4, 2002, Marlin joined the Army and was sent to Boot Camp at Fort Benning, Georgia. From there, he was stationed at Fort Stewart, Georgia. On January 20, 2003, he was sent to Kuwait and eventually went on to serve in Iraq as part of Operation Iraqi Freedom.

Mr. President, for as much as Marlin Rockhold loved the Army, he loved his family even more. In fact, two days before he joined the service, on March 2, 2002, he married the love of his life, DaVonna. Marlin was thrilled to begin his family with her and her daughter,

Therashia. He loved them both with every ounce of his being. They meant the world to him. He devoted his life to them.

Mr. President, while he was in Iraq, Marlin often wrote letters to his wife and to his family. In one letter to his grandmother, he wrote that no one wants to fight a war, but sometimes you do what you have to do. Through his service in the Army, Private First Class Marlin Rockhold was doing what he believed in. He didn't want to leave his family. He didn't want to fight in a war. But, Mr. President, Marlin Rockhold did what he felt he had to do. He was, as Reverend Lonnie Napier said at Marlin's memorial service, "He was willing to join the fight for the hopeless so that they might be free."

Marlin Rockhold was a good soldier. He was a good man. Marlin's sister Brooke said that he, "Always was determined to be happy. Now he's with the Lord. He's happy."

Mr. President, I attended Marlin's funeral and am grateful to have had the chance to hear his family talk about the "Rocko" whom they so deeply loved and admired. At the service, Marlin's brother Derrick said that, "My brother is a hero, my hero, our hero. He is my inspiration. My brother's legacy will live forever in our hearts." Without question, Mr. President, Marlin Rockhold is a hero and his legacy will live on through all who knew him and loved him.

In addition to his wife and daughter, left to cherish his memory are his mother, Mary; his father, Gary; his stepmother, Joan; his grandmother, Eileen; his four brothers, Keith, Derrick, Gregory, and Anton; his two sisters, Brooke and Kara; his in-laws, Dorothy and Clarence and Demery and Patrici; and several aunts and uncles and nieces and nephews. I know they will miss Marlin deeply. My thoughts and prayers are with them all.

Mr. President, I'd like to close with something that Marlin's wife DaVonna said. She said this:

"I just want Marlin to be remembered -- that he [won't] be forgotten. I'll never forget him."

Mr. President, we, too, will never forget Marlin Rockhold. We will always remember him because, as President Reagan said at the conclusion of his remarks at Arlington National Cemetery on that Veterans Day 17 years ago, "We owe a debt we can never repay. All we can do is remember [the soldiers who have died] and what they did and why they had to be brave for us. All we can do is try to see that other young men [and women] never have to join them."

The Screaming Eagles

An American hero is one who without thought of remuneration, publicity or self preservation, acts for the good of their fellow citizens. Firefighters, police officers, and the noble men and women of our nations military all fall within that esteemed category.

Chris Duehring
Costa Mesa, CA

U.S. Senator Mitch McConnell –

made the following remarks on the Senate floor regarding the contributions of the 101st Airborne (Air Assault) Division to the Global War on Terrorism.

I rise to honor the Screaming Eagles of the 101st Airborne (Air Assault) Division based at Fort Campbell, Kentucky. As we all know, two Black Hawk helicopters from the 101st Airborne collided in the night sky over Mosul, Iraq, on November 15, 2003. Tragically, all 17 soldiers on board the helicopters perished in the incident. This last Saturday, two additional soldiers from the Division were killed while they patrolled the streets of Mosul.

These tragic incidents bring the total number of Screaming Eagles lost in Iraq to 55. My prayers and deepest sympathies go out to the families and friends of these brave Americans.

Last month, in one of the most moving experiences of my career, I met with some of these soldiers in Mosul, where the 101st is responsible for keeping the peace in the northern part of Iraq.

These heroes shared with me their thoughts about America's struggle to bring peace and security to a long-oppressed nation, and their patriotism and passion for their mission shone through the dust and grime that accumulates with sustained operations far from the comforts of home.

Truth be told, I did not expect to encounter the extraordinary high levels of dedication and morale I witnessed in Mosul and elsewhere in Iraq. Throughout that country, I conversed with soldiers who witnessed first-hand the reality of war, and who knew friends injured or killed in combat.

It was obvious that the thoughtful young men and women I met in Iraq have spent long hours coming to grips with these harsh realities, yet remain committed to their mission and deeply believe that what they are doing is right and just. An example: at the 101st Airborne's headquarters in Mosul, I witnessed a video that detailed the Division's operations in Iraq. The moving video is dedicated to, and features footage of, Screaming Eagles who have lost their lives during the liberation of Iraq, and it is clear these lost heroes are never far from the thoughts of the soldiers of the 101st. Indeed, these heroes remain a source of poignant motivation for their comrades.

For our armed forces, sad memories of fallen colleagues are inescapable, but so too is the evidence that the Screaming Eagles are on the right side of history. From water coolers in Washington, D.C. to New York City newsrooms, many of us forget that our troops were present at the moment Iraq was liberated from the tortuous grip of Saddam Hussein. They have since witnessed firsthand the birth of a democratic process and the reawakening of a people enslaved for generations by fear and oppression. The Screaming Eagles have worked side by side with Iraqis to help rebuild a shattered country, and their joint success in this regard is truly remarkable.

The brave soldiers I met in Mosul know America is in Iraq for the right reasons, and that despite setbacks and tragic incidents, we are winning the peace in Iraq, just as surely as we won the war.

At one point during my visit, one of the Screaming Eagles came up to me and introduced himself as a captain who hailed from my hometown of Louisville. In the entryway of one of Saddam's former palaces, now serving as the 101st Airborne's Division Headquarters, he presented me with a flag of the Commonwealth of Kentucky, and recalled how he brought it with him as the Division left Fort Campbell and fought north from Kuwait, up through Baghdad, and on to Mosul.

This captain spoke with well-earned pride about the role he and his fellow soldiers played in liberating the Iraqi people and winning the war. And he spoke of the progress they were making in winning over the hearts and minds of these newly free people by treating the Iraqis with a level of dignity and respect they have not received for generations.

While in Mosul, I met with the newly elected governing council of Iraq's Nineveh Province, and I can tell you that the respect and appreciation these democratically elected leaders have for the U.S. efforts is ample evidence the Screaming Eagles are indeed winning the hearts and minds of the Iraqi people.

Indeed, both this democratically elected new government and that young captain would want us all to understand that America did the right thing to help 25 million Iraqis to realize a life without fear. And I can assure you that this captain and his fellow soldiers, although mindful of the great risks and danger inherent in their work, are committed to finishing the job by winning the peace and helping the Iraqis to get back on their feet.

I keep this soldier's flag, still covered in dust and dirt from its historic travels, in my office as a reminder that when America sets out to accomplish a difficult task, it finishes the job. And when I hear discouraging or saddening news from Iraq, I think of this young captain's dedication to his mission, and know that America must, and will, stay the course.

The entire Fort Campbell community grieves the loss of every single Screaming Eagle, and we long to welcome the Division home to the fertile farmland of Western Kentucky.

But when the Division returns to Kentucky, it will have left an indelible mark on the memories of the people of Northern Iraq. The 101st has treated the Iraqi people with respect and honor. They have acted not as occupiers, but as allies to the victims of Hussein's brutal reign. When the Screaming Eagles come home, Iraqis will see their legacy around every corner, in the hundreds of newly refurbished schools, in the electricity that now is available 24 hours a day, in the swimming pool renovated for Iraqi kids by the Division, in the repaired irrigation canals that bring water to the wheat fields near Mosul, in the soccer fields that are no longer killing fields, and in the proud Iraqis now patrolling the streets of a Free Iraq as policemen respectful of the human rights and dignity of their fellow citizens.

Iraq is now free, and an evil despot no longer threatens the United States and his neighbors, because of the selfless actions of the individual soldiers of units like the 101st Airborne. I pray that the families of those Americans who have lost their lives in this conflict find comfort and solace in their time of need. Their loved ones are American heroes, and I will never forget their sacrifice.

America wants to hear the story of your experience or the experience of someone you know as a fighter pilot. Share your story with us at - www.ModernDayHeroes.com

Making the United States of America More Secure

An American hero is someone who is willing and ready to put their life on the line to protect the lives and freedoms of everyone else.

Staci Drake
Circleville, OH

President George W. Bush –
addressed the troops at Butts Army Air Field at Fort Carson, Colorado [November 2003].

THE PRESIDENT: Thank you all.

AUDIENCE: U-S-A, U-S-A! [Applause.]

THE PRESIDENT: Thank you all very much. Thank you for the warm welcome. I'm honored to be in the Rocky Mountain state. I'm honored to be in Fort Carson. [Applause.] More importantly, I'm honored to be in the presence of so many fine Americans, so many great citizens who proudly wear our nation's uniform. [Applause.]

The soldiers of Fort Carson are now engaged in the largest deployment from this post since World War II. You reflect tremendous credit to the United States Army. You bring great pride to the people of the United States of America. [Applause.] The people of our armed forces are serving at a crucial period for America and for all free nations. We're at war with terrorists who hate what we stand for: liberty, democracy, tolerance and the rights and dignity of every person. We're a peaceful nation, yet we are prepared to confront any danger. [Applause.]

We are fighting the terrorists in Iraq and Afghanistan and in other parts of the world so we do not have to fight them on the streets of our own cities. [Applause.] And we will win. [Applause.] In this war, America depends on our people in uniform to protect our freedom and to keep our country safe. And all who serve depend every day on the support of your families. These are challenging times for military families. You in the Pikes Peak community know that very well. Military life makes many demands on wives and husbands and sons and daughters. You have faced hardships, and you have faced them together. And I want you to know, our whole nation is grateful to our military families. [Applause.]

America is also indebted to the men and women of the Guard and Reserve who are serving abroad. [Applause.] And to those who are called for homeland security assignments. Hundreds of reserve units across America have been activated in this time of war. Our country thanks these fine citizens, and we thank their employers for putting duty first.

I want to thank Major General Bob Wilson for his leadership and his strength of character. I want to thank General Larry Ellis, as well, for greeting me here today. It's my honor to have met General Lance Lord, Commander of the Air Force Space Command. I appreciate Colonels Orr, Terry, Wininger, and Resty for being such strong leaders and for greeting me here. It was my privilege to have lunch with Sergeant Major Mac McWilliams. [Applause.] He's the kind of guy you don't want to cross. [Laughter and applause.] He's the kind of guy you want on your side. [Applause.] I'm glad he's on my side, and I'm glad you're on my side. [Applause.]

I appreciate Bill Hybl, who is the Civilian Aide to the Secretary of the Army. I want to thank the families of the fallen soldiers who are here with us today. Our prayers are with you. We ask for God's strength and God's guidance. [Applause.] I'm honored that the great governor of the great state of Colorado is with us today, Governor Bill Owens. [Applause.]

We've got some members of the United States Congressional delegation here who are strong supporters of our military and our military families: Congressman Hefley and McInnis, Tancredo, Beauprez and Musgrave, thank you all for coming. I'm honored you're here. [Applause.] The Speaker of the House is here. Madam Speaker, thank you for coming, Lola Spradley. The Mayor of Colorado Springs and the Mayor of Fountain, Mayor Rivera and Mayor Barela are with us, as well. Thank you all for coming. I thank all state and local officials for being here. But most of all, I want to thank you all for coming. It's my honor to be here. [Applause.]

When I landed, and I got off that magnificent bird, Air Force One, I was greeted by a lady named Diane Campbell. [Applause.] She brought her family with her. [Laughter.] She's an active volunteer with the Army Family Team Building program. [Applause.] As I said, she brought her family with her. [Laughter.]

The reason I bring up Diane Campbell is, oftentimes, people measure the strength of America based upon the number of tanks and airplanes we have, or the size of our wallets. No, the strength of America lies in the hearts and souls of our citizens. You see, people like Diane Campbell are providing training and information to military spouses and families to help them adjust to the life in the Army. See, they're reaching out. They've heard the universal call to love a neighbor just like they would like to be loved themselves. The true strength of America is the American people, because we're a compassionate, decent, caring, loving people, just like Diane Campbell. [Applause.]

I want to thank Diane and all the Army Family Team Building members for your service. I ask you all to reach out a hand to somebody who hurts. I ask you to help us change our country one lonely soul at a time.

For more than 60 years, the units of Fort Carson have been known for training hard and being prepared at all times. Men and women have gone forth from this base to make history. From the Pacific Theater in World War II, to Korea, Vietnam, and Desert Storm. Many thousands who served in these causes still live here in this area. I don't blame you. [Laughter.] It's a beautiful part of our country.

Our Veterans and military retirees play their part in maintaining the greatest fighting force in the world. They kept our country free, and we are grateful to the Veterans who are with us here today. [Applause.] Today a new generation has been called to great challenges. The soldiers of the Mountain Post have been called to serve in the first war of the 21st Century.

This war began more than two years ago, on September the 11th, 2001, when America was attacked, and thousands of our fellow citizens were murdered. The events of that morning changed our nation. We awakened to new dangers, and we accepted new responsibilities. That day we saw the harm that our enemies intend for us. And last week, we saw their cruelty again, in the murders in Istanbul. Today America, Britain, and Turkey and all responsible nations are united in a great cause: We will not rest until we bring these committed killers to justice. [Applause.]

These terrorists will not be stopped by negotiations, or by appeals to reason, or by the least hint of conscience. We have only one option: We must, and we will continue to take the fight to the enemy. [Applause.]

We fight this war against terror on many fronts. Terrorists hide and strike within free societies, so we're draining their bank accounts, disrupting their plans. We're hunting them down one by one until they can no longer threaten America and other free peoples.

Terrorists need places to hide, to plot, and to train, so we're holding their allies, the allies of terror to account. [Applause.] Working with a fine coalition, our military went to Afghanistan, destroyed the training camps of al Qaeda, and put the Taliban out of business forever. [Applause.]

In Iraq, where a dictator defied the world, cultivated ties to terror, armed with deadly weapons, America led a mission to make the world safer, and to liberate the Iraqi people. And that brutal dictator's regime is no more. [Applause.] Thanks to our great military, Iraqi citizens do not have to fear the dictator's secret police or ending in a mass grave. Thanks to our military, the torture chambers are closed, and the prison cells for children are empty. Thanks to our military, we have captured many members of the former regime, and the rest of them have a lot to worry about. [Applause.]

Recently, in Operation Iron Hammer, our coalition worked with the Iraqi Civil Defense Corps and police to strike hard against the forces of murder and chaos. We countered attacks, we seized weapons, we brought cold-blooded killers to justice. We're proud of all who participated in these forceful and successful operations. And we're sending a clear message: Anyone who seeks to harm our soldiers can know that our great soldiers are hunting for them. [Applause.]

Our mission in Iraq and Afghanistan is clear to our service members, and it's clear to our enemies. America's military is fighting to secure the freedom of more than 50 million people who recently lived under two of the cruelest dictatorships on earth. America's military is fighting to help democracy and peace and justice rise in a troubled and violent region. And because we're fighting terrorist enemies thousands of miles away, in the heart and center of their power, we are making the United States of America more secure. [Applause.]

Units from this base have been vital to our campaigns in Afghanistan and Iraq. The 7th Infantry Division has done fine work preparing guard brigades for combat duty overseas, with one battalion in Iraq from the start of Operation Iraqi Freedom; preparing a brigade to deploy and a brigade now in Afghanistan; helping to train the Afghan National Army. We're grateful for the 3rd Brigade Combat Team -- [Applause] -- the 3rd Armored Calvary Regiment -- [Applause] -- the 10th Special Forces Group -- [Applause] -- the 43rd Area Support Group. [Applause.] These and other units are showing the skill and the discipline that define Fort Carson, and you're showing the courage that defines the United States Army. [Applause.]

Today, American forces in Iraq are joined by about 24,000 troops from 32 other countries. Together, we're helping the Iraqi people move steadily toward a free and democratic society. Economic life is being restored to cities of Iraq. A new Iraqi currency is circulating. Local governments are up and running. Iraq will soon begin the process of drafting a constitution, with free elections to follow. As Iraq joins -- rejoins the world, it will demonstrate the power of freedom and hope to overcome resentment and hatred. And this transformation will help make America more secure. [Applause.]

The work we are in is not easy, yet it is essential. The failure of democracy in Iraq would provide new bases for the terrorist network and embolden terrorists and their allies around the world. The failure of democracy in those countries would convince terrorists that America backs down under attack. Yet democracy will succeed in Iraq, because our will is firm and our word is good. Democracy will succeed because every month, more and more Iraqis are fighting for their own country. People we have liberated will not surrender their freedom. Democracy will succeed because the United States of America will not be intimidated by a bunch of thugs. [Applause.]

This community knows firsthand that the mission in Iraq is difficult and the enemy is dangerous. Saddam loyalists and foreign terrorists are attacking the symbols of order and freedom, from international aid workers to coalition forces to innocent Iraqi citizens. Terrorists have chosen to make a stand and test our resolve. Our resolve will not be shaken. [Applause.]

It is the nature of terrorism that a small number of people can inflict terrible grief. And here, you felt loss. Every person who dies in the line of duty leaves a family that lives in sorrow and comrades who must go on without them. The Fort Carson community said farewell to some of your best. One of them was Staff Sergeant Daniel Bader. This good man left behind his wife, Tiffany, and their 14-month-old daughter. Tiffany Bader said this to a reporter recently, "I'm going to wait until she is old enough to realize what happened, and I will tell her exactly what her daddy did for her. He died serving his country so that my little girl could grow up free." [Applause.]

The courage of that soldier, and the courage of that wife, show the spirit of this country in the face of great adversity. And all our military families that mourn can know this: Our nation will never forget the sacrifice their loved one made to protect us all. [Applause.]

By the unselfish dedication of Americans in uniform, children in our own country and in lands far away will be able to live in freedom, and know the peace that freedom brings. As Americans, we believe that freedom is not America's gift to the world, freedom is the Almighty God's gift to every person who lives in the world. [Applause.]

As men and women who served the cause of freedom, each one of you has answered a great calling. You live by a code of honor, in service to your nation, for the safety and security of your fellow citizens. You and I have taken an oath to defend America. We're meeting that duty together, and I'm proud to be the Commander-in-Chief of the greatest military, full of the finest people on the face of this earth.

God bless you all. God bless America. [Applause.]

The Iraq You Don't Know

An American hero serves out of love and loyalty not for praise of his fellow man; walks in truth not deceit; is humble not haughty.

Kathy Koenig
Costa Mesa, CA

U.S. Representative Michael C. Burgess

Recently, I returned from an official trip to Iraq where I was part of a bi-partisan government reform team whose mission was to look at the overall situation in the country since Coalition forces removed the Saddam regime. I was eager to take part in the mission so that I could see first-hand the realities of the situation in Iraq. What I witnessed is the true "shock and awe" story of Iraq. I saw the progress of a fledgling, free Iraq. I came away knowing we have every reason to be optimistic.

Since my return to the U.S., I have been watching the evening national news, and I can scarcely recognize the country and situation I have just left. The news anchor's comments are inconsistent with what I saw in Iraq; no relation to the real life situations. I believe it is important to share the true story of what I saw and experienced in Iraq.

While in Iraq, I met General James T. Conway, of the 1st Marine Expeditionary Force. He describes our effort in Iraq as "a vivid success story" both during the military operation and since the conclusion of the major combat phase. His sage remark is that most Iraqis were concerned not that we would stay too long, but that we would leave too soon.

But as with any rebuilding effort, patience, time, dedication, loyalty, and commitment are necessary. Within this past century the United States, along with her allies, have worked to rebuild nations into strong, independent countries; just look to Japan and Germany for parallel examples. In Iraq, there is a similar need to lend support and guidance to a new, free nation who must fight boldly to recover from past hardships and ward off new insurgents.

One of my first impressions was how the Iraqi people are simply enjoying a normal, everyday life. The markets are bustling, traffic jams in the cities, and satellite dishes dot the rooftops of Baghdad. School children had just finished classes and are preparing for a new year to begin. Electrical lines are now lighting up rural areas and fields of wheat are being harvested after decades of lying dormant. The atmosphere reflects a return to normal life.

To ensure that the Iraqi quality of life continues to improve, a new civil structure needs to be installed. After years of oppression by Saddam Hussein, the Iraq people are beginning the long, arduous process of learning to trust not only outsiders, but also each other. United State's military and Coalition forces have made great headway in helping the Iraqis on this and many fronts.

Thirty years of Saddam Hussein destroyed all sense of community. There was hardly a civil society left in Iraq, but since the fall of the regime, 90 percent of the towns and cities have created governing councils. The new governing council has been drawn from all regions of the country and is currently planning for a preparatory convention that will pave the road for a constitutional convention. After an Iraq constitution has been established, they will hold elections. The birth of democracy in Iraq is a pivotal moment in world history, and it is a moment only made possible by Coalition forces remaining to help stabilize the country.

To add security and strength to the new governance, Iraqi citizens are actively participating in rebuilding efforts. Over 50,000 Iraqis are contributing to the own security. Many are enlisting in the local police divisions throughout the country and are being trained by former New York City Police Commissioner Bernard Kerik renown for his heralding efforts during the attack on 9-11.

Kerik has been a miracle worker. Under his direction, Baghdad went from zero precincts to 35 precinct stations in just 14 weeks. That's right, 14 weeks, not months. He has started police training academies which have been given the arduous task of transforming the Iraqi Police Force from one based on brutality and corruption to stressing police procedure, criminal investigations, human rights; in short, everything we normally take as a given with police work in a free and democratic society. Law enforcement is also now backed by a functioning judicial system. Prisons, which were emptied by Saddam Hussein at the beginning of the war to wreak havoc, are being reopened. Law and order in a free society is taking root.

As a doctor, I was particularly concerned with assessing the Iraqi health care system. I knew of the difficulties the health care system had suffered under Hussein's rule, but I was still startled to see the opulent palaces Saddam had built for himself juxtaposed against the decrepit hospitals, barely functioning, for the Iraqi people. Most of the hospitals had no nursing staff at all.

A member of the public health team of the 385th Civil Affairs Brigade, Lt. Col Michael Keller reported to me that within the library at the medical school, no text had a copyright date of later than 1984. Pharmaceuticals manufactured in Iraq were of such questionable quality that doctors would not dispense them. In fact, Coalition forces have had to rely heavily upon donations of medicine from Kuwait to make-up for the shortage. On average, Saddam's government spent 50 cents per person on health care. Since the Coalition forces arrived, that amount has increased to $45 per person. Yet, even with massive improvements, more is needed in order to restore quality health care to a long-suffering Iraqi people.

A heartbreaking scene was seeing infants in the inadequate hospitals knowing they would never survive; knowing, that if they had a health care system like the United States, these same babies would grow up to be healthy adults. Still, hope is rising. Perhaps best of all, over 4.2 million children have been immunized by U.S. forces since this May.

Before my departure to Iraq, and since my return, I have not see any of these accomplishments reported by the media here in the United States. They focus solely on military dangers and how American forces should leave. There is no doubt in my mind that the combat phase of Operation Iraqi Freedom was executed brilliantly, and the country has been liberated from a brutal regime with a minimum of military and civilian casualties. While danger remains, there is no remaining strategic threat.

Currently stabilization is the goal of our new offensive operation: we seek to root-out those who would harm our troops or innocent Iraqi citizens. Our troops continue to work to make the radical elements irrelevant. Of the dangers you hear about on the news, 80 percent of these engagements are within the so-called Sunni Triangle of northern Iraq. The majority of the country is moving forward towards a free society. We should remain a strong force proving our determination to help the country regain a stable, free nation. In one of the mess halls, a banner was strung across the hall reading, "Steadfast and Loyal." I believe that banner said it best.

Our Cause is Just

Heroes are those individuals who have counted the cost, who have determined, that even though they have a choice to turn around and go back, they will not. For heroes are the ones that know there is a dangerous and deadly force on the other side of the hill and yet, with tenacity deeply woven within their being, they charge over the hill anyway.

> Reginald L. Kyles
> Husband and Father

President George W. Bush

Under the cover of darkness, at great personal risk, the President flew to the heart of the battlefield, to the center of the beast, right into Baghdad, Iraq, to serve his men Thanksgiving dinner and to show them the gratitude of a grateful nation. [November 2003]

Thank you. I was just looking for a warm meal somewhere. [Laughter and Applause.] Thank you for inviting me to dinner. [Applause.] General Sanchez, thank you, sir, for your kind invitation and your strong leadership. Ambassador Bremer, thank you for your steadfast belief in freedom and peace. I want to thank the members of the Governing Council who are here; pleased you are joining us on our nation's great holiday: it's a chance to give thanks to the Almighty for the many blessings we receive.

I'm particularly proud to be with the 1st Armored Division, the 2nd ACR, the 82nd Airborne. [Applause.] I can't think of a finer group of folks to have Thanksgiving dinner with than you all. We're proud of you. Today, Americans are gathering with their loved ones to give thanks for the many blessings in our lives. And this year we are especially thankful for the courage and the sacrifice of those who defend us, the men and women of the United States military. [Applause.]

I bring a message on behalf of America: we thank you for your service, we're proud of you, and America stands solidly behind you. [Applause.] Together, you and I have taken an oath to defend our country. You're honoring that oath. The United States military is doing a fantastic job. [Applause.] You are defeating the terrorists here in Iraq, so that we don't have to face them in our own country. You're defeating Saddam's henchmen, so that the people of Iraq can live in peace and freedom.

By helping the Iraqi people become free, you're helping change a troubled and violent part of the world. By helping to build a peaceful and democratic country in the heart of the Middle East, you are defending the American people from danger and we are grateful. [Applause.]

You're engaged in a difficult mission. Those who attack our coalition forces and kill innocent Iraqis are testing our will. They hope we will run. We did not charge hundreds of miles into the heart of Iraq, pay a bitter cost in casualties, defeat a brutal dictator and liberate 25 million people only to retreat before a band of thugs and assassins. [Applause.]

We will prevail. We will win because our cause is just. We will win because we will stay on the offensive. And we will win because you're part of the finest military ever assembled. [Applause.] And we will prevail because the Iraqis want their freedom. [Applause.]

Every day you see firsthand the commitment to sacrifice that the Iraqi people are making to secure their own freedom. I have a message for the Iraqi people: you have an opportunity to seize the moment and rebuild your great country, based on human dignity and freedom. The regime of Saddam Hussein is gone forever. [Applause.]

The United States and our coalition will help you, help you build a peaceful country so that your children can have a bright future. We'll help you find and bring to justice the people who terrorized you for years and are still killing innocent Iraqis. We will stay until the job is done. [Applause.] I'm confident we will succeed, because you, the Iraqi people, will show the world that you're not only courageous, but that you can govern yourself wisely and justly.

On this Thanksgiving, our nation remembers the men and women of our military, your friends and comrades who paid the ultimate price for our security and freedom. We ask for God's blessings on their families, their loved ones and their friends, and we pray for your safety and your strength, as you continue to defend America and to spread freedom.

Each one of you has answered a great call, participating in an historic moment in world history. You live by a code of honor, of service to your nation, with the safety and the security of your fellow citizens. Our military is full of the finest people on the face of the earth. I'm proud to be your Commander-in-Chief. I bring greetings from America. May God bless you all. [Applause.]

In the Face of Deadly Obstacles

An American hero is one who has courage, strength, and honor; who exercises all of them without fail and without being asked to.

Fawn Yarema
Huntington Beach, CA

U.S. Representative Martin Frost

After spending several days in Iraq just before Christmas, meeting with America's top military leadership and talking to rank-and-file soldiers on the front lines, I remain convinced that we can't afford to fail in Iraq, confident in our courageous troops there and certain that we must get other nations to do their share of the dangerous and costly work.

Two instances, in particular, highlight the selflessness and bravery that America's sons and daughters are displaying in Iraq in the face of enormous and often deadly obstacles.

The first was a trip to Fallujah, northwest of Baghdad, where the soldiers of the 82nd Airborne are patrolling the area, rebuilding a school for Iraqi children, and leading other reconstruction efforts. Just to get to the school, the military had to put us in a heavily armed Humvee and race across town at top speed, with an American gunner on alert in the turret. And that wasn't just for show. A few days after our visit to Fallujah, another U.S. soldier was killed there.

The second was a flight out of Baghdad on Dec. 22. Our C-130 cargo plane carried the coffins of two more Americans killed in Baghdad. They had died just three days before Christmas. We later learned that one soldier was from Texas.

For almost a year, American troops have been doing a tremendous job in one of the world's most dangerous places. You can't help but be impressed by their skill, dedication and courage, and so I was honored to be able to visit them. On behalf of the American people, our bipartisan congressional delegation personally thanked the 4th Infantry Division, which is based in Fort Hood, for finally bringing Saddam Hussein to justice.

All of America's sons and daughters in Iraq represent our country well, but their job is a very difficult one. Nor will it be over anytime soon. It is clear that at least 100,000 American troops will be based in Iraq for the next year. And we could have a significant military presence there for some time after that, depending on the attitude of the new, democratically elected Iraqi government when it assumes control over the next two years.

Like all Americans, I wish more of our allies had joined the war last spring. But they didn't, and I supported President Bush's decision to go into Iraq. I believe the United States was right to take the lead in ending the murderous dictatorship of Saddam Hussein.

But it is time that the rest of the world began to share the cost, in troops as well as treasure, for building a stable, secure and democratic Iraq. And so it seems to me that the administration was hasty in telling some of our allies that they can't participate in reconstruction contracts because they didn't commit troops to the initial battle.

Instead, I would like to see the administration tie those reconstruction contracts to the commitment of countries like France and Germany to send significant numbers of their troops to Iraq now. That way, we can internationalize the reconstruction and bring more of our troops home at a faster rate.

In my 25 years of working for a stronger military, I always have had tremendous faith in the ability of our troops. After three days in Iraq, I am even more confident in them. But we shouldn't ask them to do the job alone. Now that America has rid the world of Saddam Hussein's threat, let's get the rest of the world to do its part to help bring democracy to the new Iraq.

How do you define an American hero?
Share it with us at -
www.ModernDayHeroes.com

God Gave Us a Son

We often describe an American hero in extremely dramatic terms. I applaud any description of hero.

However, to me, an American hero is quite simply being a good dad. Giving support and love to my kids so one day they can take the baton and contribute something great to our nation.

Your #1 responsibility in life is to be a hero to your kids.

> Jon Gray
> Orange Coast Jeep/Chrysler
> President

By Tony DiRaimondo – a Father

On June 2nd, 1981, God gave us a son, Michael, and made our family complete. What I didn't know that day was that he was not ours to keep. God had a plan. God knew that on January 8th, 2004 Michael's purpose on Earth would be complete and he would be called back to Him.

So, here we are today, profoundly sad at his passing. But for those of us who had the privilege of knowing Mike, we know that he would not tolerate us being sad. Is there anyone in this church who can remember Mike without that big smile on his face? I don't think so. He was about having fun. He was about living and enjoying life. He was about helping people who were hurt. So this eulogy is not about sadness. It is about the happiness and goodness that Mike brought to our world. If I were to mention only half the things Michael did, we'd be here for days. So allow me to share just a couple with you. This will take only ten minutes of your time.

When Mike was about 12 or 13 years old, he and I went on our first-ever camping trip, alone. It was a "guys only" camping trip to Twin Lakes, up near Mammoth Mountain. We borrowed a tent, had a couple of sleeping bags, some fishing gear and a lot of enthusiasm. What we didn't have was a lot of camping knowledge!

We got there, set up our campsite and off we went to catch some trout for dinner. We had a ball and caught a lot of fish. We got back to the campsite, cleaned all the trout, cooked them up in a pan and *that's* the moment we realized that neither one of us liked trout, especially not partially uncooked, partially burnt trout filled with bones. So we did the macho thing. We packed away all our fishing gear, went into town and had a delicious dinner at Kentucky Fried Chicken and swore that we would tell everyone how good the trout was.

But the adventure didn't end with dinner. Remember what I said, we were a little short on camping expertise. For instance, it isn't too smart to clean trout in your campsite and it isn't too smart to leave the smell of food on your campsite's table. It has a tendency of attracting certain types of large, furry animals. Later that night, Michael woke me up and said very quietly, "Dad, there's a bear in our campsite." Being a typical father who didn't over react and make a big deal of things, not to mention being half asleep, I said: "Is he trying to get into our tent?" Mike said, "No, he's trying to get into our food." So I woke myself up just enough to look outside the tent and see the bear vigorously attacking our food supply. I crawled back into my sleeping bag and said to Mike, "Okay here's what we do. When we get back home, we don't tell mom about the bear or she'll never let you go camping with me again."

A year or two later, we went back to Twin Lakes, but this time we hit a spring snow storm. We tried in vain to put up our tent in a blizzard. On top of that, it was freezing cold, and our chances of catching trout were next to none. And what difference would it make? We wouldn't eat them anyway. It became obvious that we weren't going to do traditional camping that weekend. Michael said that we should check out the ski slope at Mammoth and see if it was open. To my surprise and his delight, they were open and Michael got to go snowboarding for four hours and I got to get warm and have hot chocolate.

For those of you who don't know Mammoth, there is a very nice lodge at the base of the ski slope. So when Mike was finished snow boarding, I went to see what kind of a deal I could get on a room. The place was practically empty and the young lady at the front desk was eager to make a deal. Michael was eager to make a deal of his own because she was pretty cute and he had that gleam in his eye even though he was only 14. She must have thought he was pretty cute too because we ended up with a two-bedroom, bi-level suite for about 50 bucks! I remember calling home that night. Carol asked how we were doing and I told the truth. I said that the weather was really bad but we were making the best of it. Two seconds later, Michael blew my story as he told his mom he had a great time snowboarding while dad stayed in the lodge all afternoon, having lots of cocktails by the fireplace.

I think my favorite Michael story was the tree and the car. Mike was about 16 or 17 years old. He called me about 11 o'clock one night and said, "Dad, I just got hit by a tree." I didn't think I heard him right so I asked him to repeat himself. He said, "I got hit by a tree." I said, "Don't you mean you hit a tree?" He said, "No, I got hit by a tree limb. I was riding down this street behind a truck that was hauling a cut-up tree when this huge branch fell off and was bouncing on the road. I tried to avoid it but couldn't." This was too bizarre to imagine so I got in my car and went to where he was. Sure enough, there was this tree limb sticking out of the car. It had gone through the bumper, through the radiator, shattered the alternator and was only stopped by the engine block. You couldn't move this limb. It was in there like spear in a rock.

The next day the tow truck came and took the car. When I went back to the body shop a couple of days later, all over the wall of the body shop, there were pictures of the tree sticking out of the car. I asked the guy why all the pictures were on the wall and he said, "There are some things that you just can't believe without a picture and this is one of them."

It was a pretty funny story, and I've told it many times over the last six years. But two nights ago while Kyle and Matt and Rion and Tyler and Nick and all the guys were drowning their sorrows at my house with beer and wine, Kyle, said, "Mr. DiRaimondo, would you like to know what really happened with the tree?"

It turns out, the guys were all up in the hills as they often did, off-roading and having fun except that Mike was driving a Ford Probe not an off-roading truck. There *was* a dead tree on the ground and it had a big limb on it but it wasn't bouncing around. The Probe was bouncing around with Mike and Tyler in it and he didn't see the limb and crashed right into it. Mike's first thought was that "My father is going to kill me." So he and his band of pirate friends pushed the car about ¾ of a mile out of the hills, onto the street and concocted this incredible story. We laughed and laughed about it and I'm sure Mike was laughing with us.

The last Mike story was a little more serious but had a happy ending. Michael had started taking EMT classes. On this occasion he and his friends were snow boarding up at Mountain High when Mike saw a skier go off the trail into the woods. He knew he was in trouble. When he got to the man, he was very seriously hurt. Mike sent his friends to get the paramedics while he stayed and administered first aid. When the paramedics got there, he knew that his job was done and he should turn things over to them. When they saw how well Mike had treated the victim, they asked him to stay and continue helping them saying that he obviously knew what he was doing. The man survived the injury thanks to the treatment he received from the paramedics and from Mike. Michael's purpose in life was starting to take shape.

To further enhance his chances of becoming a Paramedic Firefighter, Michael joined the US Army three weeks before 911, when the world was a safer place. He trained as a Combat Medic and was stationed at Ft. Carson in Colorado Springs. There he was assigned to the 3rd Air Calvary Regiment. He worked as a Medic but was bored handing out aspirin and treating people for colds in a clinic. What he wanted was to treat people with injuries.

Last April, the 3rd ACR was deployed to Iraq. There he didn't treat colds anymore. The wounds were combat related and Michael thrived. He could now use his skills and ability to treat wounds and combine it with his life-long compassion for people. He excelled. His purpose was becoming more clear to him. He was so good at what he did that he was recruited to join the 571st Medical Company. He was going to become a Flight Medic. To put it in perspective, a Flight Medic is about ten levels above a Combat Medic and they are very selective in who joins their ranks. The mission of the 571st is Medivac: To go in and rescue people who were wounded in combat; to give aid and to get them out, even when they are under enemy fire. The 571st put him through a training program that usually takes several months to complete. He completed it in 41 days! His

Commander told me last Saturday that they never met anyone who picked it up as fast as Mike did. I remember so many conversations with him about his training and how much he was studying to become better and better at what he was doing. When he successfully completed the training program in late November, he was the proudest soldier in the US Army. He told Carol that, "These guys are the best. I love being a part of this unit and I love the work I am doing." He said, "Regardless of what you read or hear, Mom, we are making a difference out here."

The news media doesn't talk about it nearly enough anymore but there is far more fighting going on in Iraq than the public is aware of. The 571st have several missions every day. As many of you heard yesterday, Mike saved 10 lives the day the Chinook Helicopter was shot down on November 3rd. (He was nominated for the Air Medal for his actions that day, which was posthumously awarded to him.) Every day he administered aid to people who were either shot or hit by a rocket propelled grenade or some other awful thing. He made life and death decisions on the battlefield. And often did so under fire. With his hands and his heart, he kept soldiers alive without much regard for his own life. He loved the work that he did. The purpose of his life had now become crystal clear to him. He said to me in a conversation, "Dad, I think God intended for me to be a medic and to help people who are hurt. I feel great about the job I am doing."

The Flight Medic puts himself or herself at personal risk in order to save the lives of their victims and patients. Michael DiRaimondo, along with all Flight Medics serving in Iraq and Afghanistan, saved lives every day and risked his own life in doing so. If that isn't the definition of an American Hero, I don't know what a hero is.

Michael died on one of those missions when an Iraqi insurgent fired a missile at their unarmed helicopter. We grieve for him, but as sure as I stand here, I know our son and brother would not want us to do that. He would want us to celebrate the good times; to laugh and be happy that he lived and not be sad that he died.

For that reason, we are establishing the Michael A. DiRaimondo Foundation. One hundred percent of the money collected by the foundation will go to support scholarships for individuals who want to pursue a career as a paramedic but may not have the financial means to do so. If each year those scholarships can help one person become a paramedic, and that person can save just one life a year, then Michael's purpose will go on; his life will continue to have great meaning, and his legacy will live forever. So I ask you to support this effort, not only with a donation, but with your personal effort to raise money within your own circle of business associates, professionals, and friends.

Michel was on the promotion list to be a sergeant and was posthumously promoted and given the Purple Heart and Bronze Star. *Sergeant* Michael A. DiRaimondo lies here as an American Hero. To borrow the words of song writer Kris Kristofferson, "Loving him was easier than anything I'll ever do again." I love you Son. Please be there to guide me, your mother, and sisters in continuing your dream of helping people.

The Michael A. DiRaimondo Foundation's purpose is to provide scholarships to individuals who aspire to be paramedics but don't have the financial means to do so. Many who desire to become emergency medical professionals do not have the financial means necessary to pay the tuition of $3-$8,000 per year due to the fact that student loans cannot be applied to this type of program. The Foundation has created a permanent endowment with earnings to be directed to support these types of scholarships. In sponsoring other potential paramedics, Michael's dream of helping people with his "healing hands" will live on forever.

Ventura County Community Foundation is a 501(c)(3) organization and your gift is tax deductible to the fullest extent of the law. VCCF's tax id number is 77-0165029.

Donations can be sent to:
Michael A. DiRaimondo Foundation
P.O. Box 1265
Simi Valley, CA 93062

Additional information is available at this web site:
www.MichaelADiRaimondoFoundation.org
or link to it at
www.ModernDayHeroes.com

Hero Street, USA

An American hero is a person who puts his life on the line for the safety and security of others without praise.

Michelle Wait
Gardena, CA

U.S. Representative Luis V. Gutierrez

I rise today to announce the introduction of my bill, the "Fairness for America's Heroes Act."

Currently, there are more than 37,000 non-citizens on active duty in our military and each year approximately 7,000 new non-citizens join the armed forces.

These brave men and women are willing to die defending our nation, and it is imperative that we recognize their selflessness and spirit, not only when someone is killed in battle, but from the moment they are called up for combat duty.

We need laws that reflect non-citizen soldiers' heroism and their patriotism. That say we are grateful for your sacrifice; we understand the risks and dangers of combat duty; and to honor your dedication and devotion, we are granting you citizenship. This is a right that these men and women have earned and deserve. Throughout history non-citizen soldiers have stood shoulder-to-shoulder with native-born Americans in defense of our nation. They fight with vigor and valor to protect the American dream, and they risk their lives everyday for the safety and security of our country.

All of those who serve, regardless of race, regardless of gender, regardless of country of origin, are without hesitation recognized as America's heroes. The legislation I am introducing today will allow them, rightfully and justly, to also be recognized as

Americans. This is a distinction they have certainly earned and deserve.

The "Fairness for America's Heroes Act" grants citizenship automatically to non-citizen soldiers assigned to combat duty.

The legislation says that no soldier will ever again have to come home in a body bag to be recognized as an American. No soldier's family will ever again have to sort through mounds of paperwork so their loved ones can receive citizenship posthumously. It also says that no soldier will ever again have to be preoccupied or worry what will happen to their family's immigration status if they are killed in battle.

It enables immediate family members of servicemen and servicewomen to receive expedited processing of their immigration status, and, perhaps most important, it honors the enormous contributions immigrants make to our military and to our society every day.

To understand these contributions, you have to look no further than the young men who heroically and valiantly served their adopted country in the war against Iraq: Lance Corporal Jose Gutierrez, Corporal Jose Garibay, Private First Class Francisco Martinez-Flores, Lance Corporal Jesus Suarez del Solar.

These brave young men, barely in their twenties, died fighting for our country, but the ideals and principles they fought for must not. Those ideals can be summed up most eloquently with the words of Lance Corporal Gutierrez' brother, who said that Jose joined the Marines, "To pay a little back of what he'd gotten from the U.S."

These young men, many of whom left war-torn, war-ravaged countries, understood that America is the type of place that permits you to dream as big as your heart will allow. They were willing to fight and die for that dream, and our immigration system should reflect and respect that sacrifice.

You see, Mr. Speaker, immigrants' presence in our military is nothing new. Immigrants have fought in every war since the American Revolution. In fact, immigrants account for 20 percent of the recipients of the Congressional Medal of Honor.

In Silvis, Illinois, just west of Chicago, Ill., there is a street called Hero Street U.S.A. This street stands as a tribute to honor eight young Latino men who lost their lives courageously defending our country during World War II and Korea. They went to war without hesitation even though people often ignored them or treated them as second-class individuals. The sacrifice and strength of these young men sparked an unrivaled and unmatched wave of service in their community.

The Department of Defense has documented that no street of comparable size has sent as many men and women to serve in the Armed Forces.

While tributes like these are important, and speeches are moving, we must back up our rhetoric with action. The swift passage of this legislation is an important place to begin.

It will say to these heroic young service members that we recognize and respect your contributions; we honor your spirit and your service; and that you personify the pride and patriotism that makes this nation so great.

I urge my colleagues to properly recognize these brave men and women by supporting the "Fairness for America's Heroes Act."

America wants to hear the story of your experience or the experience of someone you know in the military. Share your story with us at - www.ModernDayHeroes.com

Chapter 9

Dare to Become a Hero

Your Chosen Profession

First, I want to say to the teachers who work in the school, and all throughout New York, how much we appreciate the courage that New York teachers showed [on 9-11]. ...there's a lot of talk about heroes in our society. A hero is somebody you look up to, of course. And the teachers of New York City were very heroic.

President George W. Bush

U.S. Representative Bob Filner –

gave the commencement speech to the Department of Education graduation for San Diego State University on May 22, 1999. Representative Filner had been a professor at SDSU for 20+ years.

It is wonderful to be back here on the SDSU campus, where I taught for over 20 years. There is something very special about a college campus vibrant with young people, vibrant with learning, and today, vibrant with the joy of graduation!

And I can feel the excitement, at long last, you are ready to start, really start your chosen profession.

And what a noble and critical profession you have chosen, to be a teacher, to be involved with young people in the 21st century, and through this work, you are going to determine the future of our nation, the future of our planet.

What an exciting future is in store for you!

I can still feel my own excitement, my own idealism, when I began my teaching career at San Diego State almost 30 years ago, and the excitement of my own daughter, who has been teaching at middle school for 6 years now.

I was a history professor and I tell you, there is nothing, nothing, so rewarding or satisfying as:

- the flash of understanding in a student's eyes when he understands why it is important to understand the rise and fall of the Roman Empire.

- or the letter from a now successful young lady who tells you it was your class that inspired her to embark upon her career path.

I know you will have many such moments!

But let's be honest, there are probably some things going on around us that may make you wonder whether you have made the right choice for your career.

You look at salary schedules, and wonder why society seems to have so little respect for such an important profession.

You see politicians bash teachers, and may wonder how long they would last in a classroom with 25 or 35 or 45, 14 year olds.

You watch some very paradoxical situations, for example, when crime rate goes up people demand more cops and more resources for law enforcement. But when test scores go down, people want to punish teachers, and want to take resources away from education. How can society, you may wonder, be so short sighted?

But things are changing in California and in the nation. And you will be a part of that change.

Voters are passing school bond issues to build new schools.

State legislators are devoting real resources to decrease class size. In Washington, both political parties have put education at the very top of their agenda. Everywhere, higher standards are being set and teachers are being rewarded for excellence.

The new student boom (out pacing the famous baby boomers after WW II) means that we will hire 2.2 million new teachers in this nation over the next ten years.

With your spirit, your energy, and your skills in the incredible new internet and other technologies, you will increase the standing of teachers in our society.

Yes, you have made the right choice of career!

Even more important, you have made the right choice because our kids need you --they need you.

A lot has been written about Columbine High School in Littleton, CO, and will be written about Heritage High School near Atlanta, GA, (gun control violence in the media) but one thing is clear:

Not just those who excel, and not just those who need special attention to learn. ALL KIDS. We need to get EACH CHILD AND EACH YOUNG PERSON involved in activities, in learning, in fun. Especially the ones who may sit quietly, who may not demand attention, who may not excel, who may not get involved.

In a recent op-ed column, my friend, William Raspberry wrote:

"...the sad fact (is) that there are people who, for too many of us and often for themselves, don't matter. There are people in our schools, in our offices, on our streets, who know they don't matter to the rest of us, who exist, if at all, as objects of ridicule and derision: as nerds, as nobodies, as fatties, shorties, and blackies, as crips, as dummies, as losers.

Probably all of as spend some small portion of our lives not mattering, though most of us have refuge in places (home, workplace, church or social group) where we matter a great deal. But some of us have no such refuge apart from our fellow non- matters. And of that sad group, same will make sure they matter in the time tested way of mattering: through violence. The tendency is for the rest of us to respond to the violence and think we've dealt with the problem. We institute new rules or new dress codes, remind ourselves of the signs to be watched out for and forget that they re still people who don't matter.

The hardest point to absorb is the need to start paying attention to those who see themselves as 'outcasts', not just because it may prevent violence, but because there simply should not be human beings who don't matter."

You have the spirit, the energy, and have chosen the right profession to turn this around, to let every child know that they do matter.

In a society where kids are often latch key kids, where kids and parents often watch different tvs even when they are in the same house, where we come and go in our neighborhoods without speaking, it is the understanding teacher that can matter. Yes, it "takes a village to raise a child" but you can lead our village into a healthy future.

Yes, you have chosen the right professions and I can't wait to see you take charge of the next millennium. Congratulations to all of you!

Wei-Ji
(Translated:
Danger & Opportunity)

An American hero is a person that is not prideful but humble enough to do whatever is asked of him by his nation's leaders

Therese Anderson
Fountain Valley, CA

George J. Tenet
Director of Central Intelligence Agency
Remarks by the Director at the University of Oklahoma Graduation Ceremony on May 10, 2003.

President Boren, Regents, Officers, Deans, faculty and staff of the University of Oklahoma, families, friends and - most importantly - members of the class of 2003:

What money is to Wall Street, what celebrity is to Hollywood, talk is to Washington DC. There, words are a major export - speeches are a way of life. But I have been to this state and school often enough to know that here, when it comes to concluding remarks like these, there is a rule that everyone appreciates: Sooner is better.

For most students, graduation is a welcome celebration. For a few, it is a pleasant surprise. To all, it should be a source of enduring pride. You made it - through the courses, the papers, the exams - even the parties.

When Sooners fix their sights on a goal, there are very few forces that can keep them from it. Just ask the defensive line from Washington State or-better yet-ask the University of Texas.

For all the reasons that make this great university what it is - its constant pursuit of excellence in academics, research, the arts, and athletics, and its powerful sense of identity and community - I am privileged to be associated with this class. If it is true that we are judged by the company we keep, I cannot hope to do better than I have this morning.

In your years at OU, you have been tested and you have tested yourselves. You have extended what you know - about the world and about yourselves. This is not a place that teaches you what to think, but rather how to think. How to deal with different points of view. How to work through problems. How to absorb new knowledge, and to recognize that there is always more to know.

OU has a second purpose, no less important: to prepare you for service - to your community, your state, your country, and beyond. In this, you are especially fortunate to have as a university president a man who combines a commitment to excellence with a commitment to others.

David Boren is my lifetime mentor and friend-the man whose example of service and values I have chosen to follow. He taught me that when it comes to our nation's security, there are no Republicans or Democrats; there are only Americans.

His central legacy is the rebuilding of this great university in the heartland of the United States, and his relentless determination to build a safer America and a more secure world by being a champion of education and public service.

David Boren stands for the many, many Oklahomans who enrich the society that has in so many ways enriched all of us.

Among them are dozens of OU graduates, officers of the organization I am honored to lead - the Central Intelligence Agency. Each day, here and overseas, with passion, courage, and in anonymity, they and their colleagues rise with a single purpose: to protect Americans and their families. They are the best of the best.

Like them, you are each heir to the rich legacy of this school. It is a legacy you have earned. In long hours of study in places like Bizzell Library. And on Saturday afternoons in this stadium, with more than a few thousand of your closest friends.

Whatever the challenges, you met them head-on. But you did not meet them alone.

Always treasure the professors and teaching assistants who inspired you to dig a little deeper, or work a little harder, who opened new horizons to you or literally changed your life - not only through learning but by attentiveness, sensitivity, or simple decency.

Mom and Dad paved the way for you to reach graduation with generous amounts of care and affection. Your grandparents and siblings - your coaches, neighbors, and clergy - all had a role.

Each of you is here because some wonderful human beings took the time to make a difference in your life. They gave you a heritage to live up to. They gave you opportunities they never had. They gave you moral support and a moral compass - a set of values and a sense of possibility. They challenged you and spurred you to excellence.

Whatever you have accomplished - whatever you will accomplish - you owe in great measure to them.

And so, I think your families and your mentors, and all who love and care about you and helped you get here, deserve a big round of applause.

Today, the United States is the lone superpower, with global interests and worldwide reach - part of everyone's problem and everyone's solution.

And by this I mean more than Afghanistan and Iraq, where crises called forth from us a military response. There is another, underlying story that must be told: the story of societies and peoples who are left behind, excluded from the benefits of an expanding global economy, whose lives of hunger, disease, and displacement may become wellsprings of disaffection and extremism.

The message here may be captured best by the Chinese language, in which the word "crisis" (wei-ji [Way-gee]) is formed from two characters - one meaning "danger," the other "opportunity."

Amid the many dangers to U.S. national interests, we must never lose sight of the opportunities, places where we can make a positive difference, where hope might triumph over despair.

For the past 20 years we have lived with a global AIDS pandemic, which last year killed more than 3 million people. It threatens to rob Southern Africa of generations of leaders and workers, of farmers and educators-with devastating effects on economies and societies.

Is this a security issue? You bet it is. With more than 40 million people infected right now, a figure that-by 2010-may reach 100 million, AIDS is building dangerous momentum in regions beyond Africa. And not just the absolute poorest, either. Countries like Russia, India, and China will face major risks.

But against this dire picture, a promising counterpoint: in Uganda, Thailand, and Brazil, the epidemic has been dramatically slowed - through a combination of decisive leadership, education, and treatment. The difference is human intervention-resources and energy-and here, too, the United States plays the leading role.

In this land of plenty, we sometimes forget the 825 million people around the globe who are chronically malnourished. And food aid requirements this year will rise more sharply than other categories of humanitarian assistance, because of drought, instability, and struggling governments.

But, even here, there is optimism: The number of undernourished people in developing countries has-by some counts-dropped by 130 million since 1980. And world supplies of food are 20 percent higher than when I graduated from college.

Through these stories-and many more-there runs a common thread. A thread of hope and determination. A thread made possible in large part by the fact that Americans have opportunities to act-to make the world a better place. Not just for the strong, but for all.

In your years on this campus, you have seen us answer the greatest challenges and the gravest threats. On September 11th 2001, you saw those who despise the things for which we stand exploit the trust and openness of our society. They did so to strike at our values: freedom, opportunity, and tolerance.

America will not fight the battle against terrorism as we fought the battles of the past. Our targets are often small groups or individuals, who take shelter among the innocent. Our objective is not miles of territory to conquer, but millions of people to persuade.

This war will not end with a peace treaty. And it will not be resolved on traditional battlefields, with massed conventional armies. It will end only when global terror is broken, stripped of its support and ability to strike.

On one point there can be no doubt: We will prevail.

Those who attacked us underestimated the strength of the American people. They underestimated our daring, our resolve, and our absolute focus on one goal: to stop them from hurting American families again.

We will continue to win battles and we will lose some as well. But in the end, we and our allies around the world will triumph. We will do it with force, with intelligence, and with the strength of our values. We will do it by providing hope and opportunity.

This fight is not with Islam -- a great religion with traditions of tolerance that encompasses over a billion people and hundreds of cultures.

This struggle pits a narrow, intolerant view of Islam against a rich, open view that for centuries, made Muslim societies guardians of learning and engines of achievement.

Though this competition may seem distant, its outcome matters. We must identify with the voices of moderation. We must help them as they seek to educate new generations and create opportunities for their people-opportunities that will deny extremists the ability to manipulate the hearts and minds of the vulnerable.

In very different circumstances, Oklahoma witnessed extremism at its brutal worst. Amid your grief, with their strength and compassion, the people of this state have shown that those who love and build ultimately defeat those who hate and destroy. The courage of Oklahomans is echoed today in the valor of all who fight terror.

America faces many other pressing challenges - ones filled with danger and opportunity. But one thing links them all: Our ability-and our responsibility-to act where it makes sense to act, to act on behalf of those in this world who have fallen behind.

When we encourage tolerance, inclusiveness, and freedom - we gain far more than we spend. These values are what make America strong, but - as the foreign students graduating today can attest - their true power lies in their universal appeal.

They also lie at the core of every person dedicated to public service, every woman and man who treasures our liberties and wishes to protect and extend them. Their skill, their sacrifices, and their unwavering idealism can inspire the world.

I hope that you will consider joining their ranks - it is a calling of thousands of professions, all dedicated to helping others. In times like these, the need for heroes is clear and compelling.

Every member of this graduating class can be a hero. The possibilities are as varied as you are. No matter what the career, from diplomacy to the military, politics to law enforcement, from volunteering at a local shelter or mentoring a child who needs someone to care, the key is to contribute something of yourself.

In closing, let me share with you "George Tenet's Eight Secrets to Success." It is a formula that has worked for me, and I hope it works for you:

Tenet #1: Know who you are: Let me tell you a story. My mother escaped from southern Albania on a British submarine just as the Iron Curtain was closing - never to see her family again. My father came to the United States from Greece just prior to the Great Depression speaking no English, without a nickel in his pocket or a friend in sight. They are the two greatest people I have ever known. Imagine their courage. They dedicated themselves to educating their two sons in a new country. I talk about them with great pride to make my point. Each of you has family stories of courage and sacrifice. They tell you what your values are and who you are as men and women - never, ever forget them. They will guide you through the darkest days in your life, and sweeten your happiest moments.

Tenet #2: Honor the service and the sacrifice of men and women who protect this country and our values. As you sit in the Mont tomorrow night drinking a swirl - or if you are at O'Connell's having a beer - remember the men and women in military uniform, the law enforcement and intelligence officers working around the globe and around the clock to protect your way of life - putting their lives on the line, so that you can pursue your life's dream in total freedom. Honor their service.

Tenet #3: Follow your heart and dare to take risks. If you do not wake up every day with great passion for your work, you will be miserable. Do not just go through the motions. Never put yourself in the position of regretting what you did not try to do. Every experience, whether it is good or bad, if it is based on the passionate belief that what you are doing is something you love, will give you the will and the character to learn, grow and persevere. Stand up for yourself and your dreams. Do not lose your youthful idealism for the world.

Tenet #4: Fight hatred and prejudice wherever you see it. If there is one thing in today's world that is most responsible for the turmoil we see, it is ethnic and religious hatred. It haunts us across continents-in the Balkans, in Central Africa, in the Middle East-and even here in the United States of America. The fundamental lack of tolerance that men and women show for each other drives so much of the instability that we confront. Every one of us carries prejudice of one sort or another inside us. Purge it from your souls, get it out, and never turn a blind eye toward hatred when you encounter it-never.

Tenet #5: Laugh as much as you can. Never take yourself too seriously. Have the ability to stand back and admit your shortcomings and failures with grace and humor. This ability will help you weather any problem in your life.

Tenet #6: Take care of the people around you. If you take care of people, they will always take care of you. Many of you will rise like meteors to the top of your chosen professions. On the way up, treat the people around you with the decency and respect and generosity that have been shown to you. Have a kind word. Offer a helping hand. If and when you reach the top, show a little humility. Why? Because there will come a day when the crash occurs. When failure comes. When you plummet down the ladder. The fall will be gentle if people remember you as a caring, considerate human being, and, if they do, someone will extend a helping hand.

Tenet #7: Pray. Ask God for the guidance and strength to meet the challenges of life. Put on His armor to face the forces of evil. Manifest His goodness in caring for those who are weak and in need, showing love for others each and every day.

Tenet #8: Finally, I would say to all of you-it is a little old fashioned, but you need to hear it: Love and serve your country. In no other country in the world could someone like me, the son of immigrants, stand before you as Director of Central Intelligence. It would happen no place else. Americans are given opportunities that no other country provides. If you do not get a lump in your throat when the National Anthem is played or the flag passes by, come to your senses and recognize that you live in the greatest country in the world. Never be ashamed to be proud of this rare privilege.

When you put all these "Eight Tenets" together, they add up to one big secret for success as a human being, and it is this:

Serve someone other than yourself, serve something bigger than yourself.

Dare to become a hero.

Thank you for the honor you have bestowed on me and my family.

Congratulations to all of you. May God always bless you and your families.

The Rest of the Story

A hero is one who follows the admonition of Christ: Put your hand to the plow and don't look back. A hero is a person who believes and lives on the principle that God does not necessarily call us to be successful, but faithful. A hero is a person who continues to pursue the mission God has given him regardless of the events surrounding him or the praise or criticism received.

> Donald E. Wildmon
> American Family Association
> www.afa.net

U.S. Representative Ric Keller –
gave the following remarks at the swearing in of a new group of citizens on December 5, 2003.

Thank you very much. Good morning, fellow citizens.

They wanted to have a U.S. Congressman here to give the keynote speech today. So they first invited the smartest member of Congress to be here. He said, "No." Then they invited the most talented member of Congress to be here. He said "no." Then they invited the most handsome member of Congress to be here. I said, "Yes." I just felt guilty turning them down three times in a row.

I am honored to be here to salute your efforts to become citizens of the greatest country in the world, the United States of America. Let's have a round of applause for our new United States citizens!

On the way over here this morning, I looked at the questions on the citizenship test that you had to pass in order to become citizens of the United States. I have to tell you I was quite impressed with your knowledge of American history. You probably know more about American history than many people born in this country.

On this citizenship test, you were asked, among other things, several questions about the Declaration of Independence. Specifically, you were asked:

Who was the main writer of the Declaration of Independence?

When was the Declaration of Independence adopted?

What is the basic belief of the Declaration of Independence?

What country did we declare independence from?

As new citizens, you already know that the main writer of the Declaration of Independence is Thomas Jefferson, that the Declaration of Independence was adopted on July 4th, 1776, that the basic belief of the Declaration of Independence is that all men are created equal, and that the country we declared independence from is England.

What I would like to do today is to tell you the rest of the story. I would like to give you a behind the scenes look at what happened which lead to the signing of the Declaration of Independence on July 4, 1776. Why? Because as far as any American citizen is concerned, the most important day in this country's history was when 56 men signed their names to the Declaration of Independence because they each knew full well that they were signing their own death warrant if the United States were to lose its fight with England, which was sure to follow. It was their courage that gave freedom to all of us American citizens today.

The story begins with something that happened in Boston on March 5, 1770. The British soldiers were patrolling the streets in Boston, openly threatening our citizens by their presence. The people living in Boston were offended by their threats and they resented these armed soldiers marching all around them. They began to express their resentment openly, calling the soldiers names. Finally, the leader of the British soldiers ordered the soldiers to attack.

The battle was on. It resulted in the death and injury of many innocent folks in Boston, Massachusetts. This made two of our citizens from Boston very angry. Their names were John Hancock and Samuel Adams. Mr. Adams and Mr. Hancock began speaking up courageously against the British soldiers and demanded their withdrawal from Boston.

At the time, the governor of Massachusetts was under the control of the King of England. And he was upset with the statements of Sam Adams and John Hancock. What did the governor do? He sent a messenger to meet with Sam Adams to attempt to stop his opposition by offering him a personal bribe.

I'll quote for you exactly what the messenger said to Sam Adams. He said, "It is the governor's advice to you, sir, not to incur the further displeasure of his Majesty. Your conduct has been such as makes you liable to penalties... by which persons can be sent to England for trial for treason..., but, by changing your political course, you will not only receive great personal advantages, but you will make your peace with the King."

Sam Adams had a choice to make. He could take the bribe and cease his opposition to England, or he could continue to oppose England and run the risk of being hanged!

Sam Adams bravely reached a decision, which could have cost him his life. This is exactly what Adams told the governor's messenger, "You may tell the governor that I trust I have long since made my peace with the King of Kings. No personal consideration shall induce me to abandon the righteous cause of my country. And tell the governor it is the advice of Samuel Adams to him, to no longer to insult the feelings of an exasperated people."

When the Governor of Massachusetts received Adams' reply, he flew into a rage. He promptly announced that both John Hancock and Samuel Adams would be prosecuted for treason.

Great excitement followed. At the same time, Samuel Adams and John Hancock met up with a man from Virginia whose name was Thomas Jefferson. Mr. Jefferson was having the same problems with the Governor of Virginia. In fact, Jefferson had also recently been informed that he too would be prosecuted for treason for making statements against the King of England. Inspired by the threat, one of Jefferson's colleagues, a man named Patrick Henry, stated, "If this be treason, make the most of it." Mr. Henry also stated, "Give me liberty or give me death."

This led our patriots John Hancock, Samuel Adams, Thomas Jefferson, and Patrick Henry to form the first Congress of the United States. The head of the Congress was John Hancock. And he appointed Thomas Jefferson as chairman of a committee to draw up the Declaration of Independence.

When Jefferson was finished, the Declaration of Independence was voted upon, accepted, and signed on July 4, 1776, by the 56 men who attended the Congress.

As expected, the Revolutionary War broke out between our country and England.

And, rest assured, it was the decision of these 56 men to put their lives at risk by signing the Declaration of Independence, which was in the heart of every single soldier who fought that war and resulted in our being a free people today.

That's why those questions about the Declaration of Independence were on your citizenship test. That's why we have fireworks on the 4th of July. And that's why the name Sam Adams means a lot more than just a beer at your local pub... not that there's anything wrong with that.

Now, as an American citizen, you too will enjoy the same freedoms, rights, and privileges as our founding fathers - the right to vote, the right to obtain federal jobs, the potential to receive top-secret military security clearance, and the right to travel abroad with a U.S. passport and be protected by our government, and many other benefits.

Congratulations to all of you. You've earned it. We're proud of you. And I'm honored to call you a fellow citizen. Thank you.

To find out more information about any of the elected officials that contributed to this book, visit us at –
www.ModernDayHeroes.com

Afterword

Colonel Monty Warner (Ret.)
U.S. Army, West Point Graduate

In 1787, Thomas Jefferson would write a friend and say, "The tree of liberty must be refreshed from time to time with the blood of patriots and tyrants." This is no less true today in 2004 than it was in 1787. In fact, it might be more relevant today than ever.

Americans living in the 21st century have much to be proud of, much to remember fondly, yet also much to look forward to. As the new millennium is getting under way, America stands at the forefront of the world in technology, innovation, and personal liberty. However, one of the necessities in America's continued greatness in the future is her determination to remember and learn from her past.

America is an ideal that has been bought and paid for in blood. From the American Revolution to our current conflicts in the War on Terror, the price of liberty remains blood. Those who revel in this truth are frightening, while those who deny it are naïve. However, the truth remains constant, for good or ill, and the price must be paid.

Like no time in America's past is this truth more necessary to be mentioned and brought in to the public square. Our enemies are as numerous as they were when we were fighting the forces of fascism. Our enemies are as numerous as they were when we were fighting the forces of communism. But like every other "ism" that we've faced, the price of liberty will remain the blood of patriots.

Some in America will say that the price is too high. "Let the world contend with their evils on their side of the world," some will claim. This is nothing new. Many colonists, known as Torries, sided with the British during the American Revolution. Some Americans viewed World War I as a European squabble to be dealt with on the other side of the pond. Even the fight against fascism in WWII was not a unanimous decision by Congress or the American people. Appeasement with Hitler, appeasement with Mussolini, and appeasement with Hirohito seemed a far easier price to pay than the blood of patriots. And in truth, the price was easier. However, with respect to the views of these people, the price that liberty demands is the highest price. The scraps from the table of appeasement would not refresh the tree of liberty. A compromise with evil would not refresh the tree of liberty. Only the blood of patriots would suffice. However, the object it purchases is worth it.

As we look to the past and remember and honor our nation's fallen, we think to the ultimate price they have paid so that the tree of liberty could be refreshed for those of us who continue on. As we look to the future, we respect and praise those who willingly prepare for upcoming conflict in both the near and long term. Our current soldiers are the world's finest. An all-volunteer force, they understand better than most of us what their service may require. In addition, most military experts believe that future conflicts will not look like war from the past. The American arsenal is mighty and our enemies have learned that shock battle with the United States is a losing proposition. Instead, future engagements are likely to be asymmetrical and increasingly involving acts of terror, rather than traditional combat. Our present and future soldiers are to be lauded for their continuing commitment to preserving liberty and to their willingness to engage in fighting that is ever more dangerous because the enemy will not meet them head on.

However, our modern day heroes will meet the challenge because they know, in the immortal words of General Douglas MacArthur, "There is no substitute for victory."

It is a sad truth that the dream of lasting peace is probably of the pipe variety. Evil is a very real part of the human experience and along with it comes jealousy, vanity, and conceit. The enemies of our future are as yet unidentified. However, enemies there will be. And as long as there are enemies that threaten America and her liberties, Americans will continue to take up arms. Whether these enemies are foreign or domestic, be they despots of nation-states or fanatics operating in terrorist cells, Americans will fight. We will do this because that is our destiny, our greatest calling from the future that will judge us on how well we met the challenges of freedom. And we will do this because it is the price that liberty demands.

[Monty Warner is no stranger to the price that liberty demands. Gary McKinzy, the husband of the late Diane McKinzy, shared with us the correspondence that Monty Warner sent him after the terrorist attack against the Pentagon on September 11, 2001. Diane McKinzy was a trusted secretary of Monty Warner. She dedicated her life to supporting our Republic, and in doing so, she joined those who have given their lives for the sake of liberty. Here is that letter (originally handwritten):]

Dear Mr. McKinzy-

I was just notified that Diane was still missing after last Tuesday's attack on the Pentagon. Sir, words fail me in trying to convey the remorse that consumes me.

Diane was a wonderful person. She always gave her very best to prepare the correspondence that kept our United States Army running. Her service to the Under Secretary's office was absolutely essential to the effectiveness of operations and the efficient use of resources in our efforts to maintain peace and provide for security of our nation.

I will always remember the excitement and energy that Diane brought to our office. Her exuberance was wildly infectious and none of us could escape catching what she had. We were all the beneficiaries of her cheerful countenance. Diane's light shone upon all of us and our entire office reflected the warmth of that bright light.

Diane contributed, and she made a difference. Her thread was unique. That thread has now been woven by our heavenly father into the intricate tapestry that is these great United States. Diane's thread ties and connects us; adding color, strength, and vitality to a bolt of cloth of unbelievable beauty. Our tapestry is like none other. It is indestructible. It is human freedom. It is the revolutionary concept Christ brought to this Earth that we all stand equal before the creator. Every time old glory ripples in the blue sky, Diane will be there. The grand experiment in human freedom, Abraham Lincoln's "Last Great Hope of Mankind," is also Diane's gift to us.

One hundred thirty-seven years ago, President Lincoln wrote these words to someone who suffered unbearable loss of loved ones during our civil war. As the great emancipator's words are timeless, they are intended for you also:

"I feel how weak and fruitless must be any word of mine which should attempt to beguile you from the grief of a loss so overwhelming. I pray that the Heavenly Father may assuage the anguish of your bereavement and leave you only the cherished memory of the loved and lost, and the solemn pride that must be yours to have laid so costly a sacrifice upon the altar of freedom."

Very Sincerely,
Monroe P. Warner
Colonel, U.S. Army

Index of Contributors with Profiles

Burgess, Dr. Michael C.
U.S. Representative for Texas' 26th District (R)
Contribution: *The Iraq You Don't Know (p. 283)*

Dr. Michael Burgess is a second-generation Texas doctor from Denton County. He is a respected physician who, practiced Obstetrics and Gynecology for over 21 years in Lewisville and delivered more than 3,000 babies.

After growing up in Denton and graduating with a undergraduate degree and a Master's degree from North Texas State University, now the University of North Texas, Burgess received his M.D. from the University of Texas Medical School in Houston and completed his residency programs at Parkland Hospital in Dallas. Dr. Burgess also received another Master's degree in Medical Management from the University of Texas at Dallas. Burgess is committed to higher education.

Dr. Burgess is the founder of a private practice, Obstetrics and Gynecology Associates of Lewisville, former Chief of Staff for Lewisville Medical Center, and most recently he served as Chief of Obstetrics at Lewisville Medical Center. Also, a few years ago Burgess served as President of the Denton County Medical Society.

Dr. Burgess is dedicated to improving America's healthcare system, building a strong defense, and protecting our Homeland. He is committed to cutting wasteful spending and advocating for tax relief, while reforming the tax code into a simple, fairer system.

Dr. Burgess represents Texas' 26th Congressional District, which includes portions of DFW and Alliance airports and Highway

I-35 East and West. As a life long resident of the area, Burgess uniquely understands what issues are important to his district.

In Congress, he serves on the prestigious Transportation and Infrastructure Committee and is the only Texas Republican to serve on this Committee.

The top order of business this year will be the reauthorization of the Transportation Equity Act of the 21st Century (TEA-21). The Transportation and Infrastructure Committee has jurisdiction over Highways and Transit, Aviation, Transportation Security, Coast Guard and Maritime Transportation, Economic Development, Public Buildings and Emergency Management, and Water Resources and Environment.

Dr. Burgess also holds a seat as a member of the Committee on Science. As a member of this committee, he will oversee non-defense federal scientific research and development programs of eight federal agencies. The Committee monitors these programs to ensure that Federal tax dollars are being spent wisely and efficiently and that America's Federal science and technology enterprise maintains its world preeminence.

Dr. Michael Burgess has been married to his wife, Laura, for 30 years. They are proud parents of three grown children who are all graduates of Denton County Public Schools.

Bush, George W.
President of the United States of America (R)
(Did not contribute specifically to this book*)
Piece Used: *"God Bless America", The Story of a P.O.W. (p. 43); Not One of Them is Missing (p. 91); Enemies of Freedom (p. 161); Making the United States of America More Secure (p. 277)Our Cause is Just (p. 287)*

George W. Bush is the 43rd President of the United States. He was sworn into office January 20, 2001, after a campaign in which he outlined sweeping proposals to reform America's public schools, transform our national defense, provide tax relief, modernize Social Security and Medicare, and encourage faith-based and community organizations to work with government to help Americans in need. President Bush served for six years as the 46th Governor of the State of Texas, where he earned a reputation as a compassionate conservative who shaped public policy based on the principles of limited government, personal responsibility, strong families, and local control.

President Bush was born on July 6, 1946, in New Haven, Connecticut, and he grew up in Midland and Houston, Texas. He received a bachelor's degree from Yale University in 1968, then served as an F-102 fighter pilot in the Texas Air National Guard. President Bush received a Master of Business Administration from Harvard Business School in 1975. After graduating, he moved back to Midland and began a career in the energy business. After working on his father's successful 1988 presidential campaign, he assembled the group of partners that purchased the Texas Rangers baseball franchise in 1989.

He served as Managing General Partner of the Texas Rangers until he was elected Governor on November 8, 1994, with 53.5 percent of the vote. He became the first Governor in Texas history to be elected two consecutive four-year terms when he was re-elected on November 3, 1998, with 68.6 percent of the vote.

Since taking office, President Bush has signed into law bold initiatives to improve public schools by raising standards, requiring accountability, and strengthening local control. He has signed tax relief that provided rebate checks and lower tax rates for everyone who pays income taxes in America. He has increased pay and benefits for America's military and is working to save and strengthen Social Security and Medicare. He is also committed to ushering in a responsibility era in America and has called on all Americans to be "Citizens, not spectators; citizens, not subjects; responsible citizens building communities of service and a Nation of character."

The attacks of September 11th changed America - and in President Bush's words, "In our grief and anger we have found our mission and our moment." President Bush declared war against terror and has made victory in the war on terrorism and the advance of human freedom the priorities of his Administration. Already, the United States military and a great coalition of nations have liberated the people of Afghanistan from the brutal Taliban regime and denied al Qaeda its safe haven of operations. Thousands of terrorists have been captured or killed, and operations have been disrupted in many countries around the world. In the President's words, "Our Nation -

this generation - will lift a dark threat of violence from our people and our future. We will rally the world to this cause by our efforts, by our courage. We will not tire, we will not falter, and we will not fail."

President Bush is married to Laura Welch Bush, a former teacher and librarian, and they have twin daughters, Barbara and Jenna. The Bush family also includes their two dogs, Spot and Barney, and a cat, India.

Clinton, William J.
President of the United States of America (D)
(Did not contribute specifically to this book*)
Pieces Used: *September 11, 1998 (p. 103); American Blood (p. 107); Standing Guard for Peace (p. 113)*

President Clinton was born William Jefferson Blythe IV on August 19, 1946, in Hope, Arkansas, three months after his father died in a traffic accident. When he was four years old, his mother wed Roger Clinton, of Hot Springs, Arkansas. In high school, he took the family name.

He excelled as a student and as a saxophone player and once considered becoming a professional musician. As a delegate to Boys Nation while in high school, he met President John Kennedy in the White House Rose Garden. The encounter led him to enter a life of public service.

Clinton was graduated from Georgetown University and in 1968 won a Rhodes Scholarship to Oxford University. He received a law degree from Yale University in 1973 and entered politics in Arkansas.

He was defeated in his campaign for Congress in Arkansas's Third District in 1974. The next year he married Hillary Rodham, a graduate of Wellesley College and Yale Law School. In 1980, Chelsea, their only child, was born.

Clinton was elected Arkansas Attorney General in 1976 and won the governorship in 1978. After losing a bid for a second term, he regained the office four years later and served until he defeated incumbent George Bush and third party candidate Ross Perot in the 1992 presidential race.

Clinton and his running mate, Tennessee's Senator Albert Gore Jr., then 44, represented a new generation in American political leadership. For the first time in 12 years both the White House and Congress were held by the same party. But that political edge was brief; the Republicans won both houses of Congress in 1994.

In 1998, as a result of issues surrounding personal indiscretions with a young woman White House intern, Clinton was the second U.S. president to be impeached by the House of Representatives. He was tried in the Senate and found not guilty of the charges brought against him.

In the world, he successfully dispatched peace keeping forces to war-torn Bosnia and bombed Iraq when Saddam Hussein stopped United Nations inspections for evidence of nuclear, chemical, and biological weapons. He became a global proponent for an expanded NATO, more open international trade, and a worldwide campaign against drug trafficking. He drew huge crowds when he traveled through South America, Europe, Russia, Africa, and China, advocating U.S. style freedom.

Cunningham, Randy "Duke"
U.S. Representative for California's 50th District (R)
Contribution: *I Don't Want My Son to be a Quitter (p. 35)*

Randy "Duke" Cunningham was born December 8, 1941, in Los Angeles, California. After earning his Bachelor's degree in 1964 and his Master's in Education in 1965 from the University of Missouri, Cunningham began his career as an educator and a coach at Hinsdale (Ill.) High School. As a swimming coach, Duke trained two athletes to Olympic gold and silver medals. He later expanded his education experience as the Dean of the School of Aviation at National University in San Diego.

In 1966, at the age of 25, Cunningham joined the U.S. Navy and became one of the most highly decorated pilots in the Vietnam War. As the first Fighter Ace of the war, Cunningham was nominated for the Medal of Honor, received the Navy Cross, two Silver Stars, fifteen Air Medals, the Purple Heart, and several other decorations.

Duke's experience in Vietnam and his background as an educator prepared him well to train fighter pilots at the Navy Fighter Weapons School -- the famed "Top Gun" program at Miramar Naval Air Station. As Commanding Officer of the elite Navy Adversary Squadron, Cunningham flew Russian tactics and formations against

America's best combat fighter pilots. Many of his real-life experiences as a Navy aviator and fighter pilot instructor were depicted in the popular movie "Top Gun."

Upon his retirement from the Navy in 1987, Cunningham translated the Masters in Business Administration he earned at National University into a successful business in San Diego.

In 2002, the people of California's 50th Congressional District elected Duke Cunningham to his seventh term in the House of Representatives. As the voters returned a Republican majority to both chambers of Congress, Congressman Cunningham retained his position on the powerful House Appropriations Committee. Cunningham serves on the Labor, Health and Human Services, and Education Appropriations subcommittee, which is instrumental in providing key funding for education and medical research, two of his priorities. He also serves on the panel's Defense subcommittee, which provides funding for our national defense and armed services. At the beginning of the 107th Congress, Cunningham was appointed to the Select Committee on Intelligence. Members are chosen for this Select Committee based on their ardent interest and special expertise in dealing with national security issues.

Duke and his wife, Nancy, the Director of Administrative Support Services for the Encinitas Union School District, have three children -- Todd, April, and Carrie.

DeWine, Mike
Senator for Ohio (R)
Contributions: *To Protect and Serve (p. 73); Brave, Courageous, Fearless and Tough as Nails (p. 79); Patriotism and Love of Country (p. 241); He was a Good Man (p. 269)*

Mike DeWine was born on January 5, 1947, and grew up in Yellow Springs, Ohio. As the son of parents and grandparents who ran a small agricultural business, he spent his youth and early adult life working in the fields and in the mill, learning the value of hard work and determination. He carried those values with him first to Miami University, Oxford, Ohio, where he graduated in 1969 with a degree in Education and then to Ohio Northern University Law School, (Ada, Ohio) where he graduated in 1972 with a law degree.

Soon after, he began his career in public service -- a career that now has spanned over 30 years and has involved work at all levels of government. Firm in his belief that criminals should be brought to justice, DeWine -- at the young age of 25 -- started working as the Assistant Prosecuting Attorney for Greene County, and in 1976, he was elected Prosecutor. What he learned during those years in the Prosecutor's office stayed with him and compelled him to continue in public service in a variety of capacities. DeWine served as an Ohio State Senator, a four-term U.S. Congressman, and as Ohio's 59th Lieutenant Governor. Mike DeWine was first sworn into the United States Senate on January 4, 1995, as the first Republican U.S. Senator to represent the "Buckeye" state in more than two decades. In 2000, he was the first Republican U.S. Senator in nearly a half-century to be re-elected to serve Ohio.

Earnest in his determination to get things done for those in need, Mike DeWine has been dubbed the "bodyguard of the poor." He has developed a reputation in Washington for being hard working, honest, and solution-oriented. He has immersed himself in issues that don't necessarily grab headlines, but are vital to the well-being and prosperity of Ohioans, Americans, and citizens across the globe

Mike DeWine and his wife, Fran, who have been married for over 36 years, have eight children and eight grandchildren. As a parent, grandparent, and United States Senator, he knows that the safety and security of our children extend beyond measures to protect their immediate well-being. He knows that the world he helps to shape today is the world our children and grandchildren will inherit and he remains vigilant in his work to secure our children's future through the stabilization of countries around the world.

Diaz-Balart, Mario
U.S. Representative for Florida's 25th District (R)
Contribution: *Safer Today than Ever Before (p. 191)*

Congressman Mario Díaz-Balart was born in Ft. Lauderdale, FL, on September 25, 1961. He attended the University of South Florida in Tampa to study Political Science before beginning his public service career as an aide to then City of Miami Mayor Xavier

Suarez in 1985. Díaz-Balart was elected to the Florida House of Representatives in 1988, where he served until 1992.

In 1992, at age 31, Díaz-Balart became the youngest person ever elected to the Florida Senate. He was the first Hispanic to serve as Chair of the Combined Appropriations / Ways and Means / Finance and Tax Committee. He was also Chair in the following committees: Criminal Justice Appropriations, Banking and Insurance, and Children and Families. He was Vice-Chair of the Rules Committee.

Díaz-Balart was consistently ranked among the most effective legislators in the Florida Legislature. He developed a reputation as a budget hawk and earned the moniker "The Slasher." In 1996 he was voted "Most Effective Legislator" by the Miami Herald.

In 2002, Díaz-Balart was elected to the U.S. House of Representatives to represent Florida's 25th Congressional district, which covers portions of Miami-Dade County, Collier County, and Monroe County. He serves on the Budget Committee and the Transportation and Infrastructure Committee.

While only in his first term, Díaz-Balart has already made his presence known. He has worked in conjunction with Senate Majority Leader Bill Frist in support of Miguel Estrada's judicial nomination. He authored two amendments to protect Everglades restoration funding, which were successfully passed. He helped found the Congressional Hispanic Conference and the Washington Waste Watchers, a group which combats government waste, fraud, and abuse.

Díaz-Balart has deep roots in politics. One of his three older brothers, Lincoln, represents Florida's 21st District, and his father Rafaél served as the Majority Leader in Cuba's House of Representatives before fleeing the island. Díaz-Balart's uncle and grandfather also served in the Cuban House.

DiRaimondo, Tony
Father of Michael A. DiRaimondo
Contribution: *God Gave Us a Son (p. 293)*

The Michael A. DiRaimondo Foundation's purpose is to provide scholarships to individuals who aspire to be paramedics but don't have the financial means to do so. Many who desire to become emergency medical professionals do not have the financial means necessary to pay the tuition of $3-$8,000 per year due to the fact that student loans cannot be applied to this type of program. The Foundation has created a permanent endowment with earnings to be directed to support these types of scholarships.

In sponsoring other potential paramedics, Michael's dream of helping people with his "healing hands" will live on forever.

Ventura County Community Foundation is a 501(c)(3) organization and your gift is tax deductible to the fullest extent of the law. VCCF's tax id number is 77-0165029.

Donations can be sent to:
Michael A. DiRaimondo Foundation
P.O. Box 1265
Simi Valley, CA 93062

Additional information is available at this web site:
www.MichaelADiRaimondoFoundation.org

Dole, Elizabeth
Senator for North Carolina (R)
Contributions: *The Greatest Generation (p. 229); Terrorism Must be Torn Out by its Roots (p. 263)*

Elizabeth Dole has had a remarkable public service career, serving five United States Presidents and winning 54% of the vote in November 2002 to serve the people of North Carolina in the United States Senate. As Senator, Elizabeth Dole is focused on growing the economy and creating jobs, strengthening national security and rebuilding our military, improving education and making quality health care more affordable and accessible. Elizabeth Dole is committed to making North Carolina – and America – safer, stronger, healthier, and more successful in the months and years ahead. She serves on the Senate Armed Services, Agriculture, Banking, and Aging Committees.

Elizabeth Dole has been named consistently by the Gallup Poll as one of the world's "top ten most admired women" every year since 1996. She was the first woman to serve as the departmental head of a branch of the military, the U.S. Coast Guard, when she was

Secretary of Transportation. Elizabeth Dole currently serves in a volunteer position as the National Director of Education and Information for Hospice.

A native of Salisbury, North Carolina, Elizabeth Dole graduated with distinction from Duke University in 1958 and was a member of Phi Beta Kappa. She earned a degree from Harvard Law School in 1965 and also holds a Master's degree in Education and Government, from Harvard.

From 1969 to 1973, Elizabeth Dole served as Deputy Assistant to President Nixon for Consumer Affairs, beginning a career of dedication to public safety, for which she received the National Safety Council's Distinguished Service Award in 1989. Elizabeth Dole's resume includes six years (1973-1979) as a member of the Federal Trade Commission and two years (1981-1983) as Assistant to President Reagan for Public Liaison.

In February 1983, Elizabeth Dole joined President Reagan's Cabinet as Secretary of Transportation – the first woman to hold that position. During her four-and-a-half years at Transportation, the United States enjoyed the safest period then to date in all three major transportation areas – rail, air, and highway.

Elizabeth Dole was sworn in by President Bush as the nation's 20th Secretary of Labor in January, 1989. She worked to increase safety and health in the workplace, advocated upgrading the skills of the American workforce, and played a key role in resolving the bitter 11-month Pittston Coal Strike in southwest Virginia.

In January, 1999, Elizabeth Dole concluded her service at the Red Cross and sought the Republican presidential nomination. In her campaign for president of the United States, Elizabeth Dole became the first viable woman candidate from a major political party. She attracted thousands of first-time voters into the democratic process.

Elizabeth Dole has received honorary Doctorate degrees from 40 colleges and universities. She served on the Duke University Board of Trustees from 1974 to 1985 and Board of Overseers for Harvard University from 1990 to 1996.

Edwards, John
Senator for North Carolina (D)
Contributions: *We Will Not Forget. And We Will Act. (p. 137); Lessons of September 11th (p. 183)*

Sworn into office on January 6, 1999, Senator John Edwards has emerged as a champion for issues affecting the daily lives of regular people in North Carolina and the nation.

Senator Edwards was a chief sponsor of the Bipartisan Patient Protection Act, strong and far-reaching patient protection legislation that passed the Senate in 2001.

Senator Edwards's bipartisan accomplishments also include a major investment in America's public schools, strong anti-terrorism measures, modernization of the nation's banking system, sweeping campaign finance reform, and legislation to fight corporate corruption.

The *News & Observer of Raleigh* described Senator Edwards as, "Smart, disciplined, [and] hard-working" with "...a down-home manner." The *Wall Street Journal* called him a senator who "Impresses colleagues in behind-doors deliberations." *The Washington Post* said Senator Edwards has, "The ability to think on his feet... master complex issues and... communicate in plain language to ordinary people."

Senator Edwards serves on four committees: Health, Education, Labor and Pensions; Intelligence; Judiciary; and Small Business.

As part of his commitment to North Carolina, Senator Edwards has been to all 100 counties in the state, from Murphy (where he went to a college) to Manteo (where he honored Andy Griffith). Every week that the Senate is in session, he hosts Tar Heel Thursday, town-hall style meetings open to all North Carolinians visiting Washington.

Born in 1953, Senator Edwards grew up in Robbins, a small town in the Piedmont. His father, Wallace, worked in textile mills for 36 years. His mother, Bobbie, had a number of jobs, including working at the post office.

A product of North Carolina public schools, Senator Edwards was the first person in his family to go to college. He worked his way through North Carolina State University and graduated with an Honors degree in Textiles in 1974. He earned a law degree with Honors in 1977 from the University of North Carolina, at Chapel Hill.

He met his wife, Elizabeth, when both were law school students at Chapel Hill. They married in 1977, and have had four children. Their first child, Wade, died in 1996. Their eldest daughter,

Catharine, is a student at Princeton University. The Edwards household also includes a five-year-old daughter, Emma Claire, and a three-year-old son, Jack.

England, Gordon R.
Secretary of the Navy
(Did not contribute specifically to this book*)
Piece Used: *You Stood Watch (p. 53)*

Gordon England was confirmed as the 73rd Secretary of the Navy on September 26, 2003 and sworn in on October 1st. He becomes only the second person in history to serve twice as the leader of the Navy-Marine Corps Team and the first to serve in back-to-back terms. Prior to his return to the Navy Department, he was the first Deputy Secretary of the Department of Homeland Security. The Department of Homeland Security was established on January 24, 2003, to integrate 22 different agencies with a common mission to protect the American people.

Secretary England served as the 72nd Secretary of the Navy from May 24, 2001, until he joined the Homeland Security in January 2003. As Secretary of the Navy, Mr. England leads America's Navy and Marine Corps and is responsible for an annual budget in excess of $110 B and more than 800,000 personnel.

Prior to joining the administration of President George W. Bush, Mr. England served as executive vice president of General Dynamics Corporation from 1997 until 2001. In that position he was responsible for two major sectors of the corporation: Information Systems and International. Previously, he served as executive vice president of the Combat Systems Group, president of General Dynamics Fort Worth aircraft company (later Lockheed), president of General Dynamics Land Systems Company, and as the principal of a mergers and acquisition consulting company.

A native of Baltimore, Mr. England graduated from the University of Maryland, in 1961, with a Bachelor's degree in Electrical Engineering. In 1975, he earned a Master's degree in Business Administration from the M.J. Neeley School of Business at Texas Christian University and is a member of various honorary societies: Beta Gamma Sigma (business), Omicron Delta Kappa (leadership), and Eta Kappa Nu (engineering).

Mr. England has been actively involved in a variety of civic, charitable, and government organizations, including serving as a city councilman; Vice Chair, Board of Goodwill, International; the USO's Board of Governors; the Defense Science Board; the Board of Visitors at Texas Christian University; and many others.

Enzi, Michael

Senator for Wyoming (R)

Contributions: *Modern Day Pioneers (p. 95); Evil Will Not Stand (p. 215)*

Michael B. Enzi was sworn in as Wyoming's 20th United States Senator on January 7, 1997, replacing Alan Simpson, who retired after 18 years. Enzi has worked to balance the federal budget and see that it stays balanced. As the only accountant in the U.S. Senate, he has been a leader in the effort to create a tax system that is simple and fair to the American people. He is also the only certified Human Resources Management Professional in the United States Congress. He is working to bring more of the powers of the federal government down to their rightful place, the local level, and to create an environment of reduced regulation to spur economic growth.

Enzi was born on February 1, 1944, in Bremerton, Washington, while his father was serving our country in the naval shipyards during World War II. Enzi and his family moved to Thermopolis, Wyoming, shortly after his birth, where he attended elementary school. He graduated from Sheridan High School in 1962. He continued his education in Washington, D.C., at George Washington University. After completing his Aaccounting degree in 1966, he went on to the University of Denver where he earned a Master's Degree in Retail Marketing in 1968. Enzi is a Rapport Leadership Institute Master Grad.

After marrying Diana (Buckley) in 1969, Enzi and his wife moved to Gillette, Wyoming, where they started their own small business, NZ Shoes, with stores later in Sheridan, Wyoming, and Miles City, Montana. Gillette has been his home ever since. He served as president of the Wyoming Jaycees (1973-1974). At age 30, he was elected twice to four-year-terms as Mayor of Gillette, providing leadership as the city more than doubled in size. He served on the Department of Interior Coal Advisory Committee (1976- 1979), traveling to Washington, D.C., to give advice on coal leasing and other coal issues. He has served his county and state as a State Representative, elected three times beginning in 1987, and a State Senator (1991-1996). Enzi also served his country in the Wyoming Air National Guard (1967-1973), and he is now co-founder and chairman of the U.S. Air Force Caucus for the U.S. Senate. He was president of the Wyoming Association of Municipalities (1980-1982), a member of the Energy Council Executive Committee (1989-1993, 1994-1996), a commissioner of the Western Interstate Commission for Higher Education (1995-1996), and served on the Education Commission of the States (1989-1993). He was a member of the founding board of directors of First Wyoming Bank of Gillette (1978-1988) and an employee of a small business, Dunbar Well Service (1985-1997), where he worked as accounting manager and computer programmer. He was a director of the Black Hills Corporation (1992-1996), a New York Stock Exchange Company. Enzi was a spokesperson for WyBett, an organization which successfully opposed gambling in Wyoming. Enzi is a champion of small business and community service.

Enzi has two daughters (Emily and Amy) and one son (Brad). Enzi's wife, Diana, does volunteer work in the Senate office and travels weekends with Enzi back to Wyoming to different towns every trip. She has been the Vice President of the International Club (made up of 1/3 Congress, 1/3 ambassadors', and 1/3 business community spouses) and Treasurer of the Senate Spouses. But her biggest job has been President of the Congressional Club, a huge organization of spouses and daughters of present and former members of Congress. Diana also hosted the annual First Lady's Luncheon attended by about 3,000 members and guests. The highlight of the event for Diana was having the opportunity to visit with and introduce the First Lady.

Enzi is an elder in the Presbyterian Church and taught the high school Sunday school class for more than 10 years. Enzi's love for Wyoming grew as he became an Eagle Scout. He has been honored as a Distinguished Eagle by Scouts and Significant Sig by Sigma Chi Fraternity. He is an avid hunter, fly fisherman, bicyclist, and reader. He now co-chairs the Congressional Sportsmen's Caucus. He and his son Brad built their own canoe as a family project. He was a youth soccer coach for 10 years.

Feinstein, Dianne
Senator for California (D)
Contribution: *Americas' Armed Forces (p. 249)*

Senator Dianne Feinstein was elected to the Senate in 1992 by 5,505,780 Californians, the most votes cast for a Senator in U.S. history. Two years later, she was elected to her first full 6-year term in the Senate and won election to her second full term in 2000.

Her career has been one of firsts - she was the first woman on the San Francisco Board of Supervisors, the first woman Mayor of San Francisco, the first woman elected Senator of California, and the first woman member of the Senate Judiciary Committee.

As California's senior Senator, Dianne Feinstein has built a reputation as an independent voice, working with both Democrats and Republicans to find common-sense solutions to the problems facing our State and our Nation.

A native of San Francisco, Senator Feinstein was appointed by California Governor Pat Brown to the Women's Parole Board in 1960 at age 27. In 1969, she was elected to the San Francisco County Board of Supervisors, where she served 2 ½ terms as President of the Board.

She became Mayor of San Francisco in November, 1978, following the assassination of Mayor George Moscone and Supervisor Harvey Milk, where she immediately demonstrated a steadiness and command that calmed the city during that turbulent time.

The following year she was elected to the first of two four-year terms. As Mayor, Dianne Feinstein managed the City's finances with a firm hand, balancing nine budgets in a row. In 1987, City and State Magazine named her the nation's "Most Effective Mayor."

Filner, Bob
U.S. Representative for California's 51st District (D)
Contribution: *Your Chosen Profession (p. 305)*

Born in Pittsburgh on September 4, 1942, and raised in New York City, Bob Filner moved to the San Diego area in 1970. He and his wife, Jane Merrill, have two adult children. Their son Adam continues to live in the area with his wife Kim, and their baby daughter Madeline. Daughter Erin, married to Patrick Ryan, lives in New York.

Bob Filner is deeply committed to the battle for justice and equality. In 1961, Bob spent several months in a southern jail as a "Freedom Rider" in the Civil Rights movement. Bob is a fearless fighter and always insists that the needs of the people must come first.

During a twenty-year tenure as a Professor of History at San Diego State University, Bob challenged his students to do more than think lofty thoughts. He taught them that ideas don't mean anything unless they are put into action to help people and make the world a better place. It's a lesson he continues to demonstrate in the U.S. Congress.

Back home in San Diego, Bob's opposition to the closing of a neighborhood school led to his being drafted as a candidate for the San Diego School Board in 1979. Strong community support propelled him to a victory over a long-time incumbent.

Bob's "back to basics" approach towards education--including mandatory homework--won wide support. Under his tenure, administrators were more accountable, test scores went up, and millions of dollars in waste were eliminated.

Although Bob was the only Democrat on the School Board, his ability to work with diverse groups and win others over to his point of view, made him a leader. His colleagues elected him Board President in 1982.

In 1987, Bob Filner was elected to the San Diego City Council. In 1991, he was re-elected with more than 70 percent of the vote. His ability to work with people was seen once again when he was elected by the Council to serve as Deputy Mayor.

In 1992, Bob Filner was elected to the United States House of Representatives by a two-to-one margin. His decisive victory reflected the confidence the voters had in his ability to produce results for his city.

The 51st Congressional District is one of the most diverse areas in the nation. Encompassing the southern half of the City of San Diego, the South Bay cities of Chula Vista and National City, and all of Imperial County, the district's population is 55% Latino, 18% Anglo, 15% Filipino, and 12% African-American.

Re-elected by overwhelming margins in the next five elections, Bob has continued to demonstrate that the confidence of this diverse community is well-deserved. Beginning in his first term, when he became one of only a handful of freshman legislators to get legislation passed--in Bob's case, a critical bill amending the Clean Water Act to allow San Diego to keep its waste treatment facility and thus save billions of dollars--Bob has shown again and again that he can bring people together, create consensus, and get things done.

One of Bob Filner's early appointments upon arriving in Washington was to a seat on the Committee on Veterans' Affairs. In that capacity, Bob has been a tireless fighter for Veterans, winning the praise of thousands of individual Veterans and high accolades from national Veterans organizations.

Bob has fought to get attention to health problems affecting soldiers serving in Vietnam and the Gulf War. He has worked for more mental health care for Veterans and to ensure that GI benefits keep up with inflation. He was successful in getting better pay for VA dentists and increasing small business opportunities for Veterans.

One group that has received special attention from Congressman Filner has been Filipino Veterans from WWII. They were promised benefits in exchange for their efforts, but many were cut off from them by Congress in 1946. Outraged by this betrayal of people who fought for our country at a time of great peril, Bob has constantly brought the issue back before the Congress. He introduced legislation to restore the benefits and got Congress to hold hearings for the first time. As a result, more Filipino Veterans are receiving some benefits. Because of Bob's continuous work directly with the White House and Republican leadership, his legislation to provide access to the VA healthcare system for Filipino Veterans who reside in the United States is expected to become law in 2003. But Bob will not rest until all the Filipino Veterans get true equity and the full benefits to which they are entitled.

Frost, Martin
U.S. Representative for Texas' 24th District (D)
Contributions: *The Vision to Find It (p. 93); Peace is Best Achieved from a Position of Strength (p. 213); Defeating Tyranny (p. 255); In the Face of Deadly Obstacles (p. 291)*

U.S. Rep. Martin Frost (D-TX) is the senior Member of Congress from Texas, serving his 13th term representing the 24th Congressional District in the DFW Metroplex. In addition, Frost is the Ranking Democratic Member of the influential House Rules Committee. Frost is also the senior Southern Democrat in the U.S. House.

Congressman Frost has a long record of leadership in Congress, bringing a common sense, practical approach to a variety of senior positions. Frost served as Chairman of the House Democratic Caucus from 1999 until January 2003, and is widely respected for his ability to bring together Members with different regional and ideological backgrounds, allowing the Caucus to work toward a common agenda that addresses the real concerns of working families. A political moderate, Frost has also brought together both representatives of the business and labor communities with Democratic Members to discuss issues affecting their industries.

Congressman Frost was the leader in securing federal funding for the construction of North Texas' only national Veterans cemetery in the Oak Cliff section of Dallas. He was instrumental in keeping Northrop Grumman from moving their facility in Grand Prairie by successfully brokering an agreement between Northrop and the Navy that saved 5,000 jobs. He was also one of the leaders in the effort to keep the General Motors plant in Arlington open. And in 1985, when Grand Prairie-based LTV filed for bankruptcy and tried to cancel the health benefits of retirees, Congressman Frost stopped them by strengthening protections for all retirees. He worked to pass a law to requiring companies in bankruptcy to honor health coverage obligations to their retirees.

Congressman Frost has taken a strong stand against crime by winning passage of the Amber Hagerman Child Protection Act. Congressman Frost authored this legislation in response to the kidnapping and murder of a nine-year-old girl from Arlington, Texas. His bill created a "Two Strikes" law mandating life in prison after a second sex offense against a child. And after the success of the AMBER Alert program - which was created in North Texas by law enforcement, broadcasters and experts on missing children - Frost co-authored the bipartisan National AMBER Alert Act to bring the successful program to communities around the country.

Frost is the son of an aerospace engineer and grew up in Fort Worth, where he graduated from Paschal High School. He received both Bachelor of Journalism and Bachelor of Arts in History degrees from the University of Missouri in 1964. He received his law degree from the Georgetown Law Center in Washington, D.C., in 1970.

Prior to entering law school, Frost worked as a newspaper and magazine reporter and was a staff writer for the Congressional Quarterly Weekly Report. Following graduation from Georgetown, he served as a law clerk for Federal Judge Sarah T. Hughes of the Northern District of Texas and practiced law in Dallas until his election to Congress in 1978.

Frost, 62, has three daughters - Alanna; Mariel; and Camille - and three granddaughters, Helaine, Simona, and Esther Bach of El Paso, Texas. He is married to Major General Kathy George Frost, who is on active duty in the U.S. Army. He is a member of Congregation Beth El in Fort Worth.

Greenwood, Jim
U.S. Representative for Pennsylvania's 8th District (R)
Contribution: *The American Heroes of D-Day (p. 23)*

Congressman James C. Greenwood represents Pennsylvania's Eighth Congressional District, which currently includes all of Bucks County and portions of Montgomery and Philadelphia Counties.

Congressman Greenwood is a lifelong resident of Bucks County and a graduate of Council Rock High School. He graduated from Dickinson College in 1973 with a BA in Social Work. From 1977 until 1980, he worked as a social worker with abused and neglected children at the Bucks County Children and Youth Social Service Agency.

Congressman Greenwood served six years in the Pennsylvania General Assembly (1980-86) and six years in the Pennsylvania Senate (1986-1993). He specialized in health, environment, and children's issues.

In November of 1992, Congressman Greenwood was sworn in as a Member of the 103rd Congress. He serves on the Energy and Commerce Committee as Chairman of the Subcommittee on Oversight and Investigation. As Subcommittee Chairman, he leads investigations and holds hearings on a variety of topics from corporate governance, to bioterrorism, to the safety of nuclear power plants.

Congressman Greenwood lives in Erwinna with his wife Tina and their three children: Rob, Laura and Katie.

Gutierrez, Luis V.
U.S. Representative for Illinois' 4th District (D)
Contributions: *Unconquerable Qualities of America (p. 155); Hero Street, USA (p. 299)*

During his six terms in the U.S. House of Representatives, Congressman Luis V. Gutierrez has worked hard to establish himself as an effective legislator and energetic spokesman on behalf of his constituents in Illinois' Fourth District. He is a national leader championing the causes of the immigrant community and a tireless advocate for the economically disadvantaged. He also has secured important funding for affordable housing and transportation.

As chairman of the Congressional Hispanic Caucus' Task Force on Immigration, Rep. Gutierrez gained national recognition for his efforts to prevent the break-up of immigrants' families and led efforts to compel the INS to eliminate its massive backlog of citizenship applications.

He currently serves on the Financial Services Committee, where he is the ranking member of the Oversight & Investigations Subcommittee, and the Veterans' Affairs Committee.

Prior to being elected to Congress, Rep. Gutierrez worked as a teacher, social worker, community activist, and city official until his 1986 election as Alderman from Chicago's 26th ward. He graduated from Northeastern Illinois University in 1975. Rep. Gutierrez and his wife, Soraida, have two daughters, Omaira and Jessica, and a new grandson, Luis Andres.

Guyer, Ronnie
Vietnam Veteran
Contribution: *A Witness to the Heroism of Many (p. 39)*

As a Citizen-Activist, Ronnie Guyer has been dedicated to bringing political and spiritual clarity to others, based on his lifetime of witnessing the heroism of many in Time of War and of Peace.

The Power of the Internet and Talk Radio/TV are his weapons for that clarity, where he is known as "ALOHA RONNIE." His calls of clarity can be heard on C-Span, the Fox News Channel, and national talk radio shows like the Judicial Watch Report, Hugh Hewitt, Rush Limbaugh, Bob Dornan, Larry Elder Show, etc. He is also Co-Host for Little Saigon's Radio Free Vietnam. See: www.rfvn.com.

He has participated in many 'Support Our Troops' demonstrations during the Nation's War on Terrorism that were held by www.FreeRepublic.com, America's leading political website. The world's TV-Radio and Print Media covered these demonstrations world wide, most especially when they were demonstrating in support of the Nation's Troops outside the 2003 Academy Awards® in Hollywood, California. They were found singing "God Bless America" as movie stars arrived, while Ronnie Guyer's Vietnam Unit was spearheading freedom's arrival in Iraq.

An Associated Press photo of Ronnie in his golden yellow 1st Cavalry Jacket waving an American Flag was syndicated around the world, as was his being interviewed in support of the War by the Chicago Tribune (Article was syndicated nationwide) and by various national and international TV networks.

Shortly afterwards, some of Hollywood's anti-war activist Actors, Actresses, and their Directors felt the wrath of the American people in their pocketbooks during a time of war.

Ronnie's mid-1960's military service in the United States Army was a defining moment of his life. Trained as a Radioman and Radio Teletype Operator, he was blessed to serve in a Signal Corps Unit at Ft. Meade, Maryland, just outside Washington, D.C. This was a real blessing for this young man born and raised in California that had always wanted to experience our Nation's founding history. Little did he know that he was well on his way to witnessing more history firsthand.

President Lyndon Johnson sent his new Helicopter Air Assault 1st Cavalry Airmobile Division to stop invading Communists from taking over South Vietnam's central highlands, and then the whole country, in 1965. Ronnie received his 1st Cavalry Division orders the day after President Lyndon Johnson's White House TV announcement to the Nation. Yes sir, just like his 1964 presidential campaign slogan, Ronnie was going "All the way with LBJ."

As Lt. Col. Harold G. Moore's, and his Master Sergeant Basil L. Plumley's, first Radioman-Driver-Orderly assistant during their 1st Battalion, U.S. 7th Cavalry's (of Custer fame) first Vietnam operations, they went on to be the first American Unit to meet invading North Vietnamese Communist Army Regulars in battle, in the Valley of Death that was the Ia Drang Valley of November 1965.

By then Ronnie had become the Battalion's S-1 Personnel Clerk where he witnessed the fight at Ia Drang's Landing Zone X-Ray from our close-in artillery support Landing Zone Falcon, 3 air minutes out. Their 400 7th Cavalry Skytroopers at Landing Zone X-Ray had been surrounded by over 2,000 enemy North Vietnamese troops. But this time the 7th Cavalry won its 2nd Battle of the Little Big Horn with Air Assault tactics.

During the Battle, Ronnie carried wounded and dead from helicopters fresh from Landing Zone X-Ray to other helicopters headed to the rear hospitals at Pleiku Airstrip, while witnessing this all. After the Battle, Lt. Col. Moore hand wrote out his Letters of Condolences to the families and loved ones of all the nearly 500 U.S. 7th Cavalry's dead and wounded. He wrote them out; Ronnie typed them out for mailing back home, some going first through Mrs. Julie Moore. This took weeks with more typewriters put to work towards the end.

See the bestselling book about their battle titled *We Were Soldiers Once and Young* by now Lt. Gen. Harold G. Moore (Ret.) and Landing Zone X-Ray UPI War Correspondent Joseph L. Galloway. Also see their Battle of Ia Drang website www.lzxray.com and the outstanding Randall Wallace Film "We Were Soldiers," starring Mel Gibson, that is based on their book.

Upon his return home from Vietnam, he joined up with Matson Steamship Lines on the mainland that ships container freight and autos to Hawaii, and at the time, people on luxury liner passenger ships like the S.S. Lurline, named after Captain Matson's daughter. Over the decades he was able to encourage our Hero Soldiers who were shipping their autos and families to Hawaii while they went off to new wars or to dangerous repeat tours of duty in Vietnam. There he became known throughout the company as "Mr. Matson" for the "Aloha" Spirit he shared with the customers over the decades. An example for others to follow, just like his commanding officer Lt. Col. Harold G. Moore was for him in Vietnam, he had learned his lessons well.

After his retirement from Matson Lines, he became an administrative assistant for Judicial Watch, America's largest public-interest law firm that fights against corruption in government, a true fit.

In honor of those heroes whose names took the place of Ronnie's own on the 3rd Panel of the Vietnam Wall after the fight at Landing Zone X-Ray in the Battle of Ia Drang Valley so long ago, he has also been fighting for freedom's return to Vietnam. He has been speaking on Radio Free Vietnam and at freedom demonstrations in Little Saigon, California. He has been promoting our cities and states' adoption of the free flag of the former Republic of South Vietnam as the Official Flag for America's Vietnamese-American communities to fly next to the American Flag of freedom at their own community functions. What started out as a city by city issue in early 2003, is now a nationwide issue. This all serves to de-legitimize the flag of Communist Vietnam, bringing us closer to freedom for the enslaved people there.

And just like Ronnie's "Mr. Matson" title of old, he has now been blessed to become a symbol in the hearts of Vietnamese-Americans all across our free America for freedom's return to Vietnam.

God is God.

More information on "Aloha" Ronnie at:
www.ModernDayHeroes.com

Hoyer, Steny
U.S. Representative for Maryland's 5th District (D)
Contribution: *The Men and Women We Honor (p. 235)*

On November 14, 2002, Congressman Steny H. Hoyer of Maryland was unanimously elected by Members of the House Democratic Caucus to serve as the House Democratic Whip, the second-ranking position among House Democrats. His election as Democratic Whip makes him the highest-ranking Member of Congress from Maryland in history. Now serving his 12th term in

Congress, he also is the longest-serving Member of the U.S. House of Representatives from Southern Maryland in history.

Congressman Hoyer's experience, know-how and strong work ethic have led to increasing responsibilities within the House Democratic leadership. He served as Chair of the Democratic Caucus, the fourth-ranking position among House Democrats, from 1989 to 1994. He is the former Co-Chair (and a current member) of the Democratic Steering Committee, served as the chief candidate recruiter for House Democrats from 1995 to 2000, and currently continues to actively recruit candidates around the country. He also served as Deputy Majority Whip from 1987 to 1989.

Congressman Hoyer has secured funding for numerous important projects in the Fifth Congressional District that he represents (Calvert, Charles and St. Mary's counties and portions of Prince George's and Anne Arundel counties) and throughout the State of Maryland. He also has worked to ensure that the military bases in the Fifth District not only survived base closings in the 1980s and 1990s but grew and thrived.

On the Transportation, Treasury and General Government Appropriations Subcommittee, Congressman Hoyer is widely recognized as a national leader on issues affecting Federal employees and retirees. In addition to guiding FEPCA to passage, he fights year-in and year-out for fair pay and benefits for Federal employees and has secured funding for telecommuting centers that allow Federal workers to work closer to home and spend more time with their families.

He also is a strong proponent of Federal law enforcement efforts that fall within the Subcommittee's jurisdiction, securing funding for innovative crime-fighting projects such as the High Intensity Drug Trafficking Area Program, Gang Resistance Education and Treatment Program, and the Youth Crime Gun Interdiction Initiative. In addition, he is a long-time supporter of the COPS on the Beat Program, which has meant more than $30 million in Federal funding to hire more than 700 police officers in the Fifth District.

Congressman Hoyer also is well-recognized for his efforts to make the House more efficient and "customer friendly." He is the former Ranking Member of the Committee on House Administration, which oversees the internal operations of the House, and has played an important role on policy issues ranging from election reform and campaign finance reform to exposing fire code violations in the Capitol and enhancing the security of the Capitol complex in the aftermath of September 11. He also is a former Member of the Appropriations Subcommittee on the Legislative Branch, where he fought for pro-institution policies such as sufficient funding for the Capitol Police and cost-of-living adjustments for employees of legislative agencies.

Congressman Hoyer currently serves on the Naval Academy Board of Visitors and the St. Mary's College Board of Trustees. He and his wife, the late Judith Pickett Hoyer, have three daughters, Susan, Stefany, and Anne; and five grandchildren, Judy, James Cleveland, Lauren, Matthew, and Alexa.

Huckabee, Mike
Governor for Arkansas (R)
Contributions: *The Society (p. 47); The Flag at Half Staff (p. 143); Our States Most Pressing Needs Will Never Be Solved by Government (p. 177)*

Gov. Mike Huckabee of Arkansas is recognized as a national leader in the area of education reform. Huckabee is the chairman-elect of the Education Commission of the States, a highly respected education policy organization. He will lead the ECS from July 2004 until July 2006, succeeding Virginia Gov. Mark Warner. The ECS helps governors, legislators, state education officials and others identify, develop and implement public policies to improve student learning at all levels. The organization, which is based in Denver, was formed in 1965.

Huckabee became governor in July 1996 when his predecessor resigned. He was one of the youngest governors in the country at the time. Huckabee first was elected lieutenant governor in a 1993 special election and was elected to a full four-year term in 1994. He was only the fourth Republican to be elected to statewide office since Reconstruction. Huckabee was elected to a full four-year term as governor in 1998, attracting the largest percentage of the vote ever received by a Republican gubernatorial nominee in Arkansas, and was re-elected to another four-year term in November 2002.

In addition to his education reform efforts, Huckabee has been a leader in improving health care for Arkansans. He created the

ARKids First program, a nationally recognized initiative that provides health insurance to tens of thousands of children who previously had no access to health insurance. He also led a ballot initiative in 2000 that devoted all of the state's tobacco settlement money to improving the health of Arkansans. He has set a personal example by losing more than 90 pounds and is now planning a new statewide health initiative.

Huckabee, a fiscal conservative, pushed through the Arkansas Legislature the first major, broad-based tax cuts in state history. He led efforts to establish a Property Taxpayers' Bill of Rights and created a welfare reform program that reduced the welfare rolls in the state by almost 50 percent.

The governor is a noted speaker and author. He has given speeches on politics and public policy to groups across the country and around the world. He's a regular guest on national television and radio shows, discussing issues of importance to the states. In the fall of 1997, his book "Character Is The Issue" was released by Broadman & Holman. The book chronicles Huckabee's political career and discusses the importance of character in politics and life. The following year, Broadman & Holman released "Kids Who Kill," a book that addresses the issues of juvenile violence. His third book, "Living Beyond Your Lifetime," was released in 2000. It examines how to establish a legacy that will live on after you're gone.

The governor and his wife, Janet, have three grown children -- John Mark, David, and Sarah. Huckabee enjoys hunting, fishing, reading, and playing bass guitar in his band, Capitol Offense.

Inslee, Jay
  U.S. Representative for Washington's 1st District (D)
  Contribution: *A Foundation of Our Democracy (p. 151)*

Personal –
  • Date of Birth: 02-09-51
  • Married to Trudi Inslee since 08-27-72
  • Father of Joe, Connor, and Jack (married to Megan)
  • Education
      o Willamette University School of Law- Salem, OR.
      o Doctor of Jurisprudence, Magna Cum Laude, 1976

  o University of Washington- Seattle, WA. Bachelor of
    Arts in Economics, 1973.

Keller, Ric
  U.S. Representative for Florida's 8th District (R)
  Contribution: *The Rest of the Story (p. 317)*

    Ric Keller, 38, represents Greater Orlando in the U.S. House of Representatives.

    Congressman Keller sits on the House Education and the Workforce Committee. As the only Floridian in the House or Senate to sit on the committee, Representative Keller is the state's point man on education and the workforce issues in Washington D.C. His top priority, upon election, was to support fully funding Pell Grants, a program that helps kids from poor families go to college.

    He also sits on the House Judiciary Committee where he has played a key role in crafting anti-terrorism legislation. After the events of September 11th, Congressman Keller sponsored "The Keller Amendment", a plan that links airline passenger manifests to the FBI's Terrorist Watch List. Since the Keller Amendment's passage, airlines now do a computer check on everyone who boards a plane to make sure they're not wanted for ties to terrorist organizations.

Kind, Ron
  U.S. Representative for Wisconsin's 3rd District (D)
  Contributions: *The Forgotten War (p. 27); The History of Heroes*
        (p. 41); United Pride (p. 233); Support the Troops
        (p. 261)

    A native of La Crosse, Wisconsin, Ron Kind was first elected to represent the people of Western Wisconsin's 3rd Congressional district in November, 1996. He currently is a member of the House Education and the Workforce Committee, and the Resources Committee. In addition to serving on the full Committees, Kind holds seats on Education's Reform and 21st Century Competitiveness Subcommittees, as well as the Agriculture's General Farm Commodities and Risk Management Subcommittee. Rep. Kind is also the Senior Democrat Member on the Energy and Mineral Resources Subcommittee for the Resources Committee.

Ron Kind was born and raised in Western Wisconsin. He is the third of five children born to Greta and Elroy Kind and the fifth generation to live here. Greta formerly worked as the Assistant Director of Personnel in the La Crosse School District. Elroy had a 35-year career as a telephone repairman and union leader at the La Crosse Telephone Company.

Ron attended public schools in La Crosse and became a standout student-athlete in high school football and basketball. He accepted an academic scholarship to Harvard University, where he graduated with honors in 1985. While attending Harvard, Ron worked during the summer with Senator William Proxmire in Washington. There he helped investigate wasteful abuses of taxpayer money which provided the basis for some of the Senator's famous "Golden Fleece" awards.

Ron went on to receive his Master's Degree from the London School of Economics and his Law Degree from the University of Minnesota. He practiced law for two years at the law firm of Quarles and Brady in Milwaukee.

In September of 1995, Ron announced his intention to run for the Third Congressional District seat being vacated by 16-year incumbent Representative Steve Gunderson. More than a year later, the La Crosse native won a difficult five-person race for the Democratic nomination and went on to defeat Republican nominee Jim Harsdorf 52% to 48%. He was reelected in 1998 and again in 2000.

The Third Congressional District includes sixteen counties along the Mississippi River in Western Wisconsin. It stretches from the Illinois border in the South to the Minneapolis-St. Paul suburbs in the North. The major cities in the district include La Crosse and Eau Claire.

Ron and his wife Tawni continue to live in his hometown of La Crosse. Tawni is an official court reporter for the County Court system. The Kinds have two sons, Johnny, who was born in August, 1996, and Matthew, who was born in May, 1998.

The Kinds have remained active in their community and are members of the Immanuel Lutheran Church. Ron is a member of the La Crosse Optimists Club and a leader in the Boys' and Girls' Club and the La Crosse YMCA. He is also on the Board of Directors for Coulee Council on Alcohol or Other Drug Abuse. Tawni organizes the annual Congressional Art Competition for high school artists in Western Wisconsin.

Kohl, Herb
Senator for Wisconsin (D)
Contribution: *The Call of Duty (p. 225)*

Herb Kohl was elected to the Senate in 1988 and re-elected to a third six-year term in 2000. Kohl was born and raised in Milwaukee, where he attended public school. He earned his Bachelor's degree from the University of Wisconsin-Madison in 1956 and a Master's degree in Business Administration from Harvard University in 1958. Kohl served in the Army Reserve from 1958 to 1964.

Before coming to the Senate, Kohl helped build his family-owned business, Kohl's grocery and department stores. He served as President from 1970 through the sale of the corporation in 1979. In 1985, he bought the Milwaukee Bucks to ensure the basketball team remained in Milwaukee and is recognized as an avid sportsman.

During his time in office, Senator Kohl has been recognized as a strong advocate on children's issues. For instance, Kohl sponsored the "Child Care Infrastructure Act," a new law to encourage private companies and institutions to build on- or near-site day care centers to meet the rapidly growing demand for child care. The bill, which was signed into law on June 7, 2001, has been featured in "Working Mother" and "Parents" magazines. Kohl has also been a strong supporter for child nutrition programs. In 2003, he received the "Distinguished Service Award" from the Food Research and Action Center (FRAC), a leading organization that works to eradicate domestic hunger and undernutrition.

Senator Kohl also has focused on anti-crime legislation, especially crimes related to kids. He reauthorized juvenile justice programs in the federal government and authored laws which prevent the sale of handguns to minors and prohibit handguns from being brought into a school zone. Kohl sponsored the "Child Safety Lock Act," a bill to require the sale of safety locks with handguns to prevent accidental shootings by children.

Senator Kohl remains active in Wisconsin charitable activities. In 1990, he established the Herb Kohl Educational Foundation

Achievement Award Program, which provides annual grants totaling $100,000 to 100 graduating seniors, 100 teachers, and 100 schools throughout Wisconsin. In 1995, Kohl donated $25 million to the University of Wisconsin for a new sports arena.

Leach, James A.
U.S. Representative for Iowa's 2nd District (R)
Contribution: *Honor the Sacrifices (p. 51)*

Personal –

- Born October 15, 1942, in Davenport, Iowa.
- Resides in Iowa City with wife Elisabeth (Deba), son Gallagher, and daughter Jenny
- Education
  - 1966-68 London School of Economics, Research student in Economics and Soviet Politics
  - 1964-66 School of Advanced International Studies, Johns Hopkins University,
  - Master of Arts Degree in Soviet Politics
  - 1960-64 Princeton University, Bachelor of Arts Degree (*cum laude*) in Political Science
- Honorary Degrees
  - Iowa Wesleyan College
  - Marycrest College
  - St. Ambrose University
  - Mt. Mercy College
  - Luther College
  - Coe College
  - Virginia Theological Seminary
  - Moscow Academy of Economics

Lynch, Stephen F.
U.S. Representative for Massachusetts 9th District (D)
Contributions: *Election Day (p. 131); The Citizen-Soldier (p. 221)*

Congressman Stephen F. Lynch has represented the people of the Ninth Congressional District since he was sworn in to the House of Representatives on October 23, 2001. He first took office to finish the term of the late Congressman John Joseph Moakley, who held the seat for nearly 30 years. Congressman Lynch is honored to serve the people of the newly configured district again in the 108th Congress.

Congressman Lynch prides himself on his working class roots. The son of Francis Lynch, a union ironworker and Anne Lynch, a postal clerk with the United States Post Office, he was born and raised in South Boston.

Congressman Lynch graduated from South Boston High School in 1973. He then joined his father as a member of Boston's Ironworkers Local 7. He worked as a structural ironworker for 18 years and was eventually elected to serve as president of Local 7, the youngest president in the history of the 2,000-member union.

Congressman Lynch attended Wentworth Institute on nights and weekends, earning a Bachelor's degree in Construction Management. He later received a law degree from Boston College Law School, was admitted to both the Massachusetts and New Hampshire Bar, and continued his advocacy for working people as a labor and employment attorney.

In 1994, Congressman Lynch was first sworn in to the Massachusetts House of Representatives. After just fourteen months in office, he took office in the First Suffolk seat in the Massachusetts State Senate. In the Senate, he served as the Chair of the Committee on Commerce and Labor.

In 1999, he earned a Master's Degree in Public Administration from Harvard University's John F. Kennedy School of Government.

He continues to live in his lifelong hometown of South Boston with his wife Margaret and their four-year old daughter, Victoria.

McConnell, Mitch
Senator for Kentucky (R)
Contribution: *The Screaming Eagles (p. 273)*

On November 12, 2002, Senator Mitch McConnell was unanimously elected Majority Whip by his Republican colleagues. As Majority Whip, McConnell is the second ranking Republican in the United States Senate. He first served in leadership as chairman of the National Republican Senatorial Committee during the 1998 and 2000 election cycles. In both, Republicans maintained control of the Senate.

Senator McConnell was first elected to the Senate in 1984. That year, he was the only Republican challenger in the country to defeat a Democrat incumbent, and the first Republican to win a statewide race since 1968. Senator McConnell's landslide victory in 2002, is also one for the record books. On November 5, he won a fourth term with 65 percent of the vote – the largest margin of victory for a Republican in Kentucky history. The previous record was held by the legendary Senator John Sherman Cooper.

Born on February 20, 1942, and raised in South Louisville, McConnell graduated in 1964 with honors from the University of Louisville College of Arts and Sciences, where he served as student body president. In 1967, he graduated from the University of Kentucky College of Law where he was elected President of the Student Bar Association. McConnell gained experience on Capitol Hill working as an intern for Senator John Sherman Cooper, later as chief legislative assistant to Senator Marlow Cook, and then as Deputy Assistant Attorney General under President Gerald R. Ford. Before being elected to the U.S. Senate, McConnell served as County Judge-Executive in Jefferson County, Kentucky, from 1978 until he was sworn in to the United States Senate on January 3, 1985.

Senator McConnell is married to United States Secretary of Labor, Elaine L. Chao. Previously, Secretary Chao served as president of the United Way of America and director of the Peace Corps. He is the father of three daughters: Elly, Claire, and Porter.

Murtha, John
U.S. Representative for Pennsylvania's 12th District (D)
Contribution: *Flight 93 (p. 119)*

U.S. Rep. John P. Murtha is recognized as a bipartisan leader in Congress and an advisor to presidents from both parties because of his direct knowledge of our military and global geopolitics, and he has been visionary in focusing on non-traditional threats such as terrorism.

Born June 17, 1932, John "Jack" Patrick Murtha grew up in Westmoreland County, Pennsylvania. He joined the Marine Corps in June 1952, earning the American Spirit Honor Medal, awarded to fewer than one in 10,000 recruits. Jack rose through the ranks to become a drill instructor at Parris Island and was selected for Officer

Candidate School at Quantico, Virginia. He then was assigned to the Second Marine Division, Camp Lejeune, North Carolina, where he met and married the former Joyce Bell of nearby Richlands. In 1959, Captain Murtha took command of the 34th Special Infantry Company, Marine Corps Reserves, in Johnstown, Pennsylvania, where he ran a small business, started a family, and attended the University of Pittsburgh on the GI Bill. He graduated from Pitt with a degree in Economics and did graduate work in economics and political science at Indiana University of Pennsylvania. He volunteered in 1966-67 with the Marine Corps in Vietnam, where he was twice wounded and received the Bronze Star with Combat "V", two Purple Hearts, and the Vietnamese Cross of Gallantry. He was elected to the Pennsylvania House in 1969 and in 1974 became the first Vietnam combat Veteran elected to Congress. Jack and his wife Joyce reside in Johnstown, where they raised their three children. They have three grandchildren.

As ranking Member of the Defense Appropriations Subcommittee, Jack works hard to make sure America's men and women in uniform have every advantage possible when put in harm's way, including protective equipment and weapon systems that are both reliable and state-of-the-art. He's fought to improve computer security and our ability to respond to biological or chemical weapons. Knowing that quality personnel are our military's backbone, he's aggressively advocated better pay, pensions, health-care and quality-of-life amenities as the keys to keeping well-trained people in the service and keeping morale high.

He is known for his hands-on approach, visiting personnel on bases and during deployments to hear directly about equipment, training, conditions, accommodations, and the services available to them and their families. Visiting the troops in Iraq during Operation Iraqi Freedom in the summer of 2003, he uncovered dangerous equipment shortages that became a focus of debate over a supplemental funding bill for Iraq and Afghanistan. Because of Jack's quick action and his stature as one of the nation's foremost experts on defense, Congress added money for potentially life-saving protective body armor, critical spare parts, armored vehicles, and other equipment.

This first-hand knowledge makes him an important advisor to presidents of both parties and one of the most effective advocates for our national defense in all of Washington and the nation. He's a budget hawk, pushing to reduce costs through electronic commerce; looking at full life-cycle costs such as the environmental costs of decommissioning; promoting technologies that reduce travel costs, such as telemedicine for forward-deployed and shipboard personnel and distance learning for training; and using more reliable off-the-shelf software instead of customizing software for each weapon system.

Jack is proud to have received the Navy Distinguished Service Medal from the Marine Corps Commandant when he retired from the Marine Corps Reserves in 1990 for his 37 years of distinguished service to his country.

Myrick, Sue
U.S. Representative for North Carolina's 9th District (R)
Contributions: *The Heroes That Were Found (p. 203)*

Sue Myrick first came to Congress in 1995 and is currently in her fifth term. During that time she has risen in seniority and leadership in the House of Representatives.

A breast cancer survivor, Sue currently serves as the Co-Chair of the House Cancer Caucus and has successfully introduced and helped pass several pieces of legislation aimed at stopping this deadly disease.

Sue continues to serve on the Speakers' Drug Task Force and was personally selected to be a member of President Bush's Working Group on Iraq.

A small businesswoman herself, Sue is the former President and CEO of Myrick Advertising and Public Relations and Myrick Enterprises. She served on the Charlotte City Council and was a two-term mayor of the City of Charlotte. Sue remains the first and only female mayor in Charlotte history.

As Mayor, Sue hit the streets, going nose-to-nose with drug dealers, telling them to get the heck out of the neighborhoods.

Sue also has extensive experience in disaster relief and recovery from tornadoes, floods, and hurricanes. She knows local communities can't always depend on the federal government to help solve their emergencies. Many times, they are on their own. She also understands the role that FEMA, the Red Cross, Salvation Army and organizations like the Mennonite Disaster Service play in emergency situations, having worked extensively on site in coordination with them.

Sue is a wife and a mother of two children and three step-children. She and her husband, Ed, have 11 grandchildren and 4 great grandchildren.

Nelson, Bill
Senator for Florida (D)
Contribution: *The Risk of Life (p. 89)*

As a child growing up in Florida, Bill Nelson never imagined that one day he would both catapult into space from a NASA launch site just miles from his grandfather's homestead and go on to serve the people of Florida in the U.S. Senate. As a fifth-generation Floridian, Nelson has spent thirty years proudly serving the people of his home state as a state legislator, congressman, state treasurer, and insurance commissioner - and now as a U.S. Senator.

One of his most unforgettable experiences occurred back in 1986, when he spent six days on a NASA shuttle orbiting Earth. During his flight training and time in space, Nelson's eyes were opened not only to the importance of our nation's space program, but also to the beauty and fragility of planet Earth. Since this experience, Nelson has worked in the Senate to protect the environment by preventing oil drilling off US coastlines and restoring the Everglades, and he has been an outspoken advocate for space exploration. Nelson believes the future success of the space program depends on continued congressional support, fiscal responsibility, and the development of a long-range vision at NASA.

In Washington, he has championed issues important to Floridians. As a member of the Armed Services Committee, Nelson has kept alive the search for Navy Captain Michael Scott Speicher, a Florida native who went missing in Iraq twelve years ago during the Gulf War. On the Commerce Committee, Nelson addressed the growing annoyance of unsolicited electronic mail. He sponsored landmark legislation that would stop marketers from filling up citizens' e-mail accounts with unwanted and deceptive advertisements.

Bill Nelson has translated his mission in space and his roots in Florida into a seasoned career as an untiring public servant. Today as a U.S. Senator, Nelson is as dedicated as ever to the people of Florida and the issues they care about.

Platts, Tom
U.S. Representative for Pennsylvania's 19th District (R)
Contribution: *United We Stand (p. 187)*

Todd Platts is a Member of the United States Congress, representing the 19th District of Pennsylvania. Sworn in as a member of the House of Representatives in January 2001, Congressman Platts serves the residents of Adams, Cumberland, and York Counties.

In addition to his standing committee assignments, Congressman Platts serves on a special committee. In his freshman term, Congressman Platts was elected by his peers as their class representative on the Republican Policy Committee, and continues in that role after being unanimously re-elected by his peers for that post, again, in his second term.

A lifelong resident of York, Pennsylvania, Congressman Platts is a member of York Suburban High School's graduating class of 1980. He continued his education locally, graduating Summa Cum Laude, with a Bachelor of Science degree in Public Administration from Shippensburg University of Pennsylvania, in 1984. He then attended Pepperdine University School of Law and graduated Cum Laude with a Juris Doctorate degree in 1991.

Congressman Platts started his career as an attorney and an associate with the law firm of Barley, Snyder, Senft, & Cohen. He left the firm to begin his career in public service in 1993 when he was elected to serve the people of York County as a State Representative in the Pennsylvania General Assembly. He was re-elected to his post three times, serving in that role until his 2000 election to the United States Congress.

Congressman Platts is a devoted husband to wife Leslie, and a proud father to their seven-year-old son, T.J., and four-year-old daughter, Kelsey.

Pryor, Mark
Senator for Arkansas (D)
Contributions: *3,000 Innocent Americans Did Not Die in Vain (p. 199); The Ultimate Sacrifice (p. 237);*

On January 7, 2003, Mark Lunsford Pryor was sworn in as Arkansas' 33rd senator. As a candidate, he pledged to be a strong voice for the people of Arkansas who would always put their interests first. As a Senator, he works every day to fulfill that promise.

Five generations of public service have made the Pryor name synonymous with Arkansas politics. Susie Newton Pryor, Mark's grandmother, was the state's first woman to seek public office after being granted the right to vote. His father, David Pryor, served his country with distinction for 18 years as U.S. Senator for Arkansas.

Pryor was first elected to public office in 1990 as a member of the Arkansas State House of Representatives. In 1998 he was elected Arkansas' Attorney General, making him the youngest chief law-enforcement officer in the nation.

Pryor proved early on in his career that people matter more to him than politics. He worked with and listened to all interests to help make Arkansas a better place to live, work, and raise a family. Pryor worked with Democrats and Republicans to toughen laws against drunk drivers, enact legislation to protect children on the Internet and put in place the Morgan Nick Alert System, which helps to locate missing and exploited children.

Pryor was born in Fayetteville, on January 10, 1963, and grew up in both Arkansas and Washington, D.C. He received a B.A. in History and law degree at the University of Arkansas and worked in private practice at Wright, Lindsey & Jennings, in Little Rock, for eight years. He and his wife Jill have a son and a daughter, Adams and Porter.

Reagan, Ronald
President of the United States of America (R)
(Did not contribute specifically to this book*)
Pieces Used: *Darkest of Hours (p. 63); Slipped the Surly Bonds of Earth (p. 85);*

At the end of his two terms in office, Ronald Reagan viewed with satisfaction the achievements of his innovative program known as the Reagan Revolution, which aimed to reinvigorate the American people and reduce their reliance upon Government. He felt he had fulfilled his campaign pledge of 1980 to restore "the great, confident roar of American progress and growth and optimism."

On February 6, 1911, Ronald Wilson Reagan was born to Nelle and John Reagan in Tampico, Illinois. He attended high school in nearby Dixon and then worked his way through Eureka College. There, he studied economics and sociology, played on the football team, and acted in school plays. Upon graduation, he became a radio sports announcer. A screen test in 1937 won him a contract in Hollywood. During the next two decades he appeared in 53 films.

From his first marriage to actress Jane Wyman, he had two children, Maureen and Michael. Maureen passed away in 2001. In 1952 he married Nancy Davis, who was also an actress, and they had two children, Patricia Ann and Ronald Prescott.

As president of the Screen Actors Guild, Reagan became embroiled in disputes over the issue of Communism in the film industry; his political views shifted from liberal to conservative. He toured the country as a television host, becoming a spokesman for conservatism. In 1966 he was elected Governor of California by a margin of a million votes; he was re-elected in 1970.

Ronald Reagan won the Republican Presidential nomination in 1980 and chose as his running mate former Texas Congressman and United Nations Ambassador George Bush. Voters troubled by inflation and by the year-long confinement of Americans in Iran swept the Republican ticket into office. Reagan won 489 electoral votes to 49 for President Jimmy Carter.

On January 20, 1981, Reagan took office. Only 69 days later he was shot by a would-be assassin but quickly recovered and returned to duty. His grace and wit during the dangerous incident caused his popularity to soar.

Dealing skillfully with Congress, Reagan obtained legislation to stimulate economic growth, curb inflation, increase employment, and strengthen national defense. He embarked upon a course of cutting taxes and Government expenditures, refusing to deviate from it when the strengthening of defense forces led to a large deficit.

A renewal of national self-confidence by 1984 helped Reagan and Bush win a second term with an unprecedented number of electoral votes. Their victory turned away Democratic challengers Walter F. Mondale and Geraldine Ferraro.

In 1986 Reagan obtained an overhaul of the income tax code, which eliminated many deductions and exempted millions of people with low incomes. At the end of his administration, the Nation was enjoying its longest recorded period of peacetime prosperity without recession or depression.

In foreign policy, Reagan sought to achieve "peace through strength." During his two terms he increased defense spending 35 percent, but sought to improve relations with the Soviet Union. In dramatic meetings with Soviet leader Mikhail Gorbachev, he negotiated a treaty that would eliminate intermediate-range nuclear missiles. Reagan declared war against international terrorism, sending American bombers against Libya after evidence came out that Libya was involved in an attack on American soldiers in a West Berlin nightclub.

By ordering naval escorts in the Persian Gulf, he maintained the free flow of oil during the Iran-Iraq war. In keeping with the Reagan Doctrine, he gave support to anti-Communist insurgencies in Central America, Asia, and Africa.

Overall, the Reagan years saw a restoration of prosperity, and the goal of peace through strength seemed to be within grasp.

Rounds, Mike
Governor for South Dakota (R)
Contribution: *Freedom Isn't Free (p. 207)*

M. Michael "Mike" Rounds was sworn in as South Dakota's 31st governor on January 7, 2003. Gov. Rounds is committed to working with South Dakotans to make this state a better place to live, work, and raise a family.

Mike Rounds was born in Huron, SD, in 1954, and he is a lifelong resident of Pierre. Gov. Rounds attended South Dakota State University (SDSU) in Brookings, where he earned his B.S. in Political Science and met Jean Vedvei of Lake Preston. They were married in 1978, and have four children: Chris, Brian, Carrie, and John.

Governor Rounds is a Republican, an owner, with his shares in trust, of Fischer, Rounds & Associates Inc., an insurance and real estate agency with offices in Pierre, Mitchell, and Rapid City. His past civic leadership includes serving as Board President of the Oahe YMCA, Vice President of the Home and School Association of St. Joseph School, President of the Pierre-Ft. Pierre Exchange Club, and Exalted Ruler of the Pierre Elks Lodge. Mike is also a member of St. Peter and Paul Catholic Church of Pierre, the Knights of Columbus, and Ducks Unlimited.

The Governor is a licensed pilot with multi-engine and instrument ratings. He also enjoys spending time with his family, hunting, playing racquetball, camping, and boating.

Rowland, John G.
Governor of Connecticut (R)
Contribution: *Tuesday Morning (p. 123)*

John G. Rowland was born in Waterbury, Connecticut. He received a Bachelor's degree from Villanova University in 1979.

His public service career includes two terms in the Connecticut State Legislature, from 1981 to 1985, and three terms in the U.S. House of Representatives, from 1985 to 1991. While in Congress, he served on the Armed Services, Intelligence, and Veterans' Affairs Committees. He was elected Governor in November 1994, becoming the youngest person ever elected to this office in Connecticut. He was elected in 1998 to a second term and again in 2002 for a historic third term.

At the end of this term, he will be the longest-serving Governor since colonial times. Rowland has made responsible budgeting, economic growth, and improving the quality of life for Connecticut families his highest priorities. Business taxes and income tax rates have been cut year after year, and the welfare rolls are the lowest in almost a decade.

He is rebuilding the state's education system from the ground up with major capital investments in public schools and universities. He also has made a landmark commitment to preserve Connecticut's natural resources, from acquiring 455,000 additional acres of open space to the aggressive cleanup of Long Island Sound.

Rowland serves on several committees as an advisor to the Bush Administration, including the Advisory Committee for Trade Policy & Negotiations and the State and Local Senior Advisory Committee of the National Homeland Security Advisory Council. In the last decade, he has served as the chairman of the New England Governors' Conference three times. He currently serves on the National Governors Association Executive Committee.

Rowland and his wife, Patty, have five children between them - Kirsten, Ryan, Robert John, Scott, and Julianne.

Sensenbrenner, Jr., F. James
U.S. Representative for Wisconsin's 5th District (R)
Contribution: *A Change in Priorities (p. 189)*

F. James Sensenbrenner, Jr., (Jim), is a Republican Member of Congress, representing the Fifth Congressional District of Wisconsin. He won his race to become a Member of Congress in November of 1978, after serving ten years in the Wisconsin State Legislature. Congressman Sensenbrenner assumed the chairmanship of the House Committee on the Judiciary beginning in the 107th Congress. He has established a strong record on crime, constitutional, and intellectual property issues as a long-serving member of the Judiciary Committee. Previously, Congressman Sensenbrenner also served as Chairman of the House Committee on Science, where he solidified his reputation as an independent leader on science issues, as well as oversight.

Throughout his public life, Congressman Sensenbrenner has been at the forefront of efforts to eliminate wasteful government spending and protect the interests of American taxpayers. He has regularly been cited by the National Taxpayers Union as one of the most fiscally responsible House Members.

Sessions, Pete
U.S. Representative for Texas' 32 District (R)
Contribution: *Victory or Death (p. 31)*

A conservative community leader, United States Congressman Pete Sessions has combined hard work, innovative thinking, free-market solutions, and common sense principles and values to build a successful family, business, and congressional career.

Congressman Sessions was born on March 22, 1955, and grew up in Waco, Texas. He graduated from Southwestern University in 1978, and married Juanita Diaz in 1984. They have two sons, Bill (age 14) and Alex (age 10), and they make their home in East Dallas.

Congressman Sessions joined Southwestern Bell Telephone Company after graduating from Southwestern University. Over the next 16 years, he served at the internationally renowned Bell Labs in New Jersey and as District Manager for Marketing in Dallas. Thanks to this private sector experience, Congressman Sessions understands the need to fight bureaucracy and to utilize market-driven solutions to effectively solve problems in our communities and in government.

In 1993, Congressman Sessions retired from the private sector to seek public office. He ran unsuccessfully against Rep. John Bryant (D-TX) in 1994. He then served from 1994 to 1995 as Vice President for Public Policy at the National Center for Policy Analysis (NCPA), a Dallas-based conservative public policy research institute.

In 1996, the people of Dallas and the Fifth Congressional District sent Congressman Sessions to Washington, DC, to represent them in the United States House of Representatives. In 2002, the people of the new Thirty-second Congressional District called him back for his fourth term.

Congressman Sessions is a stalwart defender of U.S. homeland and national security interests, as well as the men and women who defend them. As the parent of a child with Down Syndrome, he is a passionate advocate for people with disabilities. Congressman Sessions also believes that taxpayers deserve to get results from government, and has pursued common-sense, market-based reforms to help government operate more efficiently.

Congressman Sessions is an Eagle Scout and a former Scout Master for 13 Eagle Scouts. He is a member of the Executive Board of the Circle Ten Council of the Boy Scouts of America. In 1999, Congressman Sessions was honored as a recipient of the National Distinguished Eagle Scout Award for service to his community as a Representative in Congress and for his commitment to furthering the role of the Boy Scouts of America in the lives of young men in the Dallas Community.

Congressman Sessions is also a member of the United Methodist Church. He is active in his community, where he is currently an honorary East Dallas Rotarian, a member of the YMCA at White Rock, and an Adopt-A-Shoreline Team Leader volunteer in the effort to maintain and conserve White Rock Lake in Dallas. As a businessman, he served as Chairman of the Northeast Dallas Chamber of Commerce.

Shelton, Henry H.
Chairman of the Joint Chief of Staff
(Did not contribute specifically to this book*)
Piece Used: *This Call to Duty (p. 111)*

U.S. Army General Henry H. Shelton was born in Tarboro, N.C., and commissioned as a second lieutenant and awarded a Bachelor of Science degree from North Carolina State University. His civilian education includes a Master's of Science from Auburn University and completion of the National and International Security Program at Harvard University. His military education includes the Infantry Officer basic and advanced courses, the Air Command and Staff College, and the National War College.

Prior to assuming his position in February 1996, Shelton served as commanding general of the XVIII Airborne Corps, Fort Bragg, N.C. Other past assignments include commander, 82nd Airborne Division, Fort Bragg; assistant division commander for operations, 101st Airborne Division (Air Assault), Fort Campbell, Ky.; and commander, Company C, 4th Battalion, 503rd Infantry, 173rd Airborne Brigade, in the Republic of Vietnam.

Shelton has also commanded the 3rd Battalion, 60th Infantry, 9th Infantry Division, Fort Lewis, Wash.; and the 1st Brigade, 82nd Airborne Division, Fort Bragg. He has served as the Joint Staff deputy for operations, J-3, Washington; chief of staff, 10th Mountain Division (Light), Fort Drum, N.Y.; division G-3, 9th Infantry Division, Fort Lewis; and brigade adjutant and operations officer, deputy division adjutant and infantry battalion executive officer while assigned to the 25th Infantry Division, Fort Shafter, Hawaii.

Shelton completed a second tour in the South Vietnam as a member of Detachment B-52 (Project Delta) and commander of

368 – Modern Day Heroes®: In Defense of America

Detachment A-104, 5th Special Forces Group. He also deployed to Saudi Arabia for Desert Shield and Desert Storm. He was joint task force commander during Operation Uphold Democracy in Haiti.

Shelton's awards and decorations include the Defense Distinguished Service Medal with oak leaf cluster, Distinguished Service Medal, Legion of Merit with oak leaf cluster, Bronze Star Medal with valor device and three oak leaf clusters, and the Purple Heart. He also has been awarded the Combat Infantryman Badge, the Joint Chiefs of Staff Identification Badge, Master Parachutist Badge, Pathfinder Badge, Air Assault Badge, Military Freefall Badge, and the Special Forces and Ranger tabs.

Shelton and his wife, Carolyn, have three sons.

Sherman, Brad
> **U.S. Representative for California's 27th District (D)**
> Contributions: *Terrorist Attacks (p. 127); We Must Wage a War (p. 147)*

Education:	Harvard Law School, J.D., Magna Cum Laude UCLA, B.A., Summa Cum Laude
Instructor:	Harvard Law School International Tax Program
Licenses:	Certified Public Accountant (*CPA*) California Attorney, California State Bar
	Certified by California State Bar as a *Tax Law Specialist*

Participated as a staff member of a big-four CPA firm in the financial audits of large businesses and governmental entities; provided tax law counsel on multi-million dollar transactions; provided tax and investment advice to entrepreneurs and small businesses; helped represent the Government of the Philippines under President Aquino in a successful effort to seize assets of deposed President Marcos. Instructor, Harvard Law School International Tax Program. Member of the Board of California Common Cause, 1985-1989.

Shimkus, John M.
> **U.S. Representative for Illinois' 19th District (R)**
> Contribution: *You Must be a Veteran (p. 55)*

John M. Shimkus (shim' cuss) was born February 21, 1958. John married Karen Muth in 1987. They have three children - David (ten years), Joshua (eight years), and Daniel (four years). The Shimkus family resides in Collinsville, Illinois.

Karen is a classically trained musician who teaches music at Holy Cross Lutheran School in Collinsville.

John received a Bachelor of Science degree in General Engineering from the United States Military Academy in 1980. He received his teaching certificate from Christ College, Irvine, California, in 1989. John is also a 1997 graduate of Southern Illinois University at Edwardsville with a Master's degree in Business Administration (MBA).

John was appointed to the United States Military Academy at West Point, New York, in 1976, by the late Congressman Mel Price (D). After graduation, he trained as an Army Ranger and paratrooper. John served as an infantry officer in the former West Germany and in the United States. He is currently a lieutenant colonel in the United States Army Reserves.

Tauscher, Ellen
   U.S. Representative for California's 10th District (D)
   Contribution: *America's Character Will Prevail (p. 175)*

Congresswoman Ellen Tauscher is currently serving her fourth term representing California's 10th Congressional district, which includes San Francisco's suburbs in Contra Costa, Alameda and Solano Counties. She is a leader on defense, homeland security, high-tech, transportation, and Veterans' issues and is one of Congress' leading experts on nuclear nonproliferation. Rep. Tauscher serves as National Vice Chair of the Democratic Leadership Council, an organization that is widely regarded as the intellectual center of the Democratic Party. As a New Democrat and Blue Dog, her fiscally responsible, bipartisan, independent brand of leadership was coined "Tauscherism" by Time magazine.

Before coming to Capitol Hill, Rep. Tauscher worked in the private sector for 20 years, 14 of which were on Wall Street. At age 25, she became one of the first women to hold a seat on the New York Stock Exchange. She later served as an officer of the American Stock Exchange.

Tenet, George J.
    Director of the Central Intelligence Agency
    (Did not contribute specifically to this book*)
    Pieces Used: *To Run to Ground a Vicious Foe (p. 133); The Pain of Injury (p. 149);An Unpayable Debt of Honor and Gratitude – The First Casualty of the War on Terror (p. 173); Wei-Ji (Translated: Danger & Opportunity) (p. 309)*

George John Tenet was sworn in as Director of Central Intelligence on 11 July 1997, following a unanimous vote by both the Senate Select Committee on Intelligence and the full Senate. In this position, he heads the Intelligence Community (all foreign intelligence agencies of the United States) and directs the Central Intelligence Agency.

Mr. Tenet served as the Deputy Director of Central Intelligence, having been confirmed in that position in July 1995. Following the departure of John Deutch in December 1996, he served as Acting Director.

Mr. Tenet previously served as Special Assistant to the President and Senior Director for Intelligence Programs at the National Security Council. While at the NSC, he coordinated Presidential Decision Directives on "Intelligence Priorities," "Security Policy Coordination," "US Counterintelligence Effectiveness," and "US Policy on Remote Sensing Space Capabilities." He also was responsible for coordinating all interagency activities concerning covert action.

Prior to serving at the National Security Council, he served on President Clinton's national security transition team. In this capacity, he coordinated the evaluation of the US Intelligence Community. Mr. Tenet also served as Staff Director of the Senate Select Committee on Intelligence for over four years under the chairmanship of Senator David Boren. In this capacity, he was responsible for coordinating all of the Committee's oversight and legislative activities, including the strengthening of covert action reporting requirements, the creation of a statutory Inspector General at CIA, and the introduction of comprehensive legislation to reorganize US intelligence.

Prior to his appointment as Staff Director, Mr. Tenet directed the Committee's oversight of all arms control negotiations between the Soviet Union and the United States, culminating in the preparation of a report to the US Senate on ``The Ability of US Intelligence to Monitor the Intermediate Nuclear Force Treaty.'' Mr. Tenet came to the Committee in August of 1985, as designee to the Vice Chairman, Senator Patrick Leahy, after working three years on the staff of Senator John Heinz, as both a legislative assistant covering national security and energy issues and as legislative director.

Mr. Tenet holds a B.S.F.S. from the Georgetown University School of Foreign Service and an M.I.A. from the School of International Affairs at Columbia University.
He is a native of New York and is married to A. Stephanie Glakas-Tenet. They have one son, John Michael.

Udall, Tom
U.S. Representative for New Mexico's 3rd District (D)
Contribution: *Every Generation of Americans Must Prove Itself*
    (p. 205)

In November 2002, Tom S. Udall was re-elected to a third term to continue to represent the people of the Third Congressional District of New Mexico. With his re-election, he became the first New Mexico congressional candidate in over two decades to run for office unopposed.

In the House, Tom Udall has earned a reputation as a thoughtful, principled, and effective legislator. He is known for reaching across party lines to find common ground, for speaking his conscience, for being an independent leader, and for getting things done for his constituents and his nation.

Probably nothing better characterizes Tom Udall's priorities than his dozens of annual town hall meetings, when he travels across his home state of New Mexico, to help him understand the diverse needs and opinions of his constituency – in a district bigger than the land mass of Pennsylvania.

The visits, he says, remind him where he came from, and why he is in Washington -- to put the priorities of New Mexico first. As a respected and accomplished leader in the nation's capital, Udall continues to put New Mexico values on the national agenda.

As part of his commitment to serving those that he represents, Tom Udall has opened six offices in New Mexico – Clovis, Farmington, Gallup, Las Vegas, Rio Rancho, and Santa Fe – to better help local communities. His staff also travels to the most remote areas of New Mexico on a frequent basis to bring the federal government to the citizens of New Mexico. Renowned for helping literally thousands of constituents and organizations cut through red tape, Tom Udall is devoted to constituent service.

In 1990, Tom Udall was elected New Mexico's Attorney General. He made an immediate and powerful impact with his tough stands on domestic violence, drunken driving, political corruption, campaign finance reform, and abuses by special interest groups. He attacked deceptive trade practices and blocked public utility rate increases. Tom fought for better education for New Mexico's children and effective protection for consumers, especially seniors.

In 1994, every daily newspaper in New Mexico endorsed Tom Udall. He was easily re-elected in a landslide victory, receiving more votes than any other candidate - either Republican or Democrat - in a contested race. He was the first New Mexico Attorney General elected to two consecutive four-year terms. During his tenure, he was elected President of the National Association of Attorneys General (NAAG).

Tom Udall comes from a family distinguished for its devotion to public service. His family pioneered the southwest in the 1800's. His roots in New Mexico run deep, with his grandmother having been born in what is now Luna, New Mexico, in 1893. His father, Stewart Udall, was elected four times to Congress before being appointed Secretary of the Interior by Presidents Kennedy and Johnson. Tom's Uncle Morris ("Mo") Udall, not only served in Congress for 30 years, but also was a major presidential contender in 1976. Representative Mark Udall (D-CO) and Senator Gordon Smith (R-OR) are Tom's cousins and current Members of Congress.

Tom Udall graduated from Prescott College in 1970. In 1975 he graduated from Cambridge University in England with a Bachelor of Law degree. That fall, he enrolled in the University of New Mexico Law School and graduated with a Juris Doctor in 1977. After graduating, Tom Udall was Law Clerk to Chief Justice Oliver Seth of the U.S. Tenth Circuit Court of Appeals. Following his clerkship, Tom's legal career included appointment as Assistant US Attorney in the criminal division; appointment as Chief Counsel to the Department of Health and Environment; and partnership in the Miller Law Firm, which has offices in Albuquerque, Santa Fe, Las Cruces, and Farmington. Tom is married to Jill Z. Cooper, and they have a daughter, Amanda. Tom and Jill live in Santa Fe. Amanda and her husband, James Noel, live in Corrales.

Vilsack, Tom
Governor for Iowa (D)
Contribution: *Real Heroes (p. 195)*

Thomas J. Vilsack was born in Pittsburgh, Pennsylvania, orphaned at birth, and adopted in 1951. He received a bachelor's degree from Hamilton College in Clinton, New York in 1972, and received a law degree from Albany Law School in 1975. Vilsack was elected mayor of Mt. Pleasant, Iowa in 1987, and was elected to the Iowa Senate in 1992. In 1998 he became Iowa's first Democratic governor in more than 30 years, and was re-elected to a second term in 2002.

Governor Vilsack has maintained Iowa's national reputation for sound fiscal management. He has worked to make Iowa a national leader in children's health care coverage, with 94% of all Iowa children having health insurance. He has helped continue Iowa's tradition of excellence in education by reducing class sizes in the early grades of elementary school for three years in a row. As a result, Iowa's fourth-graders have placed among the best in the nation in math and science progress, and reversed a ten-year decline in reading test scores. Governor Vilsack has worked to make Iowa a national leader in life sciences and value-added agriculture, boosting Iowa's economy with $265 million in value-added agricultural investment, doubling the number of ethanol plants, and supporting biotech research.

Governor Vilsack is now leading Iowa on an ambitious agenda to transform the economy. On June 19, 2003, he signed the law to establish the Iowa Values Fund, a $503 million public/private partnership with the goal of creating 50,000 high-paying high-skill jobs over the next four years.

Governor Vilsack is the incoming Chair of the Democratic Governors' Association and a member of the National Governors'

Association Executive Committee. He is a founding member and former chair of the Governors Biotechnology Partnership, and the incoming Chair of the national Jobs for America's Graduates (JAG) program, the former Chair of the Ethanol Coalition, and the Chair of the Midwest Governor's Conference. He and his wife Christie have two sons.

Wamp, Zach
U.S. Representative for Tennessee's 3rd District (R)
Contribution: *In God We Trust (p. 141)*

Now in his tenth year as a Member of the U.S. House of Representatives, 3rd District Congressman Zach Wamp serves with seniority as Tennessee's only member of the powerful Appropriations Committee.

The 46-year-old Chattanoogan was named to the important Homeland Security Subcommittee, which funds the 22 agencies now combined into the new Department of Homeland Security (DHS), under the leadership of Secretary Tom Ridge.

Congressman Wamp wrote and passed legislation to create the Moccasin Bend National Archeological District in the National Park System, to change the federal campaign finance laws increasing individual contribution limits for the first time in a generation, and to replace the Chickamauga Lock on the Tennessee River, a bill that was signed into law by President Bush in February of 2003.

Zach is well known as one of the most effective communicators in Congress. For three years, he was a regular panelist on "The News Hour with Jim Lehrer" and has appeared on NBC's "Meet the Press," ABC's "Nightline", and MSNBC's "Hardball with Chris Mathews." He has been featured in *Newsweek, U.S. News and World Report, The Wall Street Journal,* the *Washington Times,* and *The New York Times.*

In 2000, he served as president of the Bipartisan House Prayer Group and as the chairman of the National Prayer Breakfast on Feb. 1, 2001. Zach hosted the event and introduced President George W. Bush to the 4000 in attendance and to millions of television viewers around the world.

A Chattanooga native, Zach spent 12 years as a small businessman and commercial real estate broker before coming to

Congress. He and his wife, Kim, have a son, Weston, and a daughter, Coty. They are active in the YMCA, Students Taking a Right Stand (STARS), Bethel Bible Village, and the Red Bank Baptist Church, where Zach teaches a Young Adult Sunday School Class.

Warner, Monty
U.S. Army Colonel (Ret.)
Contribution: Afterword (p. 321)

Monty Warner is a native of Charleston, West Virginia where he now lives with his wife, Janie. They have two sons and one daughter.

He is an Elder in Bream Presbyterian Church of Charleston, West Virginia, where he also teaches Sunday School.

Monty is currently the President of the Square at Falling Run, a planned town center in Morgantown, WV which combines the best in housing, office, shopping, dining and entertainment. The town center will create 2,200 permanent and temporary jobs and generate $239 million in tax revenue in the first 30 years.

He has been the beneficiary of the finest leadership instruction available in the world --- the U.S. Military. For 29 years the U.S. Army shaped Monty.

Uncle Sam sent him to West Point, commissioned him, and eventually promoted him to the rank of Colonel. The nation allowed Monty to command over a thousand combat-arms soldiers in four different units.

Monty also served in the Pentagon for four years where he watched over and shepherded $12 billion in budget resources.

He also served the American People around the world and has witnessed ideas and policies that have succeeded wildly and failed dismally.

It is this lifetime of experience and knowledge that Monty is using as he transitions from a distinguished military career to one of politics as he is currently [2004] running for Governor of West Virginia.

Wise, Bob
Governor for West Virginia (D)
Contribution: *Intrepid Explorers (p. 99)*

By targeting health care, education and economic development, Bob Wise is making a difference in West Virginia.

Governor Wise championed legislation to ensure the accessibility, affordability, and stability of the health care system in West Virginia. He signed a medical liability reform bill to make West Virginia a state that has economic incentives for doctors to stay, start practices, and raise families.

He also fought to raise the tobacco tax on cigarettes to 55 cents a pack to preserve funding for the state's Medicaid program and deter its young people from smoking. He enrolled thousands of children in CHIP, signed a strong Patient's Bill of Rights and led discussions with other states to work together for lower prescription drug prices.

In 2001, Governor Wise fought for and signed legislation to fund, for the first time, the PROMISE Scholarship Program. This has helped nearly 4,000 West Virginia students stay in the Mountain State to attend college.

He has continued to promote quality education by establishing a character education curriculum in all state schools; creating the Governor's Helpline for Safer Schools to ensure our kids feel safe and secure; and twice introducing legislation for a sales tax holiday weekend, allowing parents to purchase school clothing and school supplies without paying a tax on them.

In the last legislative session, Governor Wise led the effort to rewrite the 20th century tax incentives. These new incentives lower the threshold for tax credits, expand the investment tax credit, and include a new research and development tax credit that leads the nation.

Currently he serves as chair of the Southern States Energy Board, the National Governors Association Natural Resources Committee, and the Council on the New Economy Southern Growth Policies Board.

* = Pieces were used from the public record.

The Modern Day Hero® Award

Our desire is that you read this book with a sense of pride for our modern day heroes. If you know of a story of someone who has sacrificed for the good of his fellow man, we welcome their nomination for the Modern Day Hero® Award. We accept candidates for people of all ages, political affiliations, races, and religious backgrounds.

Nominate a Candidate for the
Modern Day Hero® Award

The Modern Day Hero® Award is awarded to the candidate selected by the evaluation committee from the nominations received from people from around the nation. These award selections take place on a calendar quarter basis.

These candidate stories are the passionate true stories about people making sacrifices for the benefit of others. They are stories that exhibit the strength, honor, and pride that has made America the nation she is today. They are stories with profound significance that will cause the evaluation board to finish with awe and amazement at the caliber of person that would make such a sacrifice for others. These stories are true and are often given by others because of the level of sacrifice made by the people, will often times cost them their lives.

The most powerful stories are about people who give what Abraham Lincoln called, "The last full measure of devotion" for their country and her people. But they are not always about the sacrifice of life for others. Sacrifice comes in many forms.

Guidelines for a Modern Day Hero® Candidate Nominations:

1. A true story about a person/people in service to others.
2. The nomination story should be between 500-1500 words.
3. The nomination story should include the who, what, when, where, and why we should care about them in the story.
4. It should be told in the "story" format as you would want that story to be read to the world.
5. The story should be current, having taken place from 1950's to present.

Submission Specifications
1. Please be sure to include your name and contact information on every nomination.
2. Send only one copy of each submission.

We will not return submissions, so please don't send the original. Please feel free to submit more than one candidate nomination if you'd like.

You can submit your candidate nomination story these different ways:

Internet: www.ModernDayHeroes.com
Email: Nominations@ModernDayHeroes.com
Mail: Modern Day Heroes®
            c/o Anderson-Noble Publishing
            Attn. - Nominations
            6285 East Spring Street, Ste 387
            Long Beach, CA 90808-4000

Fax: (714) 908-8189

            With Strength, Honor, and Pride,
            Pete Mitchell and Bill Perkins

About Pete Mitchell

Pete Mitchell is the Founder of FundamentalLeadership.com, an organization dedicated to restoring the splendor and strength once possessed by America by reminding Americans the basic principals of leadership that have allowed our country to reach this level of greatness.

There was a time in American history when the White House had a pristine feel to it. Pete believes that today, the American people are distrusting of their government due to the scandals from the past 50 years involving the office of the President of the United States.

There was a time in American history when corporations were seen as a benefit to society, not the evil money leaching institutions they are seen as today by so many Americans. It is Pete's belief that the root cause of the distrust of America's most influential institutions is due in large part to a lack of the fundamental leadership skills at the top, middle, and base in these organizations.

"You can learn some of the most profound leadership principles by looking into the lives of American heroes." (Two examples below)

Fundamental Leadership Point 1
A leader must take action even when everything else around you tells you that inaction is safer (As seen in the life of Michael DiRaimondo, page 293.)
Fundamental Leadership Point 2
A leader must always lead by example, no exceptions (As demonstrated by Humbert "Rocky" Versace, page 43.)

Pete Mitchell is a graduate of Biola University and a financial advisor by trade. He is the host of a radio show in Southern California called Social Weapons (www.SocialWeapons.com) that touches on the hot topics in America while looking at them from a historical-leadership perspective. His guests are often business leaders, elected officials, and veterans. He is a sought after speaker on the topics of leadership, government and business.

For additional information about public engagements for civic organizations, please contact:

Pete Mitchell
6285 East Spring Street, Suite 387
Long Beach, CA 90808-4000
Phone: (800) 551-HERO
Fax: (714) 908-8189
www.FundamentalLeadership.com
info@FundamentalLeadership.com

About Bill Perkins

Bill Perkins was raised in a home where politics was discussed a great deal. If you were to listen to his grandmother on his father's side of the family the word was "democrat." Now if you were to listen to his father the word was "republican"; boy did that make for fun family get togethers!

When Bill was around the age of six, his father brought home a book about the Presidents of the United States and asked him to read it. Bill did as he was asked and then began years of discussions on politics and the world in which we live. He remembers asking his father what it was that the President does all day long, and his father's answer was, "He helps people." With an answer like that, Bill knew he had to look into our country's leaders more.

Since that point in his life, Bill has learned about Presidents George Washington to George W. Bush and has loved every minute of it. He has studied the works of many of the members of Congress and loved that as well. He believes in these men whether they are Republican or Democrat. He believes it to be an honor to serve in this matter. He has gained a love for this country through these studies.

"I think those who have served and those who will serve will do well in their own ways."

Bill's desire is that the hard work he put into this book will help people to understand the greatness of this country and its leaders. Bill's hope is that the reader will see that those who are elected to lead us are good men and women through their words and through their actions.

May God bless the future Presidents and leaders of this great country, those who are now serving, and you the reader.

ENJOY....

Acknowledgments

This work is a product of the dedication of many. It has been our extreme pleasure and benefit to have the opportunity to work with some of the greatest minds in the country. It has been your fervent dedication to this project that has enabled us to get these stories told.

We would like to thank-

- Julie Mitchell for the work she did in reviewing the manuscript.
- Brian McCullough for the work he did in spot checking the manuscript.
- Ronnie Guyer for his constant inspiration and belief in our project. We are better off for having known you.
- Our elected officials who contributed their time, words and effort to this project.
- The many friends we have made in the press offices of our elected officials, we will not let you down.
- The many people who contributed their definition of an "American hero" – it was not in vain.
- Jim Pidd for contributing more than the world will ever know. Your words made this book possible, for, without them, this book would not be what it is today.

Pete would like to thank:
- His wife Jami for her belief in him even when there was no good reason to have that belief. Without you, life just wouldn't be any fun. High Five.
- His father Robert Mitchell. You have taught me a great deal about life and God.
- Pete would also like to thank his mother Gaylene Mitchell. I hope that I will make you proud by the manner in which I live my life.

Bill would like to thank:

- His wife Amber. You are the best thing that has ever happened to me. You have been the source of strength and drive when I thought there was nothing left to be strong for. I love you with all my heart.
- His mother Therese Anderson for all the things that she has tried to teach him over the years.
- His father Bill Perkins for the love and support that he was to him.
- His stepfather Roy for the love and support that he is to him.
- His father-in-law Richard Rex, and his mother-in-law, Verlene Rex, for all the wisdom that they have been willing to share over the years.
- And finally to some of his wonderful friends that have believed in him from the start, Steve Lang, Gary Schaap, Aaron Bonine, Gary Monahan, Carter Hogan, and Scott Omae. If there are any left out please charge it to my head not to my heart.

Give the Gift of
Modern Day Heroes®: In Defense of America
To Your Friends, Family and Colleagues
Check Your Local Bookstore or Order Here

[] **YES**, I want _____ copies of *Modern Day Heroes®: In Defense of America* (The Red Volume) (#bob1077a) for $34.95 for each Hardbound copy and/or $27.95 for each Softbound copy.

[] **YES**, I want information on bulk orders for my organization.

Include $3.95 shipping and handling for one book, and $2.25 for each additional book. California and Nevada residents must include applicable sales tax.

Payment must accompany orders. Allow 3 -6 weeks for delivery.

For fast service, order your copies at **www.ModernDayHeroes.com**

My check or money order for $_____ is enclosed.
Please charge my [] Visa [] MasterCard [] American Express

Name_____

Organization_____

Billing Address_____

City/State/Zip_____

Phone_____E-mail_____

Card#_____

Exp. Date _____Signature _____

Phone Orders: **(800) 551-HERO** - Fax Orders: **(714) 908-8189**
Make your check payable and return to

Anderson-Noble Publishing, LLC
6285 East Spring Street, Ste 387
Long Beach, CA 90808-4000